Pearls of Comfort

Pearls of Comfort

*Experiencing divine and human comfort
at the end of life*

MARTINA HOLDER-FRANZ

Foreword by John Swinton

PICKWICK *Publications* • Eugene, Oregon

PEARLS OF COMFORT
Experiencing divine and human comfort at the end of life

Copyright © 2025 Martina Holder-Franz. All rights reserved. Except for brief quotations in critical publications or reviews, no part of this book may be reproduced in any manner without prior written permission from the publisher. Write: Permissions, Wipf and Stock Publishers, 199 W. 8th Ave., Suite 3, Eugene, OR 97401.

Pickwick Publications
An Imprint of Wipf and Stock Publishers
199 W. 8th Ave., Suite 3
Eugene, OR 97401

www.wipfandstock.com

PAPERBACK ISBN: 979-8-3852-2312-1
HARDCOVER ISBN: 979-8-3852-2313-8
EBOOK ISBN: 979-8-3852-2314-5

Cataloguing-in-Publication data:

Names: Holder-Franz, Martina [author]. | Swinton, John, 1957– [foreword writer].

Title: Pearls of comfort : experiencing divine and human comfort at the end of life / by Martina Holder-Franz.

Description: Eugene, OR: Pickwick Publications, 2025 | Includes bibliographical references.

Identifiers: ISBN 979-8-3852-2312-1 (paperback) | ISBN 979-8-3852-2313-8 (hardcover) | ISBN 979-8-3852-2314-5 (ebook)

Subjects: LCSH: Terminal care—Religious aspects—Christianity. | Church work with the terminally ill. | Death—Religious aspects—Christianity. | Attitudes to Death. | Hospice care. | Quality of life. | Pastoral care. | Grief.

Classification: BV4460.6 H65 2025 (paperback) | BV4460.6 (ebook)

08/25/25

For John, Benedict, David, Sophia, and Tim:

You not only encouraged me as a mother writing a dissertation, but were also patient when, in addition to our church work, Dan and I spent days and nights reflecting for our dissertations on different experiences which Christian people had shared with us.

May God keep you and guide you all the days of your lives.

My comfort in my suffering is this: your promise preserves my life.
—Psalm 119:50 (NIV)

Lord our God, you give us life, and then you take it away and hide it for a while in the mystery of death, in order that it may someday be brought into the light, renewed and cleansed, as our eternal life.... Teach us to consider that we must die, and let us be thankful until then for the hope that will not be brought to naught. All this we ask in the name of Jesus Christ, our Lord. Amen.
—Karl Barth, *Fifty Prayers*, 59

Contents

Foreword by John Swinton — ix

Acknowledgments — xi

1. Approaching the topic of consolation and comfort at the end of life — 1
2. Inquiring into comfort and consolation in the Bible, in literature, and in the experiences of practicing Christians at the end of their lives — 17
3. Finding "pearls of comfort": divine, human, and in creation, music, and artifacts — 69
4. Reflecting theologically around comfort and consolation in areas such as prayer, trust, peace, the body, and "things" — 143
5. Envisioning a comfort ministry for the church for those at the end of life — 193
6. Summary and closing thoughts — 209

Appendix — 215

Bibliography — 217

Foreword

It is with great joy and admiration that I introduce *Pearls of Comfort: Experiencing Divine and Human Comfort at the End of Life* by my dear friend and colleague, Martina Holder-Franz. This work, a deep and important exploration of spiritual and human experiences of comfort at life's end, reflects the depth of Martina's theological insight, her compassionate spirit, and her unwavering dedication to understanding the complex, sacred interplay between faith and human vulnerability.

Martina has always been a clear thinker and a careful listener, traits that are evident in the stories she shares throughout this book—stories gathered from those facing their final days with remarkable courage and faith. These are not just narratives; they are treasures unearthed by someone who understands that the heart of theology lies in the lived experiences of those who walk the path of faith. The title, *Pearls of Comfort*, is absolutely fitting: pearls are formed through time and under pressure. The comfort described here arises over time and under the inevitable pressure of recognizing and coping with our mortality.

Drawing on her deep roots in practical theology, Martina invites us into a space where the ordinary becomes extraordinary—where prayer, Scripture, relationships, and even simple artifacts serve as vessels of divine comfort. Her ability to weave together biblical exegesis, theological reflection, and phenomenological research is a testament to her skill as a scholar and her compassion as a minister. The insights she offers are as thought-provoking as they are deeply moving, shedding new light on the theology of comfort, particularly within the context of the Swiss Reformed Church.

But this book is more than an academic achievement; it is a labor of love, born out of decades of pastoral care and personal reflection. I see Martina's fingerprints all over this work—her sensitivity to suffering, her belief in the healing power of community, and her commitment to helping others experience God's presence even in the shadow of death. For those of us who know her, this book is not only a gift to the field of theology but also a reflection of the generous and faithful person she is.

As you journey through these pages, may you be inspired by the voices of those who shared their stories, touched by the wisdom they impart, and comforted by the assurance that God's presence is with us, even in the most challenging of times. Thank you, Martina, for this pearl of a book and for the love, care, and theological wisdom you bring to the world.

With gratitude

Prof. John Swinton
University of Aberdeen
Scotland, December 2024

Acknowledgments

MY PROFOUND APPRECIATION GOES to my supervisor, John Swinton, and to my second supervisor, Katie Cross, for their encouragement, their humor, and their skill in guiding me through my dissertation. I am particularly thankful that they encouraged me to discover the richness of qualitative research and to find my own way to integrate new findings in the analytical part of the research.

It was a great privilege for me to be so warmly welcomed at the theological faculty in Aberdeen until I finished in June 2022. I would like to express my heartfelt thanks for the interest shown in my research and the valuable exchanges over the last few years. For me, the faculty in Aberdeen was also a spiritual home, including church services and prayer times in the faculty church.

I am very grateful that I was able to meet wonderful and unique people at the end of their lives who lived their Christian faith and questioned it even in times of difficulty. I am also grateful to any number of colleagues in different churches and universities. They have supported me over many years from the time when I began to deepen my interest in Cicely Saunders and my engagement for people at the end of life in my pastoral work. I would like to thank different nurses, therapists, and doctors, who have encouraged me to take a close look at people's Christian spirituality and to learn something from it for the work of the church. I have also been greatly encouraged by my colleagues in the Swiss association "Palliative Care and Christian Responsibility."

I am indebted to my family members, my children, my parents, and parents-in-law, and friends who have supported me over the last years and whose love and prayerful support have been a source of strength and motivation for me.

I would like to mention one theological friend and companion in particular: I have been discussing and arguing with him since we met each other during our theology studies. We love and trust each other; thank you, Dan, for traveling through life together with me, always curious about what we can discover of God's presence and call.

1

Approaching the topic of consolation and comfort at the end of life

SOME REFLECTIONS ON MY PERSONAL JOURNEY AND MOTIVATION

COMFORT ("TROST" IN GERMAN)[1] is a word with which I am familiar. I grew up in the Lutheran Church tradition in Eisenach, a town in the former GDR or East Germany. It was a place where Christians were the minority in an atheistic society. In prayers, in hymns, and in preaching, the word "consolation" or "comfort" was ubiquitous. My father was an ordained Lutheran minister in this church. My mother came from a Lutheran-Reformed background ("Unierte Kirche"—United Church) in the southern part of West Germany; she had to give up her freedom (and passport) to marry my father in the eastern part of Germany in 1966. For this young couple it was hard to live with three children under these political circumstances. Daily life—like shopping, building a new church addition, or having to help people who were scared of the regime—was both an adventure and exhausting. It was not possible to talk openly in our house or at church about our faith or our problems because we were constantly being observed by the "Staatssicherheitsdienst" (Ministry of State Security) and because our telephone was tapped. A daily prayer

---

1. In English translation, "consolation" is practically interchangeable with "comfort": Shogren, "Consolation."

routine, singing, music, and living with others as devoted Christians helped my parents and us children to live with these constant difficulties and tension with a spirit of hope and joy. During those years in East Germany, I felt the comforting power of different forms of community faith praxis: the transforming power of hymns and music and art, and the richness of Christian symbols in the old church buildings of our tradition. Although I was a child and then a young teenager, I never felt that the word "comfort" ("Trost") was old fashioned or meaningless; rather, I felt strengthened by the comfort of our faith community's praxis amidst the political dangers of daily life.

Eisenach, where we lived during my childhood, was not only the place where Luther translated the New Testament, it was also the town where the renowned composer Johann Sebastian Bach was born and where in the twelfth century St. Elisabeth of Thüringen launched a ministry of comfort among the sick and dying. During my childhood, Eisenach had a bishop (the Bishop of the Lutheran Church of Thüringen) who lived there, a school for deacons, and a community of Protestant sisters (or deaconesses). For an atheistic socialist environment, it was a place where "Christian performance" was lived in a concentrated and special way. To hear or sing Bach's music, for instance, was not merely a cultural activity, it was part of a countercultural confessing event, because through music one could "hear" the gospel and the biblical story even in an atheistic environment. And this shared communal experience was very comforting at the time. In 1984, after a few years of trouble and difficulties, we were able to leave the GDR, but we did so precipitously and on condition that we never return.

After we left the GDR, I went through a period of culture shock. Because my father was not allowed to work as a minster in West Germany, he had to look for a position in another country. This was the reason that we as a family came to Switzerland. It was a time of intense introspection for us all with regard to what faith and holding on to Christ could mean in this "new world." As an East German teenager with a hunger to understand more about Christ and his calling, I was blessed to be able to work and stay in the "Schürmatt" for four years, a place where about eighty children and teenagers with special needs lived and went to school. After a year as a volunteer, I entered a training program in the education of people with cognitive difficulties. These young people with their special needs had a very open way of asking for comfort and consolation. Good food, music, special relationships, tenderness, creativity, or time for a variety of celebrations were all ways in which they found encouragement or comfort in their daily struggles.[2] I had conversations with them about God, and the meaning of life and suffering. They all had a rich spirituality. Barbara, one young lady, spent hours and hours painting when she felt sad or unstable. A young man, Nick, had to dance to feel alive and he could always move from melancholy to joy with a good strong beat and an eccentric dance form. His body movements were joyful and artistic; watching him was an encouragement for us all.

I also had "special Christians friends" with whom I shared the Christian faith tradition. One of them, Katharina, would sing church hymns for all of us on Sunday mornings. It was particularly important for her to pray, sing, and hear Bible stories recounted; she often said that this helped her to find peace and hope in the midst of difficulties and frequently also of physical pain. She and others would complain if no one was there to help them get to church on Sundays. They liked to be part of a wider community and to meet people with whom they could sing, pray, and have church coffee. When I was at church with them, I felt deeply what it meant to be part of the body of Christ. Some of these special friends were also severely physically handicapped and died at a young age. During that time of sharing in their life, and accompanying them through suffering and dying, I was struck by the difficulties many helpers had in dealing with end-of-life issues or in developing strategies to support those in need along with their family members and friends. The "Schürmatt" was a Christian organization, but the institution gave little help at that end-of-life time. In that context, the term *spiritual care* was not a familiar one, and the local ministers were not involved in our end-of-life caregiving.

During my years of theological studies at different universities, I worked the night shift on a telephone counselling ministry ("Telehilfe"). It was a completely different setting from the one with which I was familiar, speaking with suffering people whose names and faces I did not know, only voices and many questions. This phone ministry is a service funded by the Swiss Reformed and Roman Catholic Churches and available to all people, anonymously and free of charge. The service still exists

---

2. Compare here Jean Vanier's writings, for instance: Vanier, *Becoming Human* or *From Brokenness to Community*. I am aware of the serious cases of sexual abuse surrounding Jean Vanier, which have come to light after his death (see BBC News, "L'Arche Founder Jean Vanier") and do not wish to minimize these. I have nonetheless chosen to use his work given the important insights contained in them.

in different places, and is well known throughout Switzerland. Most of the callers with whom I talked had no traditional faith roots but were often very thankful to be able to share their problems with someone who would listen attentively. It was a comfort-ministry of listening, and sometimes callers were open to us praying for them on the phone.

After my theological studies and six years of practical work as a minister, I was privileged to do further courses in pastoral care and systemic counselling, and then to undertake a master's degree in pastoral care at the University of Bern in 2012, with a focus on how to share faith and life with church members and families facing death and dying. My reflections on Cicely Saunders helped me, and I started to translate two of her books into German. I also wrote a book under the supervision of Prof. Christoph Morgenthaler about Saunders's spirituality. At this time, as a minister in the Swiss Reformed Church of Switzerland in Muhen near Aarau, I was very much involved in counselling individuals and families at the end of life in my own congregation. It was likewise a particular gift to me that for eleven years I was a minister in the same community in which Katharina's mother lived. Thus, I got to know the whole family better, and they called me to be with Katharina's mother when she died. Soon afterwards I stayed with Katharina herself when the time came for her to prepare to let go of her life. Both mother and daughter had a deep love for Christ; singing and listening to church hymns and praying was how they found comfort in life and how they chose to prepare for eternity.[3] Though I could retrieve numerous examples from this period of my life upon which to reflect, here I mention only two particular people.

Sarah, a woman from church, wanted to celebrate the Lord's Supper in her flat just a few days before she died. Because this act of sharing bread and wine was so precious to her, she wanted to celebrate the Lord's Supper not only together with her daughter and two close friends but also in the room in which she spent most of her time, a room which held some of her beloved photographs and mementos. That the daughter and a friend prepared the room knowing that Sarah loved flowers, candles, and white tablecloths made me feel as if we were all guests whom someone had invited to a special occasion. Yes, there were tears, but also

---

3. Katharina's mother lost her husband when he was only sixty-seven. He had been very ill for two years. Together they had five children, three of them with a severe handicap. Two died earlier than Katharina. The two children who had no handicap stayed in contact with me. From time to time, I hear from them about how they and their families are doing. To be a so-called "heathy child" in this family was and is a challenge full of questions, suffering, grief, and also of deep love for all family members.

laughter, meditation on the psalms and Bible texts, and both silence and singing. Above all there was an atmosphere of hope and comfort in the midst of physical pain and lament, an atmosphere no doubt heightened by part of our liturgy before sharing bread and wine coming from Ps 34:8: "Taste and see that the Lord is good! Blessed is the man who takes refuge in him!" By being together in prayer for each other, and by eating and drinking together in Jesus' name, we experienced God's comfort through several of our senses, and we also experienced another dimension of life, beyond the visible, beyond death and pain. Ever since that occasion, I have found myself encouraging members of my congregation to celebrate the Lord's Supper more often and with others who share this hope in Christ, and to do so especially in times of suffering and sickness.

Then there was Ron. He was only twenty-two years old when he and his family learned that he would soon die of a brain tumor. His family were members of the Swiss Reformed Church, but they did not regard themselves as practicing Christians. They felt unable to talk with him about death, God, and all the questions he had. I visited him in hospital, and he asked me after our first encounter whether I would be willing to accompany him through his last months of life. I agreed, but those months of severe suffering and the many conversations we had about how to experience a God of love and find faith when one is dying at such a young age were challenging. He was eager to learn about Scripture, prayer, and had all sorts of philosophical questions. Christian praxis was a whole new world to him. Those new experiences of his also influenced his family, who in turn asked to speak with me about lament, suffering, and letting go. What was particularly difficult for Ron and his family was that, after being in hospital for a long time and always sharing a room with others who were not palliative patients, his last months were in a nursing home where he shared a room with an old man suffering from dementia. At that time, the first hospice group had just launched in the region, and hospitals were not yet familiar with the different aspects of palliative care and what we would now call best practices.

After eleven years, we moved to another church community in Switzerland, and it was there that I began the research contained in this thesis. I am a minister of the Swiss Reformed Church in Basel, and responsible in the parish of Riehen. In this new community, I became part of a team which brought the whole notion of palliative care to the attention of our cantonal church. I also work with an interprofessional society in the region of Basel exploring questions concerning "palliative care and Christian responsibility." For six years, a palliative care doctor and I presided over that group. During that time, together with my friend and colleague, Maria Zinsstag, I was able to interview twenty different Christians (pioneers in the palliative care field, nurses, volunteers, pastors, lecturers) to learn from them about palliative care and their motivations, experiences, and vision.[4]

Being engaged in a ministry of end-of-life care for Christians with both professionals and volunteers within my denomination, I was interested in reading more about palliative care, spiritual care, and pastoral care with regard to end-of-life issues. On reading through a great deal of literature on pastoral and spiritual care, it became clear to me that for many thinkers, psychotherapeutic models and knowledge were so central that theological reflections were secondary. At the same time, while studying the work of Cicely Saunders, I was surprised to find that theological reflections were important and indeed central for her and her work as a palliative care doctor. I discovered that both in medicine and theology this knowledge was neither widely known or discussed. I learnt from her and her theological, medical, social, and spiritual reflections that as Christians we are called to develop a better praxis for caring for the sick and dying and their families and friends. Because of her training as a nurse, social worker, and doctor, and because of her ongoing interest in theology, philosophy, and psychology, through her work at the St. Christopher's hospice she could convey her ideas and practices to people from all over the world, in so doing inspiring many of them. By the way she lived and through her writings, she communicated that experiencing community and multifaceted dimensions of comfort (physical, social, spiritual, and emotional)[5] along with spirituality, gestures, material things, and creation were all important for her patients and helped them at the end of life.

I realized then that through the achievements in palliative care and through the hospice movement, much had already been achieved in the last thirty years. Rich research supports the sick and the dying in a variety of ways and is available to educate professionals entrusted

---

4. Holder-Franz and Zinsstag, *In Beziehung sein*.
5. Saunders and the concept of "total pain" in Saunders, *Watch with Me*, 35.

with their care.[6] But I was also aware that, for example, Katharina's life and personhood were formed and developed not only by an institutional setting but also through a local community and a local church tradition to which she belonged. I became aware that Christian communities carry and perpetuate a particular lived theological praxis about which, it struck me, most people have not given much thought. Even at the end of her life, Katharina was eager to stay in contact with her church community because this community enriched her life and her spirituality. It would have been helpful if the institution in which she lived and which had been her home for many years long before her dying had been more aware of how and in which ways she experienced spiritual comfort in her suffering as a devoted Christian. Although their wisdom and knowledge about her physical and cognitive disabilities helped the staff to accompany her well, they were not well equipped to understand her spirituality and her spiritual experiences.

I became aware that the topic of comfort and consolation at the end of life was very much present in the Christian practices of the local church, and that local churches have existing links to various social networks, institutions, hospitals, and other churches. Because I am responsible for a visiting team in my church, I became interested in how the members of the team experience their ministry, how they reflect on it, what kind of self-awareness they have and how they reflect on that with each other.

As minister of a church congregation, I am also interested in speaking with Christians at the end of life, and in learning from them what it means to prepare to die and what is helping them to live faithfully through their final days on earth. Yet through being involved in many situations in which a person or a family has said their goodbyes, I also increasingly became aware that to be able to offer someone comfort one needs an awareness of the person, a faithful kind of "being with," which is often much more than words and "doing things."

I recognize that there are many approaches to deepening one's understanding of what Christian's experience as comforting and helpful at the end of their lives but surely the relational skills and human gifts of

---

6. The movement "Clinical Pastoral Training" had an enormous effect on the education for counselling, especially in hospitals or nursing homes. Later the discussion on palliative care and spiritual care had a wide influence. See for instance: Daaleman, "Exploratory Study"; Selman, "Research Priorities"; Van de Geer, "Training Spiritual Care"; Edwards, "Understanding of Spirituality"; Kellehear, "Spirituality and Palliative Care."

listening, empathy, and understanding should be central topics as regards the lives of those who are dying.

Being there for the dying and bereaved can help one to develop an attitude of thoughtful reflective attentiveness. Nicholas Wolterstorff reminded me that "being with" is a multilayered and complex engagement. He wrote in *Lament for a Son*,

> If you think your task as comforter is to tell me that really, all things considered, it's not so bad, you do not sit with me in my grief but place yourself off in the distance away from me. Over there, you are of no help. What I need to hear from you is that you recognize how painful it is. I need to hear from you that you are with me in my desperation. To comfort me, you have to come close. Come sit with me on my mourning bench.[7]

Besides such reflections and questions, I noticed that church praxis largely has to do with implementing particular faith traditions and conveying particular denominational content. I was struggling with questions like: How can we bring experience into conversation with faith and faith tradition? What does it mean to think about comfort and consolation in the context of God's triune being and the work of the Holy Spirit? What can we learn from Scripture concerning prayer, lament, and God's promise of shalom? And how can that help to deepen our trust and faith in God in the process of letting go? What is "cheap comfort" and what is "costly comfort"?[8] For people dealing with sickness, loneliness, or suffering, what is firm ground on which they can stand confidently, and what is merely shifting sand?

Wesley Nelson in his article on comfort motivated me to find out more about the deeper understanding of the topic, as he refers to central scriptural passages, both from the Old and New Testament, which are helpful in thinking ecclesiologically about comfort and consolation:

> The Christian ministry of comfort is defined both by Scripture and by human need.... God is a God of comfort (Rom. 15:5; II Cor. 1:3).... Believers are exhorted to engage in the ministry of comforting one another (I Thess. 5:14). Jesus identified himself with the ministry which is described in Isaiah 61:1-2, which was in essence a ministry of comfort (Luke 4:18-19).[9]

---

7. Wolterstorff, *Lament for a Son*, 34.

8. See Bonhoeffer and his thoughts about "costly grace."

9. Neslon, "Pastor as Comforter," 297: "The Christian ministry of comfort is defined both by Scripture and by human need. The New Testament references to comfort are

THE AIM OF AND PREPARATORY WORK FOR THIS RESEARCH

Having discussed my personal interest and practical engagement in this field, I turn now to present the framework and prerequisites of this thesis. In it, I focus on the importance of comfort and consolation at the end of life as a theological concept and as an important area of ministry for the church. To understand comfort within the context of caring for people and their families or close friends at the end of their lives, church communities can profit form new perspectives and possibilities for engaged church members, deacons and ministers. As Bonnie J. Miller-McLemore writes in her reflection on suffering,

> The cross and resurrection stand as narrative reminders of this practical theological call to witness the suffering of the world. As creatures made in the image and likeness of God, we too are called to be witnesses, martyrs in the sense of not shrinking from one another's cries of pain but entering into the costly but godly vocation of being-with.[10]

This thesis discusses comfort and consolation in the framework of a research project in practical theology and brings the topic into constructive dialogue with other disciplines. Practical theologians Seward Hiltner and Don Browning reflect on this as follows:

> Under the pressures of pluralism ... the very goals of our care often come under question; therefore, our care should be guided by a more explicitly normative discipline. Pastoral theological method needs to reconstitute under the guidance of a critical, practical ... theology, or theological ethics.[11]

---

largely derived from the verb 'parakaleo' and its noun form 'parakleisis' which, in the context of the general meaning of comfort, are usually translated 'comfort,' 'consolation' or 'encouragement.' God is a God of comfort (Rom. 15:5; II Cor 1:3). There is comfort in Christ (Phil. 2:1). The Holy Spirit is called 'Comforter' (RSV 'Counsellor') (John 14:16–17; 26; 15:26; 16:7). Comfort is promised to the believer (Matt. 5:4; II Cor 1:4; II Thess 2:16–17). There is comfort in the Scripture (Rom 15:4), and the gift of prophecy (I Cor 14:3). The apostles engaged in a ministry of comfort (I Cor 1; Eph. 6:22; Col 2:2; I Thess 2:11). The apostles were to be comforted in this ministry of comforting others (II Cor 1:7; 7:6–7); 13; I Thess 3:7–8). Believers are exhorted to engage in the ministry of comforting one another (I Thess 5:14). Jesus identified himself with the ministry which is described in Isaiah 61:1–2, which was in essence a ministry of comfort (Luke 4:18–19)."

10. Miller-McLemore, *Practical Theology*, 30.
11. Woodward and Pattison, *Pastoral and Practical Theology*, 53–54.

Humans experience comfort and consolation through concrete and specific actions. That human experience is a central source for practical and pastoral theology.[12] Zoe Bennett et al. are right in describing the importance of practical theology research as lying in its being rooted and grounded in the embodied world and taking on "the complexity of contemporary bio-social reality as an important *locus theologicus*."[13] To bring contemporary experience and theological understanding together so that they can illuminate and interpret each other will be a complex task, and I am aware that throughout this process surprises and difficulties are likely to arise. Stephen Pattison prepared me for the complexity of practical theology by noting that

> I learned that the theological world was not an enclave to be protected in its hermetic separateness, but a spacious room, full of questions and different perspectives to be vigorously explored. The God I was committed to was bigger than I had thought, and could accommodate big questions and contradictions.[14]

Indeed, special experiences do not stand alone; the individual human is not an island but part of the "web of life."[15] Moreover, as Christian humans, we interpret human experience as a

> "place" where the gospel is grounded, embodied . . . and lived out. . . . Human experience is presumed to be an important locus for the work of the Spirit. As such it holds much relevance for the continuing task of interpreting scripture and tradition and the development of our understanding of theology and faithful practising.[16]

In preparing my empirical steps, I understood the need to be clear about the sheer complexity of the "hermeneutical enterprise." As Swinton and Mowat suggest: "All research is interpretative; it is guided by a set of beliefs and feelings about the world and how it should be understood and

---

12. Miller-McLemore, *Practical Theology*, 24.
The term "living human document" is discussed in Charles Gerkin's work. See Gerkin, *Living Human Document*. The phrase is originally Anton Boisen's, an American chaplain, a leading figure in the hospital chaplaincy and clinical pastoral education movements, and himself once a patient in a mental hospital, which deeply informed his work.

13. Bennett et al., *Invitation to Research*, 12.
14. Bennett et al., *Invitation to Research*, 22.
15. See Osmer, *Practical Theology*, 16.
16. Swinton and Mowat, *Practical Theology*, 5–6.

studied."[17] Situations and experiences are "complex, multi-faceted entities which need to be examined with care, rigour and discernment if they are to be effectively understood."[18]

Accepting this epistemological position, I became more aware that as a researcher I am an active part and a "co-creator"[19] of the interpretative process. I had to train my reflexivity, which Swinton and Mowat describe as "the process of critical self-reflection carried out by the researcher throughout the research process that enables her to monitor and respond to her contribution to the proceedings."[20]

Such self-reflections involve asking questions like: What do I see? What do I not see, and why? What kind of pre-understandings are guiding me? What does this do to me? How do I feel? In what way am I engaged in this situation or conversation? Can I see the limitations of my awareness? And in which context is it sensible to discuss the various fragments of experiences within my findings? What does it mean to reflect on experiences? What does it mean to reflect on the process of engaging? Business leadership professor Tony Ghaye writes, "Reflective practice offers us a way of trying to make sense of the uncertainty . . . on the edge of chaos."[21] Such reflection clarifies that reflexivity must also acknowledge and take into account the subjectivity of every researcher. "Just as we cannot see others from an 'objective' or 'God's eye view,' [so too] we cannot see ourselves from this vantage point. Reflecting on our reflexivity will thus continue indefinitely, with no possibility to reach a final point."[22] I shall take up the theme of reflexivity further in the next chapter which deals with methodology.

There are different ways to understand and enfold practical theology in this research. I agree with the notion that practical theology can be thought of as a part of a movement of "faith seeking understanding," which recalls not only Anselm's famous words concerning *fides quaerens*

---

17. Swinton and Mowat, *Practical Theology*, 34.
18. Swinton and Mowat, *Practical Theology*, 13.
19. Swinton and Mowat, *Practical Theology*, 35.
20. Swinton and Mowat, *Practical Theology*, 59.
21. Ghaye, "Into the Reflective Mode," 7.
22. Dreyer, "Knowledge, Subjectivity," 126.

intellectum,[23] but above all that "human expression is provisional, but God comes before and is beyond all expression and all knowing."[24]

After some exploration, I found that qualitative research and in particular the hermeneutical phenomenological method are the best means by which to explore comfort experiences of Christians at the end of life. While reflecting on different epistemological approaches, I hoped that meaningful knowledge could be discovered in unique, non-replicable comfort experiences. Qualitative research describes reality not through numbers (or data) but in ways which enable one to understand the "world differently and in understanding differently begin to act differently."[25] My hope was that through this new understanding I could gain insights beyond the particularities of individuals' experiences, and that through discovering similarities in my subjects' experiences I would potentially be able to identify and describe a "transforming resonance"[26] which would be helpful in future discussions in this field of practical theology.

To take human experience seriously and to understand individual descriptions as a source of reflection entails an ongoing dialectic process. "To write is to reflect; to write is to research."[27] This qualitative phenomenological hermeneutical study includes semi-structured interviews with fourteen Christians in the Swiss Reformed Church who either were over eighty-five years old or who were diagnosed with a terminal illness. I asked them about comfort-experiences and how they are experiencing aspects of comfort in their lives as Christians.

To prepare for the qualitative research and the interviews, I used the phenomenological concepts promoted by Max van Manen and Linda Finlay. I asked the interviewees about the comfort meaning of personal belongings, and because all of the interviewees told me how meaningful some of their personal "things" were (including photos, paintings, symbols, crosses, and other objects), I decided to study practical theologian Stephen Pattison's book *Seeing Things*,[28] Gillian Rose's *Visual*

---

23. It is the theological method stressed by, for example, Augustine (354–430) and Anselm of Canterbury (ca. 1033–1109) in which one begins with faith in God and on the basis of that faith moves on to further understanding of Christian truth. Anselm uses this expression for the first time in his *Proslogion* (II–IV). It articulates the close relationship between faith and human reason.

24. Ward, *Introducing Practical Theology*, 29.

25. Swinton and Mowat, *Practical Theology*, 46.

26. Swinton and Mowat, *Practical Theology*, 47.

27. Van Manen, *Phenomenology of Practice*, 20.

28. Pattison, *Seeing Things*; Pattison, "Stuff Pastoral Theology," 154.

Methodology,[29] and to reflect on Daniel Miller's anthropological work and on the dimensions of the comfort that things and relationships bring.[30] The work of philosopher and phenomenologist Hans Blumenberg deepened my understanding about comfort and consolation as a human category.[31] Though he does not focus particularly on end-of-life issues, Blumenberg reflects on different aspects of comfort and consolation experiences because humans are mortal and the consciousness of experiencing the world, self, and others in time and culture touches significantly on my research topic. His main work on comfort is entitled *Description of a Human*. It not only broadened my horizons to understand comfort as a human phenomenon but also encouraged me to bring some of the aspects of his philosophical concept into my theological reflection. Along with these concepts and reflections, the introduction to practical theology and qualitative research by Swinton and Mowat,[32] Osmer's description of the four tasks of practical theology,[33] Ward's *Introducing Practical Theology*,[34] and Bennett et al.'s *Invitation to Research in Practical Theology* together helped me to structure the process of this thesis and informed me about the field of qualitative research.[35]

To deepen my understanding of practical theology in general, I read—and in the process became fascinated with—the different ways of explaining the meaning of practical theology as a theological and ecclesiastical discipline. One way of articulating the essence of practical theology is Browning's description in his *Fundamental Practical Theology*.[36] There, he suggests that practical theology is an exercise in understanding and interpreting the practice of the church, and that we have to ask: What shall we do? And how shall we live? Out of these two questions numerous other questions arise. For instance: What are the sources and authorities for what we are doing and what we should doing? What are the reasons, ideas, and concepts we should use to interpret and understand praxis?

---

29. Rose, *Visual Methodologies*. Rose is especially useful here in laying out ethical and systematic guidelines around the coding and presentation of visual images.
30. Miller, *Comfort of Things*; Miller, *Comfort of People*.
31. Blumenberg, *Beschreibung des Menschen*, 623–56.
32. Swinton and Mowat, *Practical Theology*.
33. Osmer, *Practical Theology*, 4.
34. Ward, *Introducing Practical Theology*.
35. Bennett et al., *Invitation to Research*, 6–46.
36. Browning, *Fundamental Practical Theology*, 10.

Another interpretive model can be seen in what Osmer calls the four tasks in practical theology. He describes the tasks as: the descriptive-empirical task (What is going on?), the interpretive task (Why is this going on?), the normative task (What ought to be going on?), and the pragmatic task (How might we respond?). I find both authors' concepts helpful, but also recognized some potential problems with them in relation to my research project. Both concepts can be useful for church praxis, but perhaps have a tendency to encourage a simplification of processes and experiences which are always actually multi-dimensional and complex. A strength of Osmer's concept is, as John Klaasen formulates it, that he puts ecclesial and public practice at the center of his tasks. "In this stage we find . . . the postfoundationalist approach, in which we are forced to listen to the narratives of the people in real life situations."[37] In phenomenological hermeneutics these tendencies are not ignored but the targets are more modest and the outcome uncertain.

Kathleen Cahalan and James Nieman are critical of the model of seeing-interpreting-judging-acting,[38] and envisage a danger in any model that shoehorns practical theology narrowly into one stage in a process. I agree with Swinton and Mowat that practical theology appropriately uses the "language of themes and patterns, rather than systems and universal concepts, seeking to draw us into the divine mystery"[39] of complex situations and contexts.

A further discussion within the field of qualitative research and especially within phenomenological approaches concerns the validity of structuring a piece of research by beginning with a literature review of the theme being researched—in that doing so seems to preclude the possibility of finding anything unexpected in one's research. Within the iterative framework of a practice-theory-practice approach with its awareness of the hermeneutical circle, the question surrounding how much pre-knowledge of a phenomenon is helpful or not remains debatable. I have chosen to orientate myself to the conclusions suggested by Fry, Scammel, and Barker[40]—that a certain amount of transparently shown research around a phenomenon is sensible and helpful in order to enable the focus of the research to be named in a relevant way.

---

37. Klaasen, "Practical Theology," 3–7.
38. Cahalan and Nieman, "Mapping the Field."
39. Swinton and Mowat, *Practical Theology*, 46.
40. Fry et al., "Muddying the Waters," 1.

When I started to prepare my empirical research, it was autumn 2018. The context was different then. No one thought of social distancing, COVID-19 was as yet unknown, and the thought of not holding the hand of a dying person because that kind of proximity could be dangerous were not part of my reflection. The world entered into a global crisis in 2020 and its consequences are still not foreseeable. I decided to revisit some of my interviewees who were still alive in autumn 2020 to make sure that I had taken their experiences sufficiently seriously during the first lockdown in Switzerland and to ask how they had experienced that period. I describe the consequent change in the research process later in the analytical part of the thesis where I describe why this change was necessary. Some of the interviewees had died before COVID-19 changed our society and world. I consider it to be a vital and particularly interesting part of my thesis to have captured interviews just before the pandemic began and then a few weeks after the lockdown. This new situation had an impact on my research questions and helped me to deepen my perception of the comfort-dimensions in the experiences of faithful Christians at the end of their lives.

The pandemic situation also made me increasingly aware that the process of qualitative research and interviewing requires a great deal of reflexivity. It was essential to frame a research question that fit the study well and to make clear what setting is helpful and what was the exact nature of the researcher's role.[41] Before I prepared my methodological section in detail, I wanted to formulate a starting and reference point. That reference point is a definition of practical theology as:

> *A reflective and critical investigation of the praxis of the church which is part of the world. It is God's purpose to comfort and redeem his creation through his triune essence, known to us first through Scripture but also through Christian traditions and experiences. Practical theology is in critical dialogue with other disciplines in theology but also with other sources of knowledge, in a critical correlation*[42] *with other sciences.*[43] Next to hermeneutical

---

41. King and Horrocks offer helpful insights about interview work: *Interviews in Qualitative Research*.

42. See Tillich, *Systematische Theologie*.

43. Important in this discussion in the context of this study is Miller-McLemore and her thoughts of the "living human web" and Gerkin's work "Living Human Document"; also helpful is Mason, *Qualitative Research* and Silverman, *Interpreting Qualitative Data*.

> *skills and theoretical reflection practical theology is committed to faithful spirituality and church praxis.*[44]

My previous attempt to describe practical theology as a starting and reference point had focused on the influence of a specific church context, tradition, and spiritual formation—in my case of a Protestant (and more precisely of a Swiss Reformed Church) context. In my experience, faithful Christians are often trained to read Scripture and/or to regard Scripture reading as formative in their tradition. In preparing my research, I reflected on different sources of comfort and consolation in the Bible. This reflection and rereading of different Bible passages was helpful for me as a researcher.

To prepare the empirical work, I had to identify the need for further research in my field and to read what scholars in theology and other disciplines have said about comfort and consolation at the end of life.

---

44. Browning, *Moral Context of Pastoral Care*, 14.; Fowler, "Practical Theology," 149; Swinton and Mowat, *Practical Theology*, 4.

2

Inquiring into comfort and consolation in the Bible, in literature, and in the experiences of practicing Christians at the end of their lives

COMFORT IN THE BIBLE AND IN LITERATURE

REFERRING TO THE DESCRIPTION I gave in the introduction[1] concerning my understanding of the basis of practical theology, I believe it is God's purpose to comfort and redeem his creation through his triune essence, known to us first through Scripture but also through Christian traditions and experiences. Practical theology, as I wrote, is in critical dialogue with other disciplines in theology but also with other sources of knowledge, in a critical correlation with other sciences. This understanding forms the framework for the decision I made to look at the biblical sources for meanings around comfort and consolation and also the discussion of the theme in literature before I moved to the methodology for the empirical part of my research.

Also, as I wrote in the introduction, reading the Bible is a formative element of the spirituality of Reformed Christians and both the people I interviewed and I myself have been and are constantly being moulded by our reading of and reference to Scripture. As a researcher, I prepared

1. Osmer, *Practical Theology*, 16.

my research process through the study of different Bible passages which seemed to me vital for the topic of comfort and consolation in general and of comfort and consolation concerning suffering, sickness and death. Within an awareness of the discussions surrounding phenomenology within the hermeneutical circle,[2] this was necessary to help me develop a vocabulary around the theme of comfort and consolation which would be useful and relevant in preparing sensible questions for the interviews and for the conversation with the interviewees. I was aware of my need of sufficient knowledge of my theme, so that I would notice the nuances of what might being said while I listened carefully to the rich descriptions of the interviewees.

In chapter 4 I shall continue to reflect on biblical lines of thought but then as they emerge in correlation with the findings from the interviews.

In this chapter I recall first the meaning of comfort or consolation within the Hebrew and Greek language and how it is used in different texts of the Old and New Testament. Because the exegetical research on this is extensive, it is only possible to give a brief overview, which includes reflecting on some of the biblical uses of the words and the process of translating different Hebrew texts into Greek. Second, I look at different fields of research around the theme of comfort and consolation in literature.

Comfort and Consolation in the Bible

In general, one can say that the meaning of comfort or consolation only becomes evident in experiences and life situations of suffering, grief, pain, or loss. The Bible has numerous texts and narratives in which people are in need of comfort and consolation. Comfort relates to either taking away suffering or dwelling more peacefully and sustainably within it. The most frequently encountered Hebrew term is "נחם /niham" and in Greek "παρακάλεω/parakaleo"; "παράκλησις/paraklesis."[3] In both Testaments the semantic breadth of meaning is wide. There are different levels of meaning, for instance, in the active or passive use of the word: "to comfort" or "to be comforted" or the aspects of "human comfort" and "God's comfort." It can be seen as vital for the present or the future and

---

2. See the aforementioned article: Fry et al. "Muddying the Waters," 1–6.

3. See: Bauer, *Wörterbuch zum Neuen Testament*, 1223–27. The meaning of "comfort" is especially strong in the Greek word and noun "paraklesis." Bauer shows that this understanding is also vital for the Greek version of the Old Testament (LXX).

References to comfort and consolation in the Old Testament

The Hebrew root is נחם nḥm. In the Pi.-Form the verb means consoling /comforting /changing of the heart,[4] in Pu. "to be comforted," in Nif. "to repent or to let something be repented of" or "to be comforted / to have pity / to take pity for someone / to have mercy." In Hitp. the meanings are "to feel pity /to repent /to be comforted /to take revenge." In nominal formations, on the other hand, only the meaning "comfort/consolation" is relevant for my purposes.[5] The translation of the Hebrew text into a Greek version affected how comfort was understood, as I explain further in the observations concerning the New Testament.

Such divergent aspects of meaning need an explanation.[6] First of all, we can assume that both the experience of comfort and the experience of suffering were situations that evoked in a person a sense of depression and even near suffocation. The subject of נחם wants a change and is affected in different ways and aspects of their being by the suffering or the situation. Where the root נחם is used in the Old Testament, the word used evokes relief, in the case of respiratory distress, for instance, the relief which is felt when deep breaths can again be taken.

In such an instance, achieving comfort or consolation would imply again being able to breathe and thus return to life. Here, the connection between "nefesch/ נֶפֶשׁ" (often translated as "soul" but more correctly understood as "living human being"[7]) and consolation (compare Pss 77:3, 94:19) would seem to refer to the whole of a human being. Similarly, the phrase דבר עַל לֵב, "to talk to the heart," has the ultimate goal of helping to

---

4. Brown et al., *Hebrew and English Lexicon*, 636–37.

5. Riede, "Trost."

6. For such different explanatory approaches, see Jeremias, *Aspekte alttestamentalischer Gottesvorstellung*; Riede, *Trost*, 138.

7. Nefesch can be understood as a vital nucleus, as elemental potentiality. Included in this understanding of nefesch is both this one indivisible person before God as well as this person in their entire existence and basis of herself life possibilities with their physicality, sociality, past, and future. The Hebrew term "nefesch," with its 754 nominal and 3 verbal uses as well as its wide use in Old Testament literature, belongs or refers to the core words/meanings, which denote the human being in this corpus of writings. Among the concrete meanings of this term are "throat" and "breath"; see Van Oorschot, "Leben/naefaesch."

remove emotional pressure from a human being. Thus: "When the cares of my heart are many, your consolations cheer my soul" (Ps 94:19 ESV). These kinds of comfort experiences can prevent a person from "freezing" and being crushed or undone by the tightness of one's of the heart. "Relieve the troubles of my heart and free me from my anguish" (Ps 25:17 NIV).[8]

In the Hebrew texts as well as in the Greek translation of the Septuagint, the expressions of need for comfort and consolation and descriptions of experiences of comfort include divine and human aspects. This I explore in more detail in the following paragraph. Next to biblical passages on Job, Jacob, and Joseph, and passages with more political and communal contexts, descriptions and instances of individual experiences and expressions of emotions like comfort are found particularly in the texts of the psalms, and in Isaiah, especially in chapters 40 to 66.

As already mentioned, to be in the need of comfort is above all a human experience of suffering, loss, and grief. Especially on the occasion of mourning for a deceased person, the consolation of mourners, relatives, and friends are part of a lived comfort praxis. This comfort praxis is seen among the people of Israel as well as in other cultures or nations.[9] Such comfort occurs not only through the presence of others, through prayers or words, but also through, for instance, gifts of drinks and food, such as the "cup of consolation" or the "mourning bread" (Jer 16; Ezek 24, 17:22; Hos 69:4) as well as through gifts that are an expression of helping solidarity (Job 42:14). The aim of consolation is described in a holistic way as strengthening a person or persons. Especially in the book of Job, the solidarity of the friends of Job becomes visible in their willingness to mourn with him and not to leave him alone in his distress. Although particular aspects of comfort are present, Job does not experience comfort from his conversations with his friends. Thus, the comforting visit is helpful (Job 2:11–13), but the conversation (Job 4–6) of his friends, in which they resort to traditional attempts to explain Job's suffering, such as the act/consequence connection (Job 4:7), Job regards as highly unsuccessful consolation.[10] It is only through the encounter with YHWH and the consequent broadening of his horizons (Job 38:1–16) that Job experiences consolation. Given such a mixed experience, it is all the more remarkable that Job is capable of combining complaints with a confession of

---

8. See Weber, *Werkbuch Psalmen*, 132–35.

9. See for instance Kittel, *Theologisches Wörterbuch*, 778–85.

10. "I have heard many things like these; you are miserable comforters, all of you!" (Job 16:2 NIV).

trust (Job 16:18–19 NIV). Thus, he begins with the appeal, "Earth, do not cover my blood; may my cry never be laid to rest!" and the affirmation, "Even now my witness is in heaven; my advocate is on high." Remarkably, shortly afterwards he draws comfort not from those "miserable comforters" of friends, but from his own stalwart faith, declaring: "I know that my redeemer lives, and that in the end he will stand on the earth. . . . I myself will see him with my own eyes—I, and not another. How my heart yearns within me!" (Job 19:25–27 NIV).[11] It is a consoling declaration of trust *in extremis* amid lament, mourning, and doubt.

To take another example, over a period of many years Jacob is inconsolable because of the news of Joseph's supposed death (Gen 37:35). Only when he receives the news that Joseph is alive does Jacob's breath "revive" (Gen 45:27). Finally, Joseph shows himself to be a comforter to his brothers, despite all the harm they have done him, speaking kindly to them and also offering them care and much-needed life-giving support (Gen 50:19–21). By essentially forgiving them and re-instating their health and their relationship to him, he enables their lasting and peaceful coexistence.

In a larger and more political context, consolation can be an expression of good neighborly relationships, for example when neighboring states offer condolences on the death of a monarch (2 Sam 10:2). In short, besides an emotional aspect to consolation, there is also a social one, which has an important unifying and edifying effect for groups, communities, and even states.

The Bible also includes examples of consolation being needed by persons living in a foreign country (Ruth 2:13) or in exile (prophetic texts such as in Jeremiah). Not only individuals, but the whole people of Israel find themselves amidst the distress of exile, abandoned by all comforters. The book of Lamentations illustrates the hopeless situation of Jerusalem and the people of Israel in view of their destruction. Behind the statement "no one is there to comfort them" stands implicitly the question of

---

11. Redeemer: *Goël*: Bible references: Job 19:25; Ps 19:14; 78:35; Prov 23:11 (Defender in NIV, Advocate in Msg); Isa 41:14; 43:14; 44:6, 24; 47:4; 48:17; 49:26; 54:5, 8; 59:20; 60:16; Jer 50:34. The words of Job have been immortalized in Händel's *Messiah*: "For I know that my redeemer liveth, and that he shall stand at the latter day upon the earth" (Job 19:25 KJV). Similar names for God are: Our Redeemer from of old, Redeemer of Israel, and Deliverer. Six times the name "Redeemer" is linked to the Holy One of Israel (Isa 41:14; 43:14; 47:4; 48:17; 49:7; 54:5). These suggest that the terms "Comforter" and "Redeemer" are closely related, if not synonyms.

what is the attitude of YHWH, the God of Israel, towards the destiny of his people.

> Bitterly she weeps at night, tears are on her cheeks. Among all her lovers there is no one to comfort her. (Lamentations)

Such examples suggest that aspects of divine and human comfort cannot be totally separated from one another. They form aspects of an approach to human wellbeing in the Old Testament which is wholistic, an approach in which the spiritual dimension of a person's experience is not seen as separate from other dimensions. I expand upon this topic in the theological response, where I connect comfort with the biblical vision of shalom that comes out of the research and its findings.

The book of Isaiah deepens our understanding of comfort and consolation in the Old Testament writings. As a main source of such references and discussions, Isaiah is then also a central textual reference for the New Testament and the apostle Paul's epistles. The book of Isaiah reacts to the bitter situation of Jerusalem in exile and in post-exilic times, and it emphasizes God's comforting message to his people and to the city of Jerusalem, a message which gives new purpose and hope to his people (Isa 40:1 NIV, "Comfort, comfort my people, says your God."). Especially in Isaiah 40 to 66, the motive of consolation and comfort and the frequent use of the word נחם/nicham are common threads that run through the texts of Isaiah (Isa 40:1; 49:13; 51:3, 12; 52:9). Here the absolution of guilt is strongly connected to comfort. The consolation comes from YHWH himself (Isa 51:12) and apparently has significance for all of creation (Isa 49:13 NIV: "Shout for joy, o heavens; rejoice, o earth; burst into song, o mountains! For the Lord comforts his people and will have compassion on his afflicted ones.") and for all nations (Isa 52:9 NIV: "Burst into songs of joy together, your ruins of Jerusalem, for the Lord has comforted his people.").

In the last chapter of Isaiah, the consolation motif is linked to the image of a mother. On the one hand, this image refers to Zion/Jerusalem, the city that gives birth to children, nourishes them and holds them in intimate physical contact, bringing joy to the mourners.

> Rejoice with Jerusalem and be glad for her, all you who love her. Rejoice greatly with her, all you who mourn over her. For you will nurse and be satisfied at her comforting breasts, you will drink deeply and delight in her overflowing abundance. (Isa 66:10–11 NIV)

On the other hand, YHWH himself becomes the comforter who turns to Zion like a mother.[12] "As a mother comforts her child, so will I comfort you; and you will be comforted over Jerusalem" (Isa 66:13 NIV). Reflecting Isa 40–66, one can read about the comfort-ministry of the expected Messiah and find quotations that are used in the Gospels, the epistles, and in the book of Revelation in the New Testament.[13] Especially for Isaiah, comfort is both an encouraging and admonishing force against despair and destruction in the present time and one that includes an eschatological vision of God's coming. It includes a "here and now" and also "a waiting for" and can be understood as being intrinsically connected with God's promises and with faith in God as savior.[14]

In the Psalms one finds rich descriptions and expressions of personal experiences and encounters with God. They are individual and unique prayers, and their particular context, the time and situation in which they were formed, are often neither clear or obvious. They can be understood as testimonies, as experience, or as part of lived religious praxis. They are written in a poetic style and use numerous metaphors.[15] Some of the psalms describe a process of searching for divine comfort, or searching for meaning and hope for the future, especially in situations of suffering, danger, and persecution (Pss 86:14–17, 94:19). One metaphor used here is God as shepherd. Trusting God as a good shepherd, Ps 23 invites the one praying to open themselves to God's comfort, to God with us. The same psalm also shows comforting closeness, affection, and promotion of life through God in the meal, which the shepherd prepares for the person (Ps 23:5). The metaphors of eating and drinking and through that of being strengthened point to the createdness of humans and their need for both actual food, and also for spiritual nourishment. Through metaphors, the psalm as a whole reminds the reader that they are not traveling through life alone but with a God who cares and comforts in the broader

---

12. This comforting image is important for the representations of Mary and Jesus in the different church traditions. Did the radical changes in the Reformations era, especially in the reformed denominations, take away from Christians a vital precognitive comfort dimension?

13. To understand better the dimension of comfort in the book of Isaiah and the deep meaning of the expected comforter, see, for instance, Tiemeyer, *For the Comfort of Zion*; Goldingay, *Theology of the Book of Isaiah*.

14. See Bieringer, "Comforted Comforter."

15. See Seybold, *Introducing the Psalms*; Seybold, *Poetik der Psalmen*; Zenger, *Psalmen*.

understanding of the word, which includes admonishing and advocating (Ps 23:4 NIV, "your rod and your staff, they comfort me").

But in this "prayer book," there are very different psalms, used by Jews and Christians. Not only are there different genres of psalms, for example hymns of thanksgiving,[16] lament,[17] or supplication;[18] sometimes one can even find different aspects combined in one psalm as we see for instance in Ps 73. Lamenting with and before God is also a central aspect of the psalms and plays a significant role in discussions of comfort and consolation and dealing with experiences of suffering. Examples include: "Why, Lord, do you stand far off? Why do you hide yourself in times of trouble?" (Ps 10:1 NIV) and "My soul is in deep anguish. How long, Lord, how long?" (Ps 6:3 NIV). Even in a situation of utter desolation, lamentation before God can become a cry for help and comfort.[19] The prerequisite for consolation and comfort is experiencing distress and suffering. The psalms encourage the individual and the community not to be ashamed of the need of comfort but to share their concrete situations, questions, and experiences of suffering experiences with God, alone or in community. To be able to speak with God like this can enable the sufferer or sufferers to breathe new life and hope into a space of despair.[20] The Old Testament professor Walter Brueggemann writes of these breaths, these moves, like this:

> The life of faith expressed in the Psalms is focused on the two decisive moves of faith that are always underway, by which we are regularly surprised and which we regularly resist. One move we make is out of a settled orientation into a season of disorientation.... It is that move that characterizes much of the Psalms in the form of complaint and lament. The complaint psalm is a painful, anguished articulation of a move into disarray and dislocation.... The other move we make is a move from a context of disorientation to a new orientation, surprised by a new gift

---

16. For instance Ps 103.
17. For instance Ps 69.
18. For instance Ps 86.

19. This is described in more detail in the theological response in ch. 4: "Prayer, Lament and Comfort in the Experiences of Christians through the Lens of Theological Thinkers."

20. See: Brueggemann, *Message of the Psalms*; Brueggemann, *Psalms*; Brueggemann, *Spirituality of the Psalms*; Wagensommer, *Klagepsalmen und Seelsorge*; Vos, *Theopoetry in the Psalms*.

from God, a new coherence made present to us just when we thought all was lost.[21]

Another special form of divine comfort is found, for instance, in Ps 119. Here, its transmission is bound to the divine word, which unfolds its power to the worshiper or worshipers and keeps them alive in the face of distress and even restores them to life (Ps 119:50). The divine word is reminiscent of the manifold experiences of the affection and grace of God (Ps 119:76), which enforces God's righteousness in the world and God's vision of shalom (Ps 119:52). The richness of the psalms lies in the poetic language, the different images and metaphors they use to capture experience, but also in the willingness not to hide but to be open to a God who is a trustworthy foundation of life. The psalms surface lived experiences in words which often also have an aesthetic dimension of beauty and transcendence, experiences which are formed with words and at the same time are beyond words. Without going into detail about the individual metaphors and words below, the following examples show something of the richness of beauty and metaphor in the psalms:

> He drew me up from the pit of destruction, out of the miry bog. (Ps 40:2 ESV)

> You have delivered my soul from the depths of Sheol. (Ps 86:10 ESV).

> Lead me to the rock that is higher than I, for you have been my refuge, a strong tower against the enemy... Let me dwell in your tent for ever! O to be safe under the shelter of your wings. (Ps 61:2a–4 ESV)

> Be merciful to me, O God ... for in you my soul takes refuge, in the shadow of your wings I will take refuge. (Ps 57:1 ESV)

> Even though I walk through the valley of the shadow of death, I will fear no evil, for you are with me, your rod and your staff they comfort me. (Ps 23:4 ESV)

The psalms remind us that everything can be brought to speech, and every emotional disposition can be addressed to God, whom they recognize as the final reference point for all of life. In short,

---

21. Brueggemann, *Spirituality of the Psalms*, 9–11.

> The psalms are not used in a vacuum, but in a history where we are dying and rising, and in a history where God is at work, ending our lives and making gracious new beginnings for us. The psalms move with our experience.[22]

Through these references and descriptions, it becomes apparent that there is no single clear definition of comfort and consolation in the Old Testament, but a multiplicity of expressions to articulate hoping for or experiencing change or a "changing of the heart," the relief of anguish, or relief from fear or suffering.

In a biblical understanding, comfort is thus that which strengthens life. The heart and life-force of the suffering person or community are strengthened through specific aspects or expressions of comfort (see for example: Ps 71:20, 23; Ps 94:19; Isa 40:1–2; Isa 66:14). To experience comfort, this "new orientation" often entails not only a spiritual change but also a larger holistic process that provides physical, emotional, and/or social relief. It includes individual and communal aspects. Comfort experiences have an emotional and spiritual effect and often go hand in hand with gestures and embodied actions that can include signs and symbols and life-sustaining practical help (Isa 40:1, 51:19, 66:12). The different biblical texts of the Old Testament, especially the Psalms, the book of Lamentations, Job, and Isaiah, all invite us to see that being in the need of comfort and experiencing being comforted is part of our humanity, our being created in time and space. The biblical texts encourage the individual and community to address their questions, their longing, and their experiences of suffering to the God who is known as the comforter *par excellence* throughout Scripture.

References to comfort and consolation in the New Testament

Beginning in the third century BCE, the sacred writings of Israel, starting with the Pentateuch, were translated from Hebrew into Greek by Hellenistic Jews. From the middle of the second century BCE, this translation work included most of the writings that are fundamental to the faith of Israel. Work on individual Scriptures continued into era of the New Testament, particularly work on the Psalms. Even before the completion of the translation of all the Scriptures now contained in the Septuagint, collections of texts were created, and these soon became important among

---

22. Brueggemann, *Praying the Psalms*, 15.

Hellenistic Jews.²³ When Luke, Paul, or other New Testament authors quote from Isaiah or the Psalms, they also use the Greek language, and thus phrases and language which were familiar to others of the time through the Greek translations.

The New Testament generally uses the verb παρακαλέω and the noun παράκλησις to describe comfort experience. It is interesting that in the Septuagint²⁴ different verbs are used to translate into Greek the Hebrew נחם / nicham, among them παρακαλέω or παράκλησις.²⁵ Indeed, in the New Testament there are 109 occurrences of the verb παρακαλέω and 29 of the noun παράκλησις. Before I turn to specific biblical passages to illustrate this, I note some of the meanings of the Greek word and its possible translations. Similar to the various meanings of nicham/ נחם in the Hebrew Bible, the New Testament Greek Lexicon translates and explains παρακάλέω and παράκλησις with a wide range of meanings, such as: calling near, calling for help, admonition, encouragement, consolation, comfort, solace, persuasive discourse, and stirring address.²⁶

The New Testament develops the understanding and meaning of comfort along the lines of the Old Testament and God's promises. For example, Luke 2:25 describes Simeon as waiting for the "comfort for Israel" (παράκλησις).²⁷ Later in the Luke 4, Jesus himself uses the words of the prophet Isaiah to describe the centrality of "comfort ministry" and mission of the expected Messiah:

---

23. Kittel, *Theologisches Wörterbuch*, 776.

24. The Septuagint (LXX) is the Greek version of the Jewish Scriptures redacted by Jewish scholars in the third and second centuries BCE and later adopted by Greek-speaking Christians.

25. Kittel, *Theologisches Wörterbuch*, 774-75.

26. Thayer, *Thayer's Greek-English Lexicon*, 482-83.

27. Here, in Luke 2, Simeon embodies the promise of God from the prophet Isaiah: to wait for the comfort of Israel means to wait for the Messiah, the Christ (v. 26). He is the one who was promised in God's word (Isa 40:5; 52:10) to be the Messiah for Israel and for the whole world. *Comforter* also refers to the one who brings salvation, the light of the world, and the glory of Israel: "Simeon was waiting for the consolation of Israel, and the Holy Spirit was on him. It had been revealed to him by the Holy Spirit that he would not die before he had seen the Lord's Messiah. . . . When the parents brought in the child Jesus to do for him what the custom of the Law required, Simeon took him in his arms and praised God, saying: 'Sovereign Lord, as you have promised, you may now dismiss your servant in peace. For my eyes have seen your salvation, which you have prepared in the sight of all nations: a light for revelation to the Gentiles, and the glory of your people Israel.'" (Luke 2:25-32 NIV).

> The Spirit of the Lord is on me, because he has anointed me to proclaim good news to the poor. He has sent me to proclaim freedom for the prisoners and recovery of sight for the blind, to set the oppressed free, to proclaim the year of the Lord's favor. (Luke 4:18–19 NIV)

> The Spirit of the Sovereign Lord is on me, because the Lord has anointed me to proclaim good news to the poor. He has sent me to bind up the broken hearted, to proclaim freedom for the captives and release from darkness for the prisoners, to proclaim the year of the Lord's favor and the day of vengeance of our God, to comfort all who mourn, and provide for those who grieve in Zion; to bestow on them a crown of beauty instead of ashes, the oil of joy, instead of mourning, and a garment of praise, instead of a spirit of despair. They will be called oaks of righteousness, a planting of the Lord for the display of his splendor. (Isa 61:1–4 NIV)

Jesus reveals himself by referring to the prophet Isaiah and to God's promise as the comforter, the expected comforting Messiah, "Menachem,"[28] whose ministry includes salvation and healing as Simeon confesses in a prayer at the end of his life, quoting the words from Isaiah and from the psalms.[29]

The authors of the New Testament confess and experience Jesus as the promised comforter as well as the savior. For the Messiah Jesus to comfort means to help,[30] to encourage, but also admonish, and to call the individual, his people, and all of humanity into the redeeming and freeing light of God's salvation and righteousness.

In the New Testament, the messianic mission of Jesus is linked with numerous narratives, psalms, and prophetic texts of the Old Testament and God's promise to renew his "shalom," which includes God's communication with humans but also with the whole of creation. "For God so loved the world that he gave his one and only Son, that whoever believes in him shall not perish but have eternal life" (John 3:16 NIV). It is noticeable how much the understanding of comfort and consolation of the New Testament is formed by the psalms and through texts of the

---

28. In biblical times the expected Messiah was referred to as "Menachem," Comforter. See Botterweck, *Theologisches Wörterbuch*.

29. Luke 2:30–32.

30. See, for instance, Jesus' healing ministry in the gospels, especially in Luke 5, 7, 8, and 18.

prophet Isaiah. Next to the famous text in Matt 5–7, in the Sermon on the Mount, and especially in the Beatitudes where Jesus emphasizes that mourners will be comforted (Matt 5:4), Paul's letters are a particularly fruitful source of comfort and consolation.

Paul expresses in different ways that God is the source of all comfort. He sees the comfort that God gives to all believers in the framework of a charismatic gift which flows into the community and works through each person comforting the other (Rom 12:8; 1 Cor 14:3). All consolation ultimately is based in God himself, as the introductory text of 2 Corinthians emphasizes (2 Cor 1:3–5 NIV):

> Praise be to the God and Father of our Lord Jesus Christ, the Father of compassion and the God of all comfort, who comforts us in all our troubles, so that we can comfort those in any trouble with the comfort we ourselves received from God. For just as we share abundantly in the sufferings of Christ, so also our comfort abounds through Christ.

The Christian community is able both to receive comfort from God and others, and to pass on consolation to one another, thus creating a community in which comfort and consolation play a central part and through which the disciples of Christ are encouraged on their path through life. This community reacts to the various suffering experiences of its members and is there for them when in despair, need, sickness, and at the end of their lives.

As long as Christians are part of this world, they are bound, as are all humans and indeed creation itself, to the experiences of space, time, body, and mortality, and therefore the need for comfort also remains.[31] This reality Paul describes in his epistle to the Roman Christian community:

> We know that the whole creation has been groaning in labour pains until now; and not only the creation, but we ourselves, who have the first fruits of the Spirit, groan inwardly while we wait for adoption, the redemption of our bodies. (Rom 8:22 NRSV)

---

31. See Wendland, *Briefe an die Korinther*. In his hermeneutical reflection, Wendland writes that, "Paul's understanding of comfort shows that he experiences suffering and comfort to such an extreme extent, that he likes to share the experience with the Corinthian community. God's comfort is a saving power where he found himself without strength and in total despair," 169.

New Testament professor Linda McKinnish Bridges, in her article on "Paul's Words of Comfort in First Thessalonians,"[32] emphasizes that Paul not only experienced suffering, sickness, and life-threatening situations, and found God's comfort in them, but also that he was sharing in the sufferings of Christians and their communities with deep concern and engagement. One example of this comes from that letter's second chapter:

> Just as a nursing mother cares for her children, so we cared for you. Because we loved you so much, we were delighted to share with you not only the gospel of God but our lives as well. (1 Thess 2:7b-8 NIV)[33]

Paul's language here shows deep affection for the Thessalonian believers, a church community founded by the apostle Paul in his early missionary years. This text and others bring to the surface that these letters are real-life documents written to a real group of people with meaningful experiences. In reading and receiving letters from Paul, the church community is experiencing comfort, the letters and their expressions of comfort being a substitute for Paul's physical presence in his absence.[34] McKinnish Bridges sees the relationship between Paul and the community as a friendship. That means Paul in writing wanting to comfort others, to share faith and faith experiences.

This comfort dimension is taken up by New Testament scholar Rudolf Bultmann who wrote in his commentary on the Second Letter to the Corinthians: "Every compassion and every comfort has its origins in God.... He is the subject of comfort and consolation."[35] And the German practical theologian Helmut Tacke reflects similarly to Bultmann on this biblical passage:

> As the "God of all consolation" God is from the outset and in himself determined by the pathos of being connected to desolate persons. Wherever suffering and desperate people are left with a trace of consolation, no matter how small, the consoling God is involved.[36]

---

32. McKinnish Bridges, "Paul's Words."

33. My own translation: "As a nursing mother, thus, having deep longing (*homeiromenoi*) for you all, we are delighted to share with you not only the gospel of God, but also our own selves, because you have become dear to us" (1 Thess 2:7b-8).

34. See Struthers Malbon, "No Need," 71.

35. Bultmann, *Zweite Korintherbrief*, 28.

36. Tacke, *Glaubenshilfe als Lebenshilfe*, "Als 'Gott allen Trostes' ist er von vorherein und in sich selbst von dem Pathos bestimmt, dem trostlosen Menschen verbunden zu

That human comfort is essential to the lives of Christians is clear to the apostle Paul and can be seen in different passages, for example at the beginning of Col 2:

> For I would that you knew what great conflict I have for you, and for them at Laodicea, and for as many as have not seen my face in the flesh; That their hearts might be comforted, being knit together in love, and unto all riches of the full assurance of understanding, to the acknowledgement of the mystery of God, and of the Father, and of Christ. In whom are hid all the treasures of wisdom and knowledge. (Col 2:1–3 KJV)

Coming back to the epistle to the Romans, the apostle Paul confesses that no power, no suffering, "nor anything else in all creation, will be able to separate us from the love of God that is in Christ Jesus our Lord" (Rom 8:37), a confession that many Christians regard as the quintessence of a faith experience of comfort.

In Rom 12, Paul teaches the church what it means to live as the body of Christ in community. In v. 8 of that chapter he writes that the charisma of comfort and consolation is an important ministry (εἴτε ὁ παρακαλῶν ἐν τῇ παρακλήσει), next to prophecy, practical service, teaching, and leading. Although it is often translated with "encourage," the Greek word παρακάλεω has a variety of meanings beyond "encourage," such as to admonish. Paul argues in 1 Cor 12:4–5 that, "There are different kinds of gifts, but the same Spirit. There are different kinds of service, but the same Lord."

Within the New Testament there are further texts important for our purposes here, for example in the Gospel of John. Jesus, the Messiah and comforter, promises (in chapter 14) that God will send the disciples the Holy Spirit, the "paraclete."

> Do not let your hearts be troubled.... I will ask the Father, and he will give you another comforter/advocate to help you and be with you forever; the Spirit of truth.... I will not leave you as orphans; I will come to you. Before long, the world will not see me anymore, but you will see me. Because I live, you also will live. On that day you will realize that I am in my Father, and you are in me, and I am in you. Whoever has my commands and keeps them is the one who loves me. The one who loves me will be loved by my Father, and I too will love them and show myself

---

sein. Wo immer Leidenden und Verzweifelten eine noch so schmale tröstliche Spur erschlossen wird, ist der tröstende Gott beteiligt," 233.

to them.... But the paraclete, the Holy Spirit, whom the Father will send in my name, will teach you all things and will remind you of everything I have said to you. Peace I leave with you; my peace I give you. I do not give to you as the world gives. Do not let your hearts be troubled and do not be afraid. (John 14:1–27 NIV, with my own translation around the word "paraclete")

These words remind us that the Holy Spirit is given and is present as a comforter in our world of troubles, grief, and suffering. The comforter, the Holy Spirit, is God's power which will not leave the earth without hope nor the church alone in despair or affliction. This is a central biblical promise and correlates with the promises of the Old Testament, which I mentioned in the previous paragraphs. The Christian hope is founded on believing and trusting that God can be thought of and experienced as the comforter and encourager, both a gentle supporting and caring divine essence and a strong and interceding power.[37]

A further narrative in the New Testament to do with comfort is the passion story of Christ. Through the different narratives in the gospels, we learn that Jesus himself shared not only the need for comfort (for instance in the Garden of Gethsemane), but also experienced desolation in his suffering–witness his quoting Ps 22 on the cross. The different texts of the gospels portray Jesus' suffering in the face of his death and dying, and his own need for comfort being very present. This we see especially when Jesus asks some of his close friends to stay and pray with him the night before his crucifixion. Jesus asks for their presence, their prayers–to minister to him in his suffering with comfort. But his friends are too tired to stay with him and not able to support him by offering him their comfort in his extreme suffering and fear.

> Then Jesus went with his disciples to a place called Gethsemane, and he said to them, "Sit here while I go over there and pray." He took Peter and the two sons of Zebedee along with him, and he began to be sorrowful and troubled. Then he said to them, "My soul is overwhelmed with sorrow to the point of death. Stay here and keep watch with me." Going a little farther, he fell with his face to the ground and prayed, "My Father, if it is possible, may this cup be taken from me. Yet not as I will, but as you will." Then he returned to his disciples and found them sleeping. (Matt 26:36–40 NIV)

---

37. The mystic Julian of Norwich meditated on this concept of divine love in her "Showings" and could thus describe Christ as mother—meaning as the source of comfort. See Julian of Norwich, *Showings*. See Hall, *Laughing at the Devil*.

Three times Jesus prayed in great distress, twice returning to his friends and to ask for support and comfort, but each time finding them asleep. In praying to God and longing for the consolation of friends, Jesus shows that he is in need of divine and human comfort in his suffering. In his suffering and dying, Jesus experienced not only the failure of human comfort but also the seeming unattainability of closeness to God.

In summary, we can see that the themes of comfort and consolation in the New Testament are connected to that of the Old Testament, and that the presence of the Messiah and the Holy Spirit are an answer to the expected comforting and helping presence of God for Israel and the world. Although the disciples of Christ experience the presence of God in Jesus, by that point the full promise of God's shalom is not yet fulfilled. The New Testament takes this up in its eschatological vision of the coming kingdom. This kind of vision allows the faithful to understand their experiences of trouble and suffering but also of joy and reorientation as part of God's journey with them and with creation towards the fulfilment of all things.

The New Testament describes why and in which way Jesus Christ can be seen as the expected comforter and savior. This saving dimension is seen and rooted in the story of Christ, his life, passion, death and resurrection. Because the authors of the New Testament have faith in Jesus as the promised comforter of Israel and the world, they experience the comforting presence of the Holy Spirit, as was promised to them. Like all humans, Christians are in need comfort, but they particularly believe in the promise of God's comforting presence in life and death. The source of all comfort is God, and yet comfort is only of importance on the way towards the *telos* of the kingdom of God, where comfort and consolation will no longer be necessary—as we are reminded in the book of Revelation, which echoes Ezekiel, Isaiah, Jeremiah, and the psalms, for instance:

> And I heard a great voice out of heaven saying, Behold, the tabernacle of God is with men, and he will dwell with them, and they shall be his people, and God himself shall be with them, and be their God. And God shall wipe away all tears from their eyes; and there shall be no more death, neither sorrow, nor crying, neither shall there be any more pain: . . . I make all things new. . . . I am Alpha and Omega, the beginning and the end. I will give unto him that is athirst of the fountain of the water of life freely. (Rev 21:1–7 KJV)

Theological literature and perspectives of other disciplines on comfort

In my search for theological reflections on comfort and consolation at the end of life, I found few books specifically for Christians or for those within particular church traditions. Certainly, in reference works of pastoral care literature,[38] there is advice and commentary on the role of the pastor and about dying, funerals, and the importance of bereavement counselling. But these reflections do not explore individual Christians' experiences of comfort. There are single volumes and research works which consider the topic in more detail from the perspective of practical theology. One example is the book by Leonard Hummel, from a Lutheran tradition. In *Clothed in Nothingness*,[39] Hummel writes about what church members experience as helpful and as comforting, not only in death and dying but in a variety of circumstances in life. He helpfully describes a concrete Christian congregation and its teaching grounded in a particular church tradition. To this church tradition there belongs, for instance, a specific form of "the theology of the cross" or a specific theology of the sacraments or liturgical elements for worship. Another book *Living Well and Dying Faithfully*,[40] edited by John Swinton and Richard Payne, is an attempt at a theological answer to the rapid advancements in medicine, especially in end-of-life care. In that book, different authors from a variety of disciplinary perspectives reframe the role and the goals of medicine in the light of the mystery and power of the cross. For example:

> Christians confess that not even death can separate us from our Creator. As the apostle Paul puts it, 'I am convinced that neither death nor life . . . will be able to separate us from the love of God that is in Christ Jesus our Lord.' (Rom. 8:38–39) . . . For Christians the meaning of suffering is discerned within a specific narrative of creation and redemption, death and resurrection . . . We need to rediscover the fact that the process of dying is a deeply meaningful and spiritual human experience within which the search for God, meaning, hope, purpose, forgiveness, and even salvation should be seen as central to the tasks of end-of-life care.[41]

---

38. For example Turnbull, *Baker's Dictionary*, 297–302.; Atkinson and O'Donovan, *New Dictionary*; Migliore, "Death."
39. Hummel, *Clothed in Nothingness*.
40. Swinton and Payne, *Living Well*.
41. Swinton and Payne, *Living Well*, xvii.

This process of reflection allows church communities to rethink preparation for dying as a formative aspect of life.[42]

Although some of those authors include insights from individual experiences, upon which the reflect from a multidisciplinary angle, they do not present qualitative research on one specific church's engagement with dying Christians.

In *Dying in the Virtues*,[43] Matthew Levering discusses the theological and philosophical theme of *ars moriendi*,[44] the preparation for death, from a Roman Catholic perspective, which was a well-known topic throughout the Middle Ages and is also discussed in present times.[45] It is inspiring that Levering develops through the Christian virtues: Love, Hope and Faith a wide perspective of an *ars moriendi* for the present time where "gratitude," "solidarity," or "courage" have their place. He emphasizes, referring to the Swiss Roman Catholic theologian Hans Urs von Balthasar, that it is an important part of a Christian virtue ethic to experience living and dying as members of Christ's body. This, so Levering, has the potential to develop mindfulness and makes it possible to respect differences in church traditions.[46]

A further article discussing *ars moriendi*, in the continuing context surrounding COVID-19, is that of Bonnie J. Miller-McLemore.[47] She puts the theme of *ars moriendi* into a critical relation with the dominant medical perspective and discusses the purpose of contemporary practical theology within that perspective. Also, regarding contemporary approaches to *ars moriendi* practical theology has been influenced by the

---

42. Of interest here is the work of Hauerwas on suffering: *God, Medicine and Suffering*; Hauerwas, *Suffering Presence*; Hauerwas, *Character and the Christian Life*; Hauerwas, "Presence and Silence."

43. Levering, *Dying and the Virtues*.

44. *Ars moriendi* ("The Art of Dying") are two related Latin texts dating from about 1415 and 1450, which offer advice on the protocols and procedures of a good death, explaining how to "die well" according to Christian precepts of the late Middle Ages. It was written within the historical context of the effects of the macabre horrors of the Black Death sixty years earlier and consequent social upheavals of the fifteenth century. It was very popular, was translated into most Western European languages, and was the first in a Western literary tradition of guides to death and dying. About fifty thousand copies were printed in the years before 1501. See also Forcén and Forcén, "Ars Moriendi."

45. Resch, *Trost im Angesicht*; Schmid: "Kunst des Sterbens"; Schrock, *Consolation*.

46. Levering quotes a few theologians from the Orthodox Christian tradition. He does not discuss Protestant publications like those of Swinton and Hauerwas.

47. Miller-McLemore, "This Is My Body."

psychological and therapeutical discussion around the terms of resilience and coping. This interdisciplinary viewpoint has been helpful in the area of end-of-life care in general as the theme of comfort and consolation has been integrated as part of an approach which takes the specific situation of the person concerned seriously.[48]

The theme of comfort or consolation has been discussed in different traditions throughout the centuries. Brian S. Rosner, a New Testament scholar, shows in his book *The Consolation of Theology* that theological and philosophical questions are often intertwined within this discussion.[49] He criticizes the Enlightenment and the concept of the primacy of reason, which led theology to pay little attention to the personal and the emotional. Many important and influential theologians both pre- and post-Enlightenment (for example: Augustine, Thomas Aquinas, Luther, Kierkegaard, and Bonhoeffer)[50] in the history of the church have however emphasized the role of theology in affording genuine comfort in the face of life's difficulties, especially in suffering and dying. Rosner highlights that a historical understanding of comfort in the different theological concepts is helpful and that it can enrich reflection within the human sciences as well. Unfortunately, there is not a single woman's perspective on comfort present in Rosner's collection. No doubt mystics, like Julian of Norwich,[51] who lived through the massive destruction of the Black Death, would be an excellent source for such a perspective.

48. See Welter and Hildenbrand, *Resilienz*, 67.

49. Rosner, *Consolation of Theology*.

50. Unfortunately, two important quotations by Bonhoeffer on grief and loss are not reflected in this book:
"There is nothing that can replace the absence of someone dear to us, and one should not even attempt to do so. One must simply hold out and endure it. At first that sounds very hard, but at the same time it is also a great comfort. For to the extent the emptiness truly remains unfilled one remains connected to the other person through it. It is wrong to say that God fills the emptiness. God in no way fills it but much more leaves it precisely unfilled and thus helps us preserve—even in pain—the authentic relationship. Furthermore, the more beautiful and fuller the remembrances, the more difficult the separation. But gratitude transforms the torment of memory into silent joy. One bears what was lovely in the past not as a thorn but as a precious gift deep within, a hidden treasure of which one can always be certain" (Bonhoeffer, *Letters and Papers from Prison*, letter 89, p. 238). "We must learn to regard people less in the light of what they do or omit to do, and more in the light of what they suffer" (Bonhoeffer, *Letters and Papers from Prison*, 10). The original words here are: "Wir müssen lernen, die Menschen weniger auf das, was sie tun und unterlassen, als auf das, was sie erleiden, anzusehen." *Widerstand und Ergebung*, 83.

51. Julian of Norwich, *Revelations of Divine Love*. She wrote these revelations after a longer period of severe suffering. She was convinced that she was preparing for death at this time.

In the area of German speaking theology, I found a few different thinkers. They show that reflections on comfort are important for pastoral care and practical theology. The presented works are helpful in deepening our understanding of comfort and consolation. Stefanie Reumer wrote a dissertation in practical theology in Basel with a focus on aspects of comfort in the context of funerals.[52] Her starting point was the first question of the Heidelberger Catechism: What is your only comfort in life and in death?[53] She deepens the understanding of comfort through a phenomenological study in which she researches the comfort dimensions of funeral services in the Swiss Reformed context.

The German professor for practical theology, Christoph Schneider-Harpprecht,[54] combines various questions about counselling and comfort and reflects in different ways how one can combine theological understanding with psychological knowledge. It is helpful that in his dissertation the different aspects of "comfort" are discussed with regard to counselling. Yet his work does not include reflection on aspects of comfort at the end of life.

Volker Weymann,[55] also a professor of practical theology, tries to connect biblical and secular literature on comfort. His particular focus is the critical reception of comfort in the work of Sigmund Freud and Karl Marx.[56] This book helps to understand the negative reception of the word "Trost" (comfort) in philosophical, psychological, and theological discussions but does not suggest much regarding how people might fulfil their need for comfort in suffering or dying.

Sibylle Rolf,[57] a professor of systematic theology, in her dissertation discusses the question of how pastoral care and counselling can support those who are suffering. After discussing theological anthropology and different psychoanalytical paradigms, she defines comfort in the Christian faith tradition, especially in the Protestant churches, as something happening *extra me* and as an essential part of God's being present with and for us. As a protestant theologian, she analyses Luther's understanding of

---

52. Reumer, "Was ist dein Trost."
53. Ursinus, "Heidelberger Catechism 1563."
54. Schneider-Harpprecht, *Trost in der Seelsorge*.
55. Weymann, *Trost?*
56. "Ich beuge mich Ihrem Vorwurf, dass ich keinen Trost zu bringen weiss," Sigmund Freud quoted in Marcuse, *Sigmund Freud*, 58, quoted by Blumenberg, *Beschreibung des Menschen*, 642.
57. Rolf, *Vom Sinn zum Trost*.

"Trost" and the consequence of the doctrine of justification through faith. Dying and the end of life are not the focus of her study, however. What I found helpful in her work is that she tries to think through and discuss the limits of the "search for meaning" and that she discusses the correlation between different psychotherapeutical and theological approaches.

In January 2022 the journal *Spiritual Care* published a thematic volume dealing with the topic of consolation from a theological, philosophical and psychotherapeutic point of view in which comfort is described from different disciplines as "Beziehungsgeschehen" ("a relational event") which has a spiritual dimension for all humans.[58] The German Catholic theologian and professor for spiritual care Eckhard Frick reminds his readers in his article that Christian consolation has its center in hope, which is itself grounded in the resurrection of Christ and which also takes suffering and lament seriously. For him "Trost" or comfort has in its relational orientation towards Christ a different focus of understanding than just a search for meaning and he underlines this by referring to the consolation letters of the reformer Martin Luther who is for him very near in his understanding of comfort and consolation to Ignatius of Loyola.[59]

The distinction between "search for meaning" ("Suche nach Sinn") and comfort and God's emphasis in comforting his people and the individual through his word and through his grace in Jesus Christ is the focus of the German Reformed practical theologian Helmut Tacke's work.[60] In his two volumes *Glaubenshilfe als Lebenshilfe* ("Help for Faith as Help for Life") and *Zur rechten Zeit mit den Müden reden* ("Talking to Those Who Are Tired at the Right Time")[61] he underlines the importance of skilled,

---

58. Frick, "Zwischen Vertröstung und Trost," 10: "In German the word 'Trost' has the same etymological root as 'trust.' Expressing sorrow and longing for consolation may be a part of the relationships toward God and other spiritual attachment figures, e.g., in prayers such as Johannes Brahms' 'tröste mich wieder mit deiner Hilfe' (Op 29,2). In Ignatian spirituality and especially in the Spiritual Exercises, the awareness for emotions ('soul movements') and individualized value judgments have a pivotal role for the 'discernment of spirits,' i.e., for distinguishing what corresponds to God's will and what is against it. The discerning persons recognize empty promises putting them off."

59. "Am wichtigsten erscheint aber bei Luther ebenso wie bei Ignatius die Zurückführung professionellen ('amtlichen') Tröstens auf den Trost, der allein von Gott selbst kommt (2 Kor 1,3f.)." Frick, "Zwischen Vertröstung und Trost," 16.

60. Tacke, *Glaubenshilfe als Lebenshilfe*; Tacke, *Mit den Müden*. Tacke died in 1988 at the fairly young age of sixty.

61. There is no translation into English of the books. (The book titles are the author's translation.)

empathetic, and faithful counselling—which includes end-of-life issues. Scripture and the mutual reflection of Scripture, says Tacke, is a central part of God's way to comfort and encourage. This reflection of Scripture as comforting church praxis is vital for Tacke's understanding of counselling as "comfort ministry."

In a time when different psychotherapeutic models in counselling were dominant in pastoral care teaching, Tacke reflects on the dangers that attend theological language in counselling becoming rare and almost non-existent. He was responsible for the training of young ministers and chaplains, and he criticized that psychotherapeutic education of ministers and chaplains had pushed aside and underestimated the power of Scripture and Christian spirituality. He refers in his writings to the Psalms, especially to the psalms of lament, to narratives and texts of the Gospels, and he endeavors to introduce the sufferer and the brokenhearted to the richness of God's promises of comfort and help in the Bible.

Christian Möller, in *Teaching Practical Theology*,[62] by introducing consolation letters written by Tacke to a wider audience, offers rich material on the skilled and gentle way in which Tacke as a Christian teacher and minister cared for those in need and despair. He himself speaks in his letters and writings of Tacke's personal doubts and fears. In his ministry of comfort Tacke, who refers to "paracletical counselling,"[63] brings into play his own vulnerability and shares his own need of comfort as a human person and Christian. In certain parts, his writing is reminiscent of those of by Henri Nouwen who reflects on human existence,[64] searching for hope, and living in this world with uncertainties and experiences of suffering.

On my research journey I understood through Tacke more of what it might mean to be engaged in a ministry of comfort within the church and the praxis of mutual comfort experiences within Christian communities. It underlines the importance of a comfort ministry as part of practical theology and church praxis not only at the end of life. Tacke often refers to the work of Martin Luther, who shaped the German use of the word "Trost" and inspired a rich music tradition embedded in a protestant understanding of grace and comfort.

62. Möller and Lauter, *Seelsorge in Einzelportraits:* Helmut Tacke.

63. Tacke speaks of "parakletische Seelsorge": Tacke, *Glaubenshilfe als Lebenshilfe*, 92–96.

64. Nouwen, *Wounded Healer*; Nouwen, *Way of the Hear*; Nouwen, *Letter of Consolation*; Nouwen, *Inner Voice of Love*; McNeill and Morrison, *Compassion*.

Gerhard Ebeling, a German Luther scholar, who wrote a large research volume on Luther's understanding of counselling by analyzing Luther's letters,[65] shows that Luther in many letters to friends, church members and church leaders, politicians and other people who asked for advice and comfort in their suffering and dying, tries to understand the individual situation, the experience and the dimensions of a question, and the different aspects of suffering and doubt. Luther brings into these conversations his own understanding of comfort, of Scripture, of belief and trust at all times in the God who is with us. What is impressive is that he reflects with care on each individual instance of suffering and mourning in his many different letters.

As a researcher I learned through the comfort letters Martin Luther wrote, that he was able to grasp and hold the whole meaning of Christian comfort, which includes such things as: being with a suffering person and taking seriously a particular situation, encouragement, help, admonition, prayer, music, and quoting Scripture. Transparent in his letters is that he tried to "feel" what a person was going through without completely dissolving into the other person. Luther's letters show compassion with the sufferer, with the individual, with a particular kind of loss, grief, or despair. Luther himself experienced deeply the need of comfort and was able to respond to the suffering of others and to comfort them by focusing on the love of Christ who was for him the source of all comfort (2 Cor 1). Comfort or "Trost" was for Luther a matter of "sich fest machen" ("holding on") in trust and hope to the belief that the suffering and resurrected Christ is the "Emmanuel," God with us. Not only through words but also through music and hymns he tried to encourage other believers. Ebeling writes, "For Luther, Paul is a witness to an experiential theology, not a *theologia speculativa*, but a *theologia practica*, which is a *theologica crucis*."[66]

Luther's awareness of people's suffering and dying during the plague and his comfort ministry during that time is part of his critical self-reflection: "I must admit that a lot what I have to do is beyond my strength."[67] Of interest here is also his translation of John 16:33 in which Luther uses the phrase "be comforted," something which is translated in the King James Version in English as "be of good cheer": "In the world you are

---

65. Ebeling, *Luthers Seelsorge*.

66. Ebeling, *Luthers Seelsorge*, 348. (This quote is the author's own translation.)

67. Letter from Martin Luther from 1538, "Todesfurcht in Pestzeiten," in Ebeling, *Luthers Seelsorge*, 323.

fearful, but be comforted, I have overcome the world." With reference to Luther, Ebeling writes the following about comfort and consolation:

> The consolation to which he holds himself to and which he passes on presupposes precisely a situation in which human weakness cannot and must not be masked, but must itself enter into faith.... But the consolation that sustains it is nothing other than the Gospel itself ... Christ's promise that his power comes to fruition in weakness (2 Cor 12:9).... Consolation in the strict sense of the word does not consist of experiencing an improvement in our weakness ... but in being turned away from ourselves to Christ through faith in the midst of our weakness.[68]

Aside from such academic literature, the word "comfort" is used in many articles and church information sheets about advanced health care directives, which have the word "consolation or comfort" in the title, but do not contain a theological anthropology or eschatology. They are intended as practical help to prepare for the final period of life and for discussing end-of-life issues with family members, church carers, and friends.[69] What is helpful in such church information sheets is the fact that thanks to the word "comfort" readers see themselves not merely as clients or patients. Theirs is not primarily a medical perspective but an anthropological way of understanding that we are all vulnerable at times and especially at the end of life, when we are dependent on care, help, spiritual or medical support. Not only in Switzerland but also in many other countries, numerous books have reflected on dying, on palliative care, counselling and spiritual care.[70]

---

68. Ebeling, *Luthers Seelsorge*, 339–40: "Ich gestehe, dass ich dennoch vieles tun muss, was über meine Kräfte geht" (Quote: Martin Luther) "Der Trost, an den er sich selbst hält und den er weitergibt, setzt gerade eine Situation voraus, in der die menschliche Schwachheit nicht überspielt werden kann und darf, vielmehr selbst in den Glauben eingehen muss.... Der Trostgrund, der ihr standhält, ist nun aber nichts anderes als das Evangelium selbst ... den Zuspruch Christi, dass seine Kraft in der Schwachheit zur Verwirklichung kommt (2. Kor 12,9).... Trost im strengen Sinne besteht nicht darin, eine Aufbesserung unserer Schwachheit zu erleben ... vielmehr darin, mitten in unserer Schwachheit durch den Glauben von uns selbst weggekehrt zu werden zu Christus hin." (Quote: Gerhard Ebeling).

69. See, for instance, "Umsorgen—Begleiten—Trösten," Hospizarbeit: "Umsorgen, belgeiten, trösten"; Palliative Betreuung am Lebensende, Baden, Hospital Switzerland;. "Wenn ein naher Mensch stirbt, Trauer—Trost," Graubünden Switzerland.

70. See, for instance, Peng-Keller, *Klinikseelsorge*; Roser, *Spiritual Care*; Weiher, *Geheimnis des Lebens berühren*; Smeet, *Spiritual Care*; Cobb, *Dying Soul*.

It is striking that numerous publications in the last years consider suffering and coping strategies or suffering and resilience together. Resilience refers to a person's motivation, to the mental toughness and perseverance that enables them to go through difficult events or phases of life.[71] The research has insights into palliative medicine and wider care disciplines. Though some of the studies value the importance of religious attitudes or practices, they do not focus on Christians and their particular spiritual formation and understanding as members of a church or as a worldwide community.[72]

There is a substantial literature on spiritual care that focuses on end-of-life issues.[73] Especially important are different works of research in the nursing field.[74] Kirsten Anne Tornøe, Lars Johan Danbolt, Kari Kvigne, and Venke Sørlie, for example, explore comfort-dimensions in palliative care. Their research work, published in 2015, "The Challenge of Consolation: Nurses' Experiences with Spiritual and Existential Care for the Dying; A Phenomenological Hermeneutical Study," shows that the nurses noted that it was challenging to uncover dying patients' spiritual and existential suffering because it usually emerged as elusive entanglements of physical, emotional, relational, spiritual, and existential pain. The nurses' spiritual and existential care interventions were aimed at facilitating a more peaceful death. One of the results was that the nurses experienced that they had been able to convey consolation when they managed to help patients to find peace and reconciliation in the final stages of dying. The nurses experienced it as emotionally challenging to be unable to relieve dying patients' spiritual and existential anguish, because it activated feelings of professional helplessness and incapacity.

The study shows that nursing has a lot to do with comfort in general, but that the work of spiritual comforting can't be done without skills and inner beliefs. The field of medicine and nursing care recognizes the importance of religious experience at the end of life. Regarding the ongoing discussion in this field, the article, "Comparing Nurses' and Patients' Comfort Level with Spiritual Assessment" by Tove Giske and Pamela

---

71. See, for instance, Welter and Hildenbrand, *Resilienz*; Garg and Chauhan, "Coping Styles."

72. De Sousa Matos et al., "Quality of Life." Van Laarhoven et al., "Coping, Quality of Life."

73. One particularly well-known pioneer was Kübler-Ross. For example, Kübler-Ross, *On Death and Dying*. See also Piper, *Gespräche mit Sterbenden*. Piper was one of the first German theologians to publish interviews with dying patients.

74. Tornøe et al., "Challenge of Consolation."

Cone is helpful,[75] as is that of Suvi-Maria Saarelainen, Auli Vähäkangas, and Mirja Sisko Anttonen, "Religious Experiences of Older People Receiving Palliative Care at Home."[76] The authors show that not only are human interactions important for the interviewees at the end of their lives but so too are aspects of comfort in the context of a relationship to God and questions of faith.

As I explained before, present discussions concentrate on the rediscovery of "coping strategies"[77] and different modes of "resilience" in suffering. Bruce Rumbold, Simon J. C. Lee, Harold G. Koenig, Christina Puchalski, and Allan Kellehear have done a lot of research in this area around the topics of spiritual care and end-of-life care.[78] The Swiss theologian Simon Peng-Keller, who teaches in both the medical and the theological faculties at the University of Zürich, speaks of a "process of transition and transformation"[79] in which "counselling" and pastoral care have been superseded by spiritual care—although he is aware that there is no uniform understanding of spiritual care but that a wide range of aspects is involved. In the book *Spiritual Care im globalisierten Gesundheitswesen: Historische Hintergründe und aktuelle Entwicklungen*,[80] Peng-Keller illuminates the historical development of spiritual care and the inclusion of the spiritual dimension into the definitions of health and wellbeing used by the World Health Organization. He shows well the global historical impact in modern times of the Christian faith in end-of-life care and palliative medicine.

In this context the work of the British palliative pioneer Cicely Saunders is of importance. She integrated Christian faith and practice, nursing and medical skills within her concept of caring for the terminally ill and dying.[81] For her there was no doubt that nurses, doctors, and other caregivers were part of the ministry of comfort and could help each other

75. Giske and Cone, "Comparing Nurses' and Patients' Comfort Level," 671.

76. Saarelainen et al., "Religious Experiences," 336.

77. Pinto et al., "Comfort."

78. Rumbold, "Spiritual Assessment"; Lee, "In a Secular Spirit"; Koenig et al., *Handbook of Religion and Health*; Koenig, "Integrating Spirituality"; Puchalski et al., "Improving the Quality"; Puchalski and Ferrell, *Making Health Care Whole*, 25–32; Kellehear, "Spirituality and Palliative Care"; Cobb et al., *Oxford Textbook of Spirituality*; Lazenby, et al., *Safe Passage*; Swift, *Hospital Chaplaincy*; Engelhardt and Delkeskamp-Hayes, "Geist der Wahrheit"; Bishop, *Anticipatory Corpse*.

79. Peng-Keller, "Spiritual Care."

80. Peng-Keller and Neuhold, *Spiritual Care*.

81. Saunders, *Selected Writings*, 275.

with the different dimensions involved. Saunders saw in her palliative care work a mutual comfort dimension not only for families or communities but also for society:

> The dying needs the community, its help and fellowship and the care and attention which will quieten their distress and fears and enable them to go peacefully. The community needs the dying to make it think of eternal issues and to make it listen. . . . The community of the Church has a particular responsibility . . . to meet with people dying in many different surroundings and to sustain those who sometimes have to endure in very difficult places.[82]

Saunders's emphasis on a deeper understanding of comfort or comfort ministry can be understood primarily as a result of her praxis that is embedded in the hospice movement. Next to reflecting on suffering and dying from the perspective of the dying person or family and friends, Saunders realized early on that carers are also in need of comfort. She called this "staff-pain."[83] Saunders saw the need for such a specific ministry of comfort, a spiritual component alongside medical care.

Saunders's emphasis on a multi-disciplinary approach that includes a Christian understanding of personhood is something which Peng-Keller takes up. In a more recent publication, he tried to rethink counselling in the hospital setting and to bridge theology with other disciplines.[84] From 2014 to 2016, the University of Zürich undertook an interdisciplinary research project on the individual's praxis of "prayer" in sickness and dying.[85] The project aimed to contribute to a better understanding of multi-religiously-shaped prayer reality. By taking into account previously neglected physical aspects of the prayer event, the study not only corrected the one-sided perception of the multi-layered phenomenality of prayer, but also used the example of prayer to explore the capacities and limits of a hermeneutics of lived religion. One specific church context was not the focus of the research, however. Another national study entitled *Competence Network Health Workforce* tried to work with a local

---

82. Saunders, "And from Sudden Death,"39.
83. Saunders, "Current Views," 180.
84. Peng-Keller, *Klinikseelsorge*; Roser, *Spiritual Care*, 229–34.
85. Swiss Academic Project: SNF-Forschungsprojekt, "Beten als verleiblichtes Verstehen: Hermeneutische Zugänge zum Ereignis des Gebets" (Prayer as Embodied Understanding: Hermeneutical Approaches to the Experiences of Prayer); Dalferth and Peng-Keller, *Beten als verleiblichtes Verstehen*.

church community, but did not focus on comfort.[86] And a third study concentrated on the challenges to society posed by those at the end of their lives.[87] In this research paper one thing of interest in the context of this study was that the dimension of visually imagining things while in the process of dying could be regarded as comforting. An example given was that of children drawing pictures shortly before they die.[88]

Regarding the literature in conjunction with nursing, care and medicine often the medical model is so dominant that it is difficult to focus on church and ecclesiological insights which would allow one to deepen an understanding of comfort and consolation as a Christological task and as part of church praxis. In general, one can say that often these discussions only take into account a certain kind of praxis and certain aspects of comfort. The question of how church communities might play a bigger role in the comfort ministry for Christian community members or establish a new awareness of a Christian approach of the *ars moriendi* is very rarely asked.[89] Having said that, different churches, like my own in Switzerland, attempt to train pastors, deacons, and engaged church members to become more involved in local networks such as those of palliative care in different regions of Switzerland. In Germany the hospice movement encouraged many people to become involved in places where very sick and dying people are cared for.[90]

Next to the theological and medical studies, the topic of comfort and consolation has been taken up by the anthropologist Daniel Miller. He wrote two books on comfort, *The Comfort of Things* and *The Comfort of People*,[91] as mentioned in the introduction. In *The Comfort of People* he includes observations about the networks of people who live under the threat of a serious health diagnosis and how these networks work to comfort them.[92] From his perspective as an anthropologist, he describes vital aspects of people as "social agents." Through eighteen narratives, Miller shows how people experience human comfort in different circumstances and how important relationships are. In the story of "Matt," for instance, Miller shows how digital communication and relationships in

86. Holder-Franz and Zinnsstag, *In Beziehung sein*, 122–28.
87. See Zimmermann and Steiger, *Lebensende als gesellschaftliche Herausforderung*.
88. Peng-Keller. "Symbolisierung."
89. In this regard, Murray's work is of interest: Murray, *Faith in Hospice*, 37–60.
90. See, for instance, Gerstenkorn, *Hospizarbeit in Deutschland*.
91. Miller, *Comfort of Things*; Miller, *Comfort of People*.
92. Miller, *Comfort of People*, 32–38; 81–90; 185–88.

suffering at the end of life can be very important. His phenomenological, ethnographic research underlines how essential it is to listen and observe carefully what and which relationships people experience. Although "Matt" was not a Christian, questions about meaning, the after-life, and love were part of his pilgrimage through his final days. Miller opens up vital themes of relationship and comfort as a research field, and these are helpful also in practical theology.

> When it comes to the comfort of people, there are many potential sources of support and comfort from friends.... With regard to friendship more generally, a common finding is that those who are most present when one becomes a terminal patient are not necessarily those one might expect.[93]

Miller concludes with the observation that hospice work in a secular society has the potential—thanks to its familiar setting—to be a place where relationships and comfort can grow and society can learn to develop new skills to support each other.[94] Miller also sees in his research the relevance of the spiritual dimension and that friendships and relationships help to develop a personal spirituality. Besides, the social component the study of human everyday relations with objects is interesting for research work on comfort and consolation. Often, one is confronted with "things" which have a special meaning, "symbols" with a history or memories which are located not only in cognitive memory but also in some "material" of significance.[95]

In addition to Miller's research, the work of practical theologian Stephen Pattison is of interest, as he attempts to deepen an understanding of artifacts for theology.[96] Pattison himself uses other disciplines to explore the wide field of the topic "seeing" and has developed possible ways of rethinking pastoral care. He developed as practical theological arguments to discuss the importance of visual artifacts in the field of practical theology. He suggests that artifacts and "things," such as for example paintings, souvenirs, or photographs, help to make human persons what they are in all aspects of their existence. People can enter into different kinds of relationships with things. "To ignore the relations that

---

93. Miller, *Comfort of People*, 210–11.

94. Miller, *Comfort of People*, 210–12.

95. "I sort of expected, but couldn't really fully imagine, the sadness of lives and the comfort of things." Miller, *Comfort of Things*, 402.

96. Pattison, *Seeing Things*.

people have with physical artifacts is therefore to fail to take seriously the fullness of embodied material existence," he says.[97] Pattison writes about the significance of being concerned about the nature of human beings and their relations with other human beings and the world around them.

> We are whole-body perceivers who need all our senses of we are to really gain a full grasp of what is before us . . . when people want to gain a real sense of what they are seeing, they will often automatically reach out to touch the object they are looking at. Sight is often closely related to the sense of touch.[98]

> There is a reasonable consensus that all the senses work together to produce a more or less unified perception of the world.[99]

Many items, says Pattison, are retained in the home not so much for their usefulness or aesthetic charm, but because they mirror memories of experiences or special relationships which are central to the individual. Attending more consciously to the relationship that people have with artifacts, and the meanings and reflections which emerge within those relationships, might be helpful for understanding people more fully. Often pre- or nonverbal dimensions are important as well. Some artifacts may mediate the divine or ultimate reality for a person. Pattison took up in his research the work of the social scientists Donald A. Norman. Also Mihaly Csikszentmihalyi, and Eugene Rochberg Halton helped to deepen his reflection on the meaning of things.[100] Although his focus is not on end-of-life care, Pattison's work is useful to me in deepening my understanding of the importance of "things" within a Christian framework. As he writes: "There is a need to develop a Christian theology and practice that values artefacts."[101]

From a more philosophical position one can turn to Jean-Pierre Wils, a professor of philosophical ethics and political philosophy, who published a book on the *Ars moriendi* in 2007.[102] In this book he discusses some of the phenomenological insights into pain and suffering through

---

97. Pattison, "Stuff Pastoral Theology," 7.
98. Pattison, "Stuff Pastoral Theology," 42.
99. Pattison, "Stuff Pastoral Theology," 48.
100. Norman, *Emotional Design*. Csikszentmihalyi and Rochberg Halton, *Meaning of Things*.
101. Pattison, *Seeing Things*, 258.
102. Wils, *Ars moriendi*; Wils, *Sterben*.

examples in literature.[103] "What we can (and should) agree on . . . is the need for consolation. The dying person is the most consolation-needy being there is."[104] Here he quotes Elaine Scarry, who did research work on pain and the body: "'Physical pain is an intentional state without an intentional object.'"[105] Wils argues that pain has negative and positive sides in human life and if overwhelming pain is controlled and comforted, the "person can be part of life again and find ways back to life even when illness can't be cured."[106] It is remarkable that Wils does not discuss standard teaching in palliative care on pain or the research work of Cicely Saunders on "total pain."[107] Although Wils's focus on dying as a process of recognition of dependency is vital, he makes no connection between the philosophical discussion and the Christian story of Jesus Christ.[108] *Ars moriendi* has to do for Wils first with a philosophical and humanistic tradition which we can also find in Christianity.[109]

A strong point of his book is that Wils criticizes the danger in the Christian tradition of spiritualizing and glorifying pain and suffering.[110] Taking Augustine as an example, Wils states: "What the sufferer and the dying are called to hear is: 'Just endure it!'"[111] Around the theme of comfort and endurance from the viewpoint of Christian faith, the work of Cicely Saunders is once again important. As she writes in different publications which contribute to an *ars moriendi*, she understands herself

---

103. Lenz, *Über den Schmerz*.

104. Wils, *Ars moriendi*, 228.

105. Wils, *Ars moriendi*, 102: "Worüber wir uns . . . verständigen können (und sollten), ist die Trostbedürftigkeit des Menschen. Der Sterbende Mensch ist das trostbedürftigste Wesen, das es gibt." Scarry is an American essayist and professor of English and American literature and languages. Her interests include theory of representation and the language of physical pain. See Scarry, *Body in Pain*.

106. Wils, *Ars moriendi*, 103.

107. Saunders, *Selected Writings*: "Her pain included not only her physical suffering, but also her emotional and mental suffering, her social problems and her spiritual need" (68); "The process of listening and communication referred to in the discussion of the patient's awareness is often more important than all our drugs. A dying person needs above all someone to listen and understand how he feels" (106).

108. See also the work of MacIntyre, *Dependent Rational Animals*.

109. "Es wäre angemessener von einer Tradition der humanistischen Antike und einer Tradition des christlichen Humanismus zu sprechen." Wils, *Ars moriendi*, 121.

110. The tradition of the *imitatio Christi* in the Middle Ages is one such example. More in Wils, *Ars moriendi*, 131.

111. Wils, *Ars moriendi*, 132: "Was hier dem Leidenden und Sterbenden zugerufen wird, lautet: 'Aushalten!'" (The translation into English is the author's own translation.)

as having been called to care for the dying by the love of a compassionate God who reveals himself in Christ through his cross and resurrection. She wanted to change the Christian attitude towards suffering at the end of life and to develop a "theological and medical praxis" of care, a comforting community which could care for the dying with the help of medical, nursing, and counselling resources. Saunders writes,

> The Christian imperative is to care and to heal. Healing does not only mean assisting someone to get better. It may mean easing the pains of dying or allowing someone to die when the time is come. There is a misconception that, because Christians believe in the redemptive value of Christ's suffering and the call at times to 'suffer with Him,' they do not believe in the relief of suffering; and it is asserted that, as they consider life to be a gift from God they are, therefore, convinced that they should prolong it as long as possible, even if this should mean prolonging suffering. . . . The Christian believes that the God who made this world entered in the vulnerability of the Incarnation, shared and transformed suffering.[112]

Coming back to the philosophical discussion of *ars moriendi*, the work of Hans Blumenberg is also of note in the context of this study. As a philosopher with a special interest in anthropology, his book *Beschreibung des Menschen* ("Description of a Human")[113] is important for this study because Blumenberg uses the phenomenological approach of the philosophical phenomenologist Edmund Husserl to examine experiences of "comfort and consolation" as a *conditio humana*. For Blumenberg, "the need of comfort" is a key element in his anthropology and describes what humans are and how we deal with reality.[114] One chapter of his book is entitled "Trostbedürftigkeit und Untröstlichkeit des Menschen" ("The need for comfort and the disconsolateness of humans").[115] For Blumenberg, the starting point is not what "comfort" is or seems to be for the individual but the phenomenon that the human being is capable of receiving "comfort."[116]

112. Saunders, "Problem of Euthanasia," 135.
113. Blumenberg, *Beschreibung des Menschen*, 2014.
114. He quotes *Dionysos-Dithyramben*: "Man geht zu Grunde, wenn man immer zu den Gründen geht." Blumenberg, *Beschreibung des Menschen*, 639.
115. The translation of the chapter into English is the author's own translation.
116. "Dass er ein der Tröstung fähiges Wesen ist. Trost ist eine Kategorie, deren Eigentümlichkeiten aufs Engste mit der Spezies Mensch zusammenhängen." Blumenberg, *Beschreibung des Menschen*, 623.

> The concept of consolation has a much wider, deeper meaning than one would consciously attribute to it. A human being is a comfort-seeking creature. . . . Comfort is one of the things that makes life possible after a point at which it would seem impossible to do so. It remains true: A human being is the being who is "nevertheless" able to live. Comfort and consolation are instruments of this position in the midst of negation.[117]

Blumenberg's reflections show clearly the need for comfort for humans, but as a philosopher he is careful not to step into a framework of specific religiosity or into a philosophy which underestimates anthropology and phenomenology. This I discuss more extensively in the theological response section.

Through the aforementioned literature we can see that the theological material on comfort and consolation is rich and varied, but that there are gaps. The interest in reflecting on dying and death is present in different disciplines. The international movement in palliative medicine and care (which includes the hospice movement) and the importance of spirituality promoted in this movement jump-started practical theology's reflections and writings, often in an interdisciplinary setting, on what it means to face one's own or another's dying and how spirituality, counselling, and spiritual care can support the individual at the end of life.

Having read the literature, through my experience as a pastor, and thanks to the insights of my former research on the Christian palliative care pioneer Cicely Saunders, along with a variety of discussions around end-of-life care, it became obvious to me that a study in practical theology around comfort and experiences of consolation by practicing Christians at the end of life is necessary. During my research, the crisis around COVID-19 began, confronting the world's humans with thoughts of severe illness, suffering, dying and possibly dying alone, and this in turn deepened my need to understand experiences of suffering and comfort at the end of life.

---

117. "Der Begriff des Trostes hat eine viel weitere, tiefere Bedeutung, als man ihm bewusst zuzuschreiben pflegt. Der Mensch ist ein trostsuchendes Wesen. Trost ist etwas anderes als Hilfe . . . aber der Trost ist das merkwürdige Erlebnis, das zwar das Leiden bestehen lässt, aber sozusagen das Leiden am Leiden aufhebt, er betrifft nicht das Übel selbst, sondern dessen Reflex in der tiefsten Instanz der Seele. . . . Trost gehört zu dem, was Weiterleben nach einem Punkt, der es unmöglich zu machen schien, dennoch möglich macht. Es bleibt dabei: Der Mensch ist das Wesen, welches 'trotzdem' zu leben vermag. Trostbedürftigkeit und Tröstungsfähigkeit sind Instrumente dieser Position inmitten der Negation." Blumenberg, *Beschreibung des Menschen*, 625, 633.

It will be useful for research in practical theology on comfort and consolation in the context of death and dying to be developed with the skills of practical theology and in conjunction with the insights from others disciplines. Swinton formulates this task in the following manner:

> Practical theology whilst remaining a churchly discipline, in the sense that its primary focus is on the praxis of the church, is also a discipline which is fundamental for the world which is the subject of God's redemptive mission. To examine and reflect upon the praxis of the church must be understood as a task that takes place in the world and for the world. . . . The practical theologian seeks to interpret Scripture, tradition, and praxis in order that contemporary praxis of both church and world can be transformed.[118]

For me as a researcher that also makes more urgent my need to understand myself as a Christian theologian who is involved in the world and has a part in God's redemptive mission for that world.

STUDYING THE EXPERIENCES OF THOSE AT THE END OF LIFE

Practical theology I understand as an interpretative discipline which brings new and complex insights into the Christian tradition by interpreting experiences carefully.

Qualitative Research

In order to "stay close to experience"[119] in a particular situation, I decided to study the wide range of approaches in qualitative research. Here, I found Denzin and Lincoln's definition of qualitative research to be particularly helpful because they emphasise the importance of studying people's experiences in their natural environment and of taking seriously the meaning they give to these experiences. They define qualitative research as:

> Multi-method in focus, involving an interpretative, naturalistic approach to its subject matter. This means that qualitative

---

118. Swinton, *From Bedlam to Shalom*, 8, 12.
119. Fowler, "Emerging New Shape," 26.

researchers study things in their natural setting, attempting to make sense of, or interpret, phenomena in terms of the meanings people bring to them.[120]

Through reading the work around qualitative research by the sociologists Jennifer Mason and David Silverman,[121] it became clear to me that any qualitative research should be a systematically and rigorously conducted process. The professor of counselling and psychotherapy, John McLeod, emphasizes that good qualitative research is not merely a matter of following a set of procedural guidelines. Rather "the principal source of knowing in qualitative research is the researcher's engagement in a search for meaning and truth in relation to the topic of inquiry."[122] In this search for meaning and truth, I am aware that I, as a researcher, cannot be neutral or objective or detached from any knowledge emerging from the research. As a researcher I have a role and responsibility in that process, and the very act of asking myself difficult self-reflective questions is part of the activity which qualitative researchers call reflexivity. Thus, Swinton and Mowat define reflexivity as

> the process of critical self-reflection carried out by the researcher throughout the research process that enables her to monitor and respond to her contribution to the proceedings.[123]

Within the range of qualitative research methods, it was then important to find a specific methodology which would be helpful in the particular context of my research question and research goals.

To explore the experience of comfort it was necessary for me to ask: What is this or that kind of experience like? How does the person experience comfort, and in what kind of context and life history? These are what are called phenomenological questions.

Before exploring further the relationship between phenomenology and qualitative research, it will be useful to mention very briefly what is understood by the term phenomenology and where it comes from.

Phenomenology is a philosophy of experience which attempts to get close to the way people construct meaning. Thus, the phenomenological project includes the study of structures of consciousness as experienced from the first-person point of view. It was originally developed

---

120. Denzin and Lincoln, *Collecting and Interpreting*, 3.
121. Mason, *Qualitative Research*; Silverman, *Doing Qualitative Research*.
122. McLeod, *Qualitative Research*, 55.
123. Swinton and Mowat, *Practical Theology*, 59.

in philosophy in the first half of the twentieth century by thinkers such as Edmund Husserl, Martin Heidegger, Maurice Merleau-Ponty, Jean-Paul Sartre, and Hans Georg Gadamer. The Danish psychologists Sven Brinkmann and Steinar Kvale show that the term *phenomenology* in current use is a wide term which no longer refers merely to a philosophical movement but also to a range of methodological research approaches.[124]

Phenomenology as a methodological approach in qualitative research in general refers to the study of the lifeworld and is used to gain a deeper understanding of the meaning of a certain experience. Max van Manen, a professor in research methods and pedagogy who has written extensively in the field of phenomenology and pedagogy, develops this phenomenological understanding in his work. According to van Manen, "phenomenology does not offer us the possibility of effective theory with which we can now explain or control the world, but rather it offers us the possibility of plausible insights that bring us into more contact with the world."[125] Phenomenology attempts to uncover and describe the structures and the internal meaning of structures of "lived experience." It is also a way of "seeing" how and in which contexts phenomena present themselves to humans through experiences.

But what does "lived experience" mean? Van Manen describes phenomenological research as "oriented to the lifeworld as we immediately experience it—pre-reflectively, rather than as we conceptualize, theorize, categorize, or reflect on it."[126] To try and get close to this experience, van Manen refers to the basic method suggested by the philosopher Edmund Husserl, called *the reduction*, which he explains as follows:

> The reduction consists of two methodical opposing moves that complement each other. Negatively it suspends or removes what obstructs access to the phenomenon—this move is called the epoché or bracketing. And positively it returns, leads back to the mode of appearing of the phenomenon—this move is called the reduction.[127]

There is, however, always a critical element within the dynamic of the epoché and the reduction as, however hard one tries, one is never quite able to capture fully the moment of experience. Van Manen writes,

---

124. Kvale and Brinkmann, *Learning in the Craft*.
125. Van Manen, *Researching Lived Experience*, 9.
126. Van Manen and Adams, "Qualitative Research," 449.
127. Van Manen, *Phenomenology of Practice*, 215.

> Phenomenology is the project that tries to describe the pre-reflective meaning of the living now. However, phenomenology is also aware that when we try to capture the "now" of the living present in an oral or written description, then we are already too late. . . . No matter how we try, we are always too late to capture the moment of the living now.[128]

This being the case, van Manen understands phenomenology in general to mean "hermeneutic or interpretive-descriptive phenomenology"[129] as there is always an element of interpretation involved in the process, on which it is necessary to reflect. Hermeneutic phenomenology thus is the attempt to get close to a phenomenon through the dynamic of epoché and reduction while practicing a reflective awareness of one's own involvement in interpreting what is happening and being described.

Next to van Manen's work the work of Linda Finlay regarding hermeneutic phenomenology is instructive. As an integrative psychotherapist she is committed to a pragmatic approach which allows therapists and counsellors to deepen their understanding and sensitivity in using phenomenological methodology. She emphasizes the researcher's attitude, which can be seen as a kind of "dance" between the reduction and reflexivity. The world of phenomenology remains for her one of uncertainty, controversy, and competing diverse interests. She argues that in hermeneutic phenomenology any description of lived experience has to be seen in the context of a person's life situation. The interpretations are filtered through a spatial-temporal lens and arise out of particular cultural and historical contexts.[130] For the research process Finlay underlines the importance of moving beyond what might be regarded as the literal meanings of an experience and to offer, if possible, a provisional range of meanings, what we might call the implicit meanings.[131]

Further, Finlay suggests that the phenomenological project needs to pay special attention to the body. "Our body is the vehicle for experiencing, doing, being and becoming."[132] Personhood with the meaning given

---

128. Van Manen, *Phenomenology of Practice*, 34.
129. Van Manen, *Phenomenology of Practice*, 26.
130. Finlay, *Phenomenology for Therapists*, 112.
131. Finlay, *Phenomenology for Therapists*, 16.
132. Finlay, *Phenomenology for Therapists*, 29.
"The body stands before the world and the world upright before it, and between them there is a relation that is one of embrace." Merleau-Ponty, *Visible and the Invisible*, 271.

to it and body are intertwined. In the context of this study, involving people at the end of their lives and with terminal illnesses, this aspect of the methodological approach is especially relevant.

It is clear that phenomenological research places emphasis on the particular and that while interpreting experiences it tries to suggest different levels of meanings. Although the field of phenomenology is wide, there are some principles shared by different researchers. Finlay sums these up and illustrates them in six facets of what it means to be "doing phenomenology."[133] These six facets are useful for my research:

1. **A focus on lived experience and meanings.** Phenomenologists in general look at particular, specific situations involving a phenomenon. Then, through in-depth analysis, they attempt to get to the essence of those experiences and what they might mean, both expressly and implicitly. Within my research project the particular, specific situation is that of people at the end of life who understands themselves as Christians within the Swiss Reformed Church and the phenomenon I am studying is the experience of comfort and consolation which they describe.

2. **The use of rigorous, rich, resonant description.** Rich descriptions are essential in any form of phenomenology, as the description of the experience is "prized above any kind of explanation or theorising."[134] It is the challenge of phenomenology to provide "fresh, complex, rich descriptions of phenomena as concretely lived."[135] Indeed, such is the importance of language within the methodology that the boundaries between science (empirical studies) and art (literary evocations) can become blurred, and yet it is within this blurring that qualitative research emerges. For my study it was important to find people who were willing and capable of formulating their experiences of comfort and consolation in a rich and nuanced way.

3. **A concern with existential issues.** Van Manen refers to four basic existential concepts for research, which all have to do with the way things are felt and experienced; lived space, lived body, lived time and lived relations.[136] These can involve existential feelings which

---

133. Finlay, *Phenomenology for Therapists*, 15–18.
134. Finlay, *Phenomenology for Therapists*, 18.
135. Finlay, *Phenomenology for Therapists*, 173.
136. Van Manen, *Researching Lived Experience*, 102–8.

are not so much directed to something, but rather woven into our perception of the world, such as feeling fulfilled or feeling distant. Such existential issues are close to the surface with people who realize that they are in process of letting go and preparing for dying as they experience that "lived space, lived body, lived time and lived relations" are coming to an end in the form they know.

4. **The assumption that body, self, and world are intertwined.** Phenomenology in general works through a holistic approach which refuses to confine itself to a dualist split between the mental and the material, and is aware of the immensely complex interconnection between the physical and the mental. Similarly to what I wrote in point three a holistic approach regarding the intertwining of body, self and world appears to be an existential experience for those coming to the end of their lives, where physical, mental and spiritual aspects are interconnected.

5. **The application of the "phenomenological attitude."** Like Aristotle,[137] van Manen and other phenomenologists write about an attitude of "wonder" which allows the researcher to discover new things and be open to life in all its diversity and complexity: "Phenomenological research begins with wonder at what gives itself and how something gives itself. It can only be pursued while surrendering to a state of wonder."[138] Within this wonder an awareness of one's own involvement in the phenomenon being researched is paramount to the "phenomenological attitude." Intersubjectivity is recognized and reflexivity welcomed. Within my research I was aware of the "wonder" of talking to people who were willing to describe to me their experiences of comfort and consolation in connection with their Christian faith. Feeling this "wonder" however, I consciously attempted to take into account how involved I was myself within the ongoing conversation. This involved a sharpening of my own reflective process in taking on the "phenomenological attitude."

6. **A potentially transformative relational approach.** The transformative character of the process of engaging research is something which belongs to "doing phenomenology." Such a reflective,

---

137. McKeon, *Basic Works of Aristotle*, 692: "For it is owing to their wonder that men both now begin and at first began to philosophize."

138. Van Manen, *Phenomenology of Practice*, 27.

collaborative process is something which can be experienced by both participant and researcher, and can indeed touch and move us in ways we did not expect. Throughout my study project I became aware of how the learning of the "phenomenological attitude" was interwoven with my experience as a pastor. Through the depth and comprehensiveness of the whole research process in interviewing people at the end of life I was aware of the privilege of coming close to people in light of their suffering and comfort experiences. This is something which has had a transforming quality for me as a researcher but also with regard to my ministry as a Christian pastor.

In hermeneutic phenomenology, these six described facets help us to understand the process whereby both phenomenology and hermeneutics come together, with the aim of providing a rich description of lived experiences along with an interpretative perspective on that experience.[139] Although initially the "objectivity" of phenomenological bracketing, which might seem to aim for a detached view of the phenomenon, would seem to be at odds with a hermeneutic stance which celebrates subjectivity and self-reflection in finding meaning emerge from the study of a phenomenon, Finlay describes well how these might be brought together:

> The challenge here is to juggle the contradictory stances of being "scientifically removed from," "open to" and "aware of" while simultaneously interlacing with research participants in the midst of their own personal experiencing.[140]

The bringing together of these layers, as described by Finlay, is something which seems to me necessary and good as part of the process of research using hermeneutic phenomenology and I have attempted to practice this within my research study.

Hermeneutic phenomenology is thus a process and a methodology which can lead to a deeper understanding of the phenomenon being researched, especially when this is related to particular feelings and experiences that people have. Regarding the theme of my research around comfort and consolation at the end of life, it was clear to me that it would be necessary to use a research methodology capable of coming to grips with the complexity of individual comfort experiences as expressed by people near the end of their lives or with terminal illnesses. My research

---

139. Swinton and Mowat, *Practical Theology*, 109–15.
140. Finlay, *Phenomenology for Therapists*, 23.

question required a methodology which placed a high value on subjective understanding and would keep close to the experience being expressed and described. In order to explore how Christians experience God's benevolent "carrying of them" at the end of their lives and how they describe divine and human comfort experiences, hermeneutic phenomenology seemed to me a most helpful methodology.

Of special interest within my research was the growing understanding of the importance of the holistic approach to phenomenology, which Finlay takes up in her fourth facet: the assumption that body, self, and world are intertwined. While studying the literature around comfort, the work of the anthropologist Daniel Miller[141] and that of the practical theologian Stephen Pattison[142] regarding relations with visual artifacts struck me as useful for my study. Pattison refers to Merleau-Ponty and his emphasis on whole body perception and the way people relate to things they encounter with the senses.[143] Thus, I realized that my research, besides relationships with people, also needed to take seriously visual things and people's relations to them. Considering my research question, it was important to ask the participants how they engage with the visual dimension of material existence. While artifacts like paintings or sculptures easily draw the attention, I wanted to ask which objects or "things" have a comfort dimension for the individual at the end of their lives. Some of the interviewees allowed me to take photographs of some of the "things" which had a comfort quality for them. In doing that, I was aware of my own influence in choosing the scope of the visual images. Rose and Pattison[144] emphasise that the social sciences do not look at images and artifacts carefully enough, and they give advice how to do this in the social sciences and practical theology. "Not having a critical awareness of relationships with visible artefacts does not mean that these relationships do not exist."[145] The ability to appreciate "things" is part of human life. Perception is not only focused on the visual world: it is a whole-body phenomenon. The world is known to us through hearing, seeing, touch, and other senses. Because my research is within the sphere of practical theology, I am interested in the relationship between belief

---

141. Miller, *Comfort of Things*.

142. Pattison, *Seeing Things*.

143. "Perceived things are 'encountered by the body as animate, living powers that actively draw us into relation.'" Pattison, *Seeing Things*, 45.

144. Pattison, *Seeing Things*.

145. Pattison, *Seeing Things*, 2.

and practice. I am deeply concerned with the nature of human beings and their relations with others, God, and the world around them.

In the contemporary Western world, and especially with philosophical assumptions such as Descartes's (on the animate and inanimate world),[146] sight and vision have often been treated as separate from the other senses. Pattison explains through examples in church history that this was not always like that. "Gregory of Nyssa in ascribing tactile qualities to the eyes in gaining the vision of God—the eyes, inner and outer, physical and spiritual, touch the divine."[147] He identifies an approach to perception which includes "haptic vision" not as something new, but as a recovery of old wisdom.

Although different thinkers and researchers value this approach of a holistic perception, there are limits and difficulties. There is still a tendency for words and images to be placed in opposition to each other. "Visual images, in particular, are often presented as an alien threat that must be reduced to words to be taken seriously."[148] I decided to present certain "things" both with a verbal description and as photographs in the main body of the thesis. To add to my research method, the study of artifacts of the interviewees means also having to be aware of the difficulty of interpreting those as a researcher. I decided to refer only to visual things within the main body of the thesis when the interview participant was describing dimensions of it in the context of my research question.

---

146. Descartes (1596–1650), *Discourse on the Method* (1637). His rationalistic thinking is also called Cartesianism. One of his famous sayings is: *"cogito ergo sum"* ("I think, therefore I am") which forms the basis of his metaphysics, but he also introduced self-confidence as a genuinely philosophical topic. The assumption that the thinking soul is the origin of knowledge has three implications: First, the source of all knowledge is no longer to be sought in the tracing of the thoughts of God; second, the thinking ego makes the body an object of the physical world like others (the body-soul dualism); third, laws of movement apply in the area of the body, which are not broken by any interference of the soul in the event (a mechanistic world view). However, questions remain as to how the world of the body affects the thinking ego via the sense organs and how the will can affect the body world. He distinguished between the natural world including an immaterial mind that, in human beings, was directly related to the brain; in this way, Descartes formulated the modern version of the mind–body problem.

147. Pattison, *Seeing Things*, 43.

148. Pattison, *Seeing Things*, 99.

Research design

How was this research project designed and conducted? As previously mentioned, the guiding framework is hermeneutic phenomenology. There are two main components to the design of this study: data collection and data analysis (in two steps).

To interview people of very old age and at the end of their life needs critical consideration. Although I am an ordained minister and trained to reflect on my work, I was grateful to have three practical experiences in palliative care units before my research project started, two in Switzerland (Basel and Winterthur), and one in England (Oxford). These gave me a wider understanding of how important respect for human dignity and personal integrity at the end of life is. As a researcher, I have a responsibility to protect personal integrity in vulnerable circumstances and preserve individual freedom and self-determination as much as possible. It is important to show respect to each interviewee in their choice of how to answer a question (or not) and to protect participants' confidentiality.[149] This included using codes and pseudonyms to protect the identity of participants. I informed all of them how I would use the interview material and that any quotations or information would appear in association with a pseudonym. I sent an application for ethical approval to the University of Aberdeen to explain the planned interview process and the ethical reflections being involved. They accepted my considerations and gave me permission to start the interview process in autumn 2018.

Phenomenological research working with interviews requires that participants be capable of providing rich accounts of their experience.

All of the interviews apart from one were in German or in Swiss dialect. The fourteen participants from different parts of Switzerland lived at home or in a nursing home. One person had lived in Australia for many years and decided to talk to me in English. I transcribed the interviews in two steps: first from Swiss dialect into German, then from German into English.

In light of the coronavirus crisis beginning in 2020, I decided (after discussing this with my supervisor) to revisit some of the interviewees. I wanted to ask them if their experiences of comfort had changed or developed during the lockdowns, as I had noticed as a pastor who is in frequent contact with other people that the crisis had affected them in

---

149. Mason, *Qualitative Researching*, 79–81.

various ways. Not all of the interviewees were still alive. I was able to revisit eight people who had earlier taken part in the research project.

My sample selection, in which I attempted to recruit participants who might each "throw light on meaningful differences in experience"[150] in relation to the research topic, was based on the following criteria for inclusion:

- Persons who see themselves as Christians
- Persons who are over eighty-five years old and have serious health problems or adults with a life-threatening serious illnesses
- Persons who were willing and capable of providing rich verbal accounts of their experience

The interview process included travelling. One difficulty was that some of the interviewees had to change the week or day of the interview because of their health condition or an unplanned time in hospital for a special treatment. I planned the time for the interview process carefully. I made sure that I arrived at least twenty minutes early to have time to prepare myself; that included prayer, writing notes, or having a few moments of silence or a drink in my car. After the interview, I typically made a few notes and used the time travelling back home to reflect on the interview process. All together it took me four months to conduct the interviews.

As I mentioned in the previous section, I revisited seven of the interviewees in 2020. Because I had time to sit with the interview material, I was familiar with the content of the first interview and reflected in different ways on the sentences I had transcribed. Before we planned the date for a visit, I spoke to each interviewee on the phone, wanting to listen carefully to how they had experienced the lockdown and the last few months during the COVID-19 crisis. Before revisiting them the second time, I re-read the first interview. During two conversations, I took notes by hand and I made audio recordings of the conversations.

---

150. King and Horrocks, *Interviews in Qualitative Research*, 29–43.

Fourteen Interviews

Pseudonym (with notes of the special life situation)	Age (Age second interview)	Where the interviews took place
Marion (she had been a social worker with children with disabilities; she lost her mother when she was young, and after working a few years she had to look after her sister who had been suffering from depression for years; she never married but lived with a female friend in a big flat for over twenty years before both moved into a nursing home; she suffers from Parkinson's disease)	87 (89)	Nursing home
Frank (he lived in Germany for many years and was a theologian. After his wife died, he moved to Switzerland)	85	Flat
Richard (he was a scientist who lived in different countries, including for many years in Australia and Asia; he was always engaged in different churches; he had been a member of a Swiss Reformed church for over twenty years; extreme weakness led to admission to a nursing home after his wife died)	87	Nursing home
Heidi (she lost her father when she was nine years old; she was married and lost her husband to an illness many years ago when they still had young children; she lives with her dog; she doesn't go to church very often but had contact with the church through concerts and cultural activities; she suffers from extreme physical weakness, which was diagnosed as leukaemia shortly after the interview)	86	Flat
Ruth (she lost her husband early on young and suffered from depression for years herself; she sought peace in nature; she does not go to church very often)	89	At the daughter's flat

INQUIRING INTO COMFORT AND CONSOLATION IN THE BIBLE 63

Pseudonym (with notes of the special life situation)	Age (Age second interview)	Where the interviews took place
Alice (she is a widow; she has children; one suffers from MS and is very weak; she always had close contact with the church)	86 (88)	Flat
Anne (she lost her husband many years ago; she hosted a Christian house group for many years)	89	Flat/Nursing home
Lydia (she became a deaconess in the Swiss Reformed Church; she painted a lot in her years as a deaconess; she suffered from cancer and has been in hospital often during her last year)	64	Flat
Aaron (he had a Jewish mother and a German father; his father died in the war when he was seven, he suffered as child under the terror of the Nazi regime; he was married to a Swiss wife and was active in the Swiss Reformed Church; his wife suffers from dementia; according to what he told me, his heart was only working at 10 percent)	87 (89)	Flat (his wife moved during COVID time into a nursing home)
Paul (he worked in Africa for many years as a school teacher; after being in Africa with his family, he was a minister in a Swiss Reformed church; he was in a wheelchair and almost deaf)	89 (91)	Flat; Nursing home
Sally (she had a difficult childhood and had to look after her ill mum and her younger brother; she lost her husband years ago; she loves music)	98 (99)	House
Margaret (she suffers from a broken back which cannot be cured; she is constantly in physical pain; she enjoys reading the Bible alone)	86	Nursing home

Pseudonym (with notes of the special life situation)	Age (Age second interview)	Where the interviews took place
David (he lost his wife and tries to stick to a daily routine which includes going to church on Sundays and prayer times; when he was seven, his father died)	88 (90)	Flat
Daniela (she was a nurse and became a deaconess in the Swiss Reformed Church; she worked in different nursing positions in Switzerland and Africa)	88 (90)	Nursing home; Garden of the nursing home

The interviews were semi-structured interviews,[151] and were based on five questions which focused on human and divine experiences of comfort:

- *Opening question: Are there things or symbols that you consider to be helpful or important for your wellbeing? And can you describe how they make you feel?*

- *What is important for your Christian spirituality and faith (e.g., prayer, reading Scripture, taking part in services and the Lord's Supper or hearing music) and how do you experience comfort through these different spiritual practices?*

- *What kind of relationships are comforting and helpful at the moment and why?*

- *Do you and how do you experience comfort through creation, music, and art?*

- *What would be important or vital for you concerning the comfort ministry of the church at the end of your life?*

I was allowed to take photographs of some of the objects but decided not to take photographs of images with people on them to protect the participants' confidentiality.

After the interviews, it took another three months to transcribe and translate the audio material.

---

151. King and Horrocks, *Interview in Qualitative Research*, 182–95.

Data analysis

Data analysis methods for this study were adapted from different researchers, such as Swinton, van Manen, Finlay, and Pattison.[152] The goal of data analysis in hermeneutical phenomenology is to maintain the uniqueness of each person's lived experience, while at the same time allowing for an overall understanding of the meaning of the phenomenon itself. Next to pursuit of this balance, Osmer reminded me as a researcher that to interview Christians about their experiences also requires a spirituality of presence. He describes this attitude as "openness, attentiveness and prayerfulness."[153] Phronesis, wisdom, is part of various disciplines, but for me as a practical theological researcher I know that wisdom comes from God and that the Old and New Testaments speak in a certain way about living and dying. The New Testament portrays the crucified and risen Jesus Christ as more than just God's wisdom for the world but as one who was truly human and at the same time divine, one who came into this world to proclaim God's shalom to humankind.

Data analysis was not a linear process. Regardless of what "step" I was finding myself at, I often found the hermeneutic concept of the "fusion of horizons" and of the hermeneutical circle to involve a challenging and difficult process. At the beginning of the process of analysis I wrote in my diary after a discussion with my supervisors of the methods of data analysis available to me:

> I reread the transcripts for the first time all together. This is overwhelming. Where to start, where to begin? . . . I am standing at the seafront in Aberdeen, meditation stones. There are a lot of stones, innumerable. They are all different, in size, form, colour. They are all at a different place and have a certain history. I just have to pray for wisdom to get a kind of order in this chaos, or should I say in these "pieces of deep beauty."[154]

The focus of all phenomenological analysis is on pulling out explicit and hidden meanings through iteratively examining the data. Engaging this process involves "dwelling" with the data, examining it, and progressively deepening different aspects of understanding and meaning. As Finlay notes, "the analysis process can be a messy one, involving both

---

152. Swinton and Mowat, *Practical Theology*. Van Manen, *Phenomenology of Practice*; Finlay, *Phenomenology for Therapists*; Pattison, *Seeing Things*.

153. Osmer, *Practical Theology*, 34.

154. Personal notes 2019.

imaginative leaps of intuition as well as systematic working through of many iterative versions."[155] Although van Manen argues that phenomenology "does not let itself be seductively reduced to a methodical schema or an interpretive set of procedures,"[156] it is helpful to acknowledge the worth of certain steps for the analytical process.

Helpful steps in the analysis of the data include:

Transcription and photos—The interviews were digitally recorded and transcribed. The texts and the photos represented the material for the analysis. Reflective analytical and personal memos were taken throughout the entire research process.

"Dwelling" in the data—The texts were read through several times in order to get familiar and connected with the participants' stories and experiences. By dwelling in the data, the process of analysis became an "embodied lived experience in itself."[157] When I was immersed in the data, I was also responding and resonating with it rationally, spiritually, and bodily. This process nurtured the awareness and understanding of a person and their experiences.

Coding—Coding was done in four, or in some cases five, cycles or passes. The first cycle involved marking important texts which were salient to the research question: *"How do Christians in the Swiss Reformed Church experience comfort and consolation at the end of life?"* The second cycle required a more analytical and conceptual interaction with the data. By revisiting the data and going through the different markings, a deeper understanding began to surface. The second cycle was a process of going back and forward; because of the richness of description, I had to go through different texts a few times. The third cycle involved pondering the photographs. I collected the photos with the transcriptions. Then I brought photos together which seemed to have a special relevance to the content of the interview and to the comfort experiences. After dwelling with the visual material, I decided to design a collage out of the different photographs. The fourth cycle involved a special focus on suffering experiences mentioned in the interview and how they were related to individual descriptions of comfort and consolation. Then I returned to the second cycle and the analytical approach to deepen my understanding with the material of the photographs I had taken and the interaction of suffering and comfort experiences. The fifth cycle was possible with

---

155. Finlay, *Phenomenology for Therapists*, 228.

156. Van Manen, *Phenomenology of Practice*, 22.

157. Finlay, *Phenomenology for Therapists*, 229.

half of the interviewees. Through revisiting eight interviewees after the first COVID lockdown in 2020 and taking their experiences seriously, I was able to compare and deepen the individual comfort dimensions.

Analysis of each transcript—From each transcript a detailed thematic analysis was constructed. This was done using different colors, and through notes and tables. I was able to capture thick, rich descriptions, and these gave me a better understanding of the intertwined relationship between suffering and comfort.

Categorizing—This step involved a deep reflection on the codes and themes as a way of developing a thematic organization of the data. All codes were collected with different colors, printed out, and cut into pieces. Then I grouped the small slips of paper by hand, according to their similarities, differences, and relationships. Related themes I clustered together. I also drew data information on paper by hand and used signs and symbols to order the material. In this process I also searched for constitutive patterns which unified the different texts and data. This was difficult, and I found drawing mindmaps to be a helpful way to make sense of the patterns.

Fusion of Horizons—The different themes which emerged from my dwelling on the data also arose through a process in which the participant's viewpoints and my own perception and understanding were interacting. In short, deeper understanding of the phenomenon came through an interaction of my own and the interviewee's perspectives. This was not only part of the analytical process but also part of the entire process of engagement with the other person: the preparation of the interview, the interview, etc.

Validation of data—Some of the participants asked me if I could discuss the validation of the data with them. A few of them wrote and mailed special notes to me because they thought they had not answered the research question fully in the interview. I decided not to discuss the interview data with the participants. I realized that this might be another interpretative step and could bring up other questions of how to integrate the procedure in the research process. I also wanted to be free in my own journey as a researcher and to bring my theological horizon as a practical theological researcher into that process.

Through regular discussions with my supervisors, I tried to search for integrity and faithful understanding. Their feedback and guiding questions, and sometimes their irritating or persistent comments, made me aware once again that there is no straightforward or linear way of doing qualitative research, and that it takes time to develop strategies for one's own research project.

3

Finding "pearls of comfort": divine, human, and in creation, music, and artifacts

APPROACHING THE PRESENTATION OF MY FINDINGS

THE FOLLOWING CHAPTER PRESENTS the themes developed through the process of data analysis as described in chapter two. One of the main findings in this study was that all participants shared thick prayer descriptions which were significant for their spiritual wellbeing besides suffering, illness, loss, and various limitations. The three major themes and fourteen related sub-themes will be illustrated and thoroughly reviewed. In an attempt to preserve the significance of the uniqueness and diversity offered in their accounts, I use the metaphor "pearls of comfort." This expression came out of one interview in which a person shared thoughts about the New Jerusalem:

> Oh yes, to stay in the picture, the heavenly Jerusalem has twelve gates—that moves me deeply! . . . And I find it very exciting: these gates have pearls. And you know that pearls are formed in shells when sand gets in. The sand means pain for the shell and around this pain this precious thing, a special pearl, is formed over the course of time! (Lydia)

With the individual comfort experiences in mind as "pearls," I would like to view the phenomenon of comfort as "going through or being carried through." Human and divine comfort can be experienced very differently at the end of life; it depends on one's circumstances, personhood, health issues, relationships, life story, etc.

I have chosen to order the findings from the interviews under three major themes, which emerged from them. These three major themes of comfort and consolation at the end of life can be represented as: spirituality and faith; relationships with family and friends; and relationships with "things"/appreciation of creation, music, and art. In other words, comfort experiences include the feeling of:

- *being carried through the relationship with God;*
- *being carried through relationships with others (including animals); and*
- *being carried through the appreciation of "things" and the appreciation of beauty and brokenness in creation, music, and art.*

How spirituality, relational aspects, and creativity are intertwined is shown, for instance, in this interviewee's words:

> I need a lot of friendships (he laughs). I had a lot of friends in F., unfortunately I am now living here in W. and in this nursing home, but I still have people who are in contact with me from my church. . . . Last Sunday was a very good service, first class! I liked the singing and the sermon: that gives me energy for the week. (Richard)

Richard needs lots of friendships (relationships with friends), he felt the service at church was good and liked the sermon (spiritual aspect), and he enjoyed the singing (appreciation of music).

Having now introduced the three major themes of comfort and consolation which emerged from the interviews, I now return to the approach of "hermeneutic phenomenology." Given that my chosen framework by which to present the findings follows the guidelines of this specific methodology, I have to remember that this understanding includes the fact that the aim of the process of analysis is not first and foremost to arrive at or structure a generalizability of the findings. Instead, the aim is to present how the participants experienced their world in the context of the phenomenon being explored. I recognize that another researcher might interpret and present the findings in a different way than I did.

I made every attempt to preserve each interviewee's unique experience. I explicated and constructed common themes in response to my interpretation of the meaning and significance of the research question. All the interviewees described and reflected experiences at different levels and mentioned that the interviews themselves were an intense experience, spiritually, mentally, and bodily. I chose to give voice to certain core patterns in the data material which I found to be particularly insightful and essential to a phenomenological construction and interpretation of what it means to live with human and divine comfort at the end of life. Some interviewees' statements were very clear, others full of multidimensional metaphors, and still others hinted at important experiences that the interviewees were not able to describe fully but nonetheless tried to share. Sometimes I extracted and assembled data from across an individual's transcript in order to form a longer quotation. This was done to enhance the readability of the data and to illustrate the depth with which a person discussed a given aspect throughout the semi-structured interview.

Sometimes lived experience of the themes of the research topic overlapped and interconnected. Rather than conceiving of each of them exclusively, it was useful to picture them together and bring them together to form a larger unit. I decided to underline different parts of the data according to the level of intensity with which the interviewee spoke in the interview. As mentioned in chapter two, I quote or refer to each person using a pseudonym.

The following results, which I have put into the form of a table to make the three dimensions of the findings in the research more accessible, give an overview of key themes which I describe in the following pages:

Spirituality and Faith	Relationships	Appreciation of, creation, "things," music, and art
Prayer:	Family:	Creation:
Prayer as spiritual and creative praxis; Prayer and friendship with God; Prayer and the Holy Spirit; The transforming power of prayer; Prayer and creation; Prayer and thanksgiving; Prayer and suffering; Prayer as crying to God—looking for help; Prayer and lament; Prayer and mourning	Relationship with a spouse; Family bonds and comforting one another	Creation and a psalm; My blue stone; Comforted by a singing bird; Experiencing spring in the COVID era
Scripture:	Friends:	Music:
The Bible as a book; The Bible as a teacher; The Bible texts which belong to my life; The Bible and the "big story" of salvation; The Bible—appreciating the Old and New; Testaments together; The Bible and the Psalms; The Bible and the metaphor of the shepherd	Remembering a good friend; Death of a spouse, and experiencing a friend as comforter; The pastor as friend; When friendship hurts; When good friends die; Spiritual friends; My dog as a friend	A comfort hymn for life; Singing inwardly; Songs of comfort; Enjoying music
Worship services and the Lord's table:		Comfort of things:
Church services; The Lord's Supper		"Things warm us"; Sheep and shepherd; My furniture
		Art:
		"My resurrection cross"; Crucifixion painting; "My own painting"

FINDING "PEARLS OF COMFORT"

For all the participants, all three themes belonged together in different ways. One interviewee, for instance, said:

> The feeling of being carried and having contact with other people, this is what comfort is.... I also find it very beautiful when I find encouragement through psalms composed as music. It touches me deeply and gives me the feeling of connectedness with God, creation, and people all at the same time. (Paul)

He then started reflecting on human relationships first and from there added spiritual dimensions.

SPIRITUALITY AND FAITH

The word spirituality covers a wide range of understandings and is defined in many and various ways. One very general way of seeing the two terms together comes from the National Cancer Institute: "Spirituality means the way you look at the world and how you make sense of your place in it. Spirituality can include faith or religion, beliefs, values, and 'reasons for being.'"[1] However, it seems clear to me that spirituality and faith are interwoven. In the interviews, all of the participants talked about their spirituality in terms of their Christian faith and the concrete forms which that faith takes in their lives. Because all interviewees described prayer experiences, I decided to start with that topic. During the interview, I asked openly about different forms of spirituality.

Prayer

In the following subchapters I suggest that different themes have emerged through the data analysis in the context of prayer.

Prayer as a spiritual and creative praxis

Daily prayer was important for all the participants. Some of them had a "prayer rhythm" or routine.

> In the morning and evening, "quiet times" help me, simply for regaining strength through the Bible, or in the verses of daily light ("Losungen"). (Alice)

---

1. National Cancer Institute, "Faith and Spirituality."

> But we must not forget that certain occasions also teach us to pray: happiness, misfortune, etc. But there is also the everyday prayer, I have no special feelings or visions, I am rather sometimes just happy when the "business" [of prayer] is finished. But I am thankful because I have kept something up with regularity. ... The habit of praying builds me up. (Frank)

Some liked to pray freely; others preferred using biblical texts.

> During my praying of the Lord's Prayer, I like to imagine what it means. I see a picture for instance of Jesus, being there with his disciples. I reflect during praying what Jesus did for us. It's more than praying in words, it is also a picturing of what it means, to reflect and meditate. (Richard)

> I am very happy when I can say prayers that others have prayed before me. I find Psalms very helpful. For me it is always important that I am a "fellow in prayer." My living and dead brothers and sisters have "warmed up" the language. . . . I step into a space and a form with the prayer of others that is shaped by the faith of those others. That is helpful for me. I "swim" in their faith. With the Psalms I experience this again and again. (Frank)

Music and art played a role in prayer praxis. Three of the participants mentioned that they pray with the help of particular hymns or songs. Another four interviewees showed me pictures and paintings in their rooms which helped them to pray.

> When I hear this song, I feel that I have to pray this song inwardly. (Aaron)

> I like to pray with the Bible verse which is hanging as a picture on the wall: (Gal 2:20 Christ lives in me). (Daniela)

The Christian prayer praxis of which the interviewees spoke has a lot of creative forms. Some of the participants wrote prayers themselves, gave prayers as an encouragement to other people, or prayed with others on the phone.

> One can also pray on the phone. . . . I like writing letters to comfort people and I pray before I start writing. (Marion)

> I like to write prayers, for example: "Lord give me inner peace, give me a joyful happiness in all things, even in the smallest [of

things]. Give me the fire of true love and most important: give me forgiveness." (Sally)

During prayer times, some of them experienced a kind of connectedness with friends who were far away and were not able to respond or get into contact with them easily. Daniela had a very dear friend in Germany who was now so fragile that she couldn't get on the phone or talk to her anymore. She says:

> It is so strengthening that we are connected through the words of comfort from Scripture. Sometimes we don't know how God works . . . The Holy Spirit helps us. (Daniela)

Lydia understood her activity of painting often as prayer or connectedness with God. She was always surprised that God could use these painting for the good for others. Often, she was not very enthusiastic about her painting, and she never saw herself as an artist. Yet for her, painting was a time and an opportunity to find peace.

> The more I have forgotten myself in the painting process, the more I have understood that praying and painting can meet. (Lydia)

Prayer and friendship with God

In different ways the participants gave expressions to their connectedness with God in prayer. The way some of them described it resonates with the experiences expressed by the mystics. Theresa of Avila, for instance, wrote: "Prayer is nothing but an intimate conversation between friends; it means conversing frequently and alone with him who we know loves us."[2]

> Then I simply talk to God . . . it is very simple—my thoughts come to me and I share them with God. (Margarete)

> Praying is like staying with Jesus. (David)

> God hears, and God also speaks. . . . Because I trust God I can pray. (Lydia)

> My dear saviour is my consolation. You know, Rev. B. once told me that Jesus said to his disciples in the Bible: "You are my

---

2. Houston, *Transforming Friendship*, 267.

> friends!" That is why we can call him friend! And then I also pray: You are my best friend, my greatest consolation! (Sally)

In each of these responses the participants were trying to put into words something about their faith that within prayer they experience a closeness with God which is similar to being with a friend who offers consolation.

Prayer and the Holy Spirit

After my initial interview in December 2018, I revisited Alice in September 2020 after the experience of the first Covid lockdown.[3] She was very eager to explain to me that the triune God, especially the Holy Spirit became more important in her spiritual life during lockdown and afterwards. She had a lot of time to reflect on the question which already came up in the first interview, that she wondered how God could not only be present but also working "in us."

> I learned during lockdown that the Holy Spirit is such a strong comforter. The Spirit is not only there when I go to church or when I am active or when I am visiting people. The Holy Spirit is also in me, so close, and I have been experiencing that.
>
> Researcher: How does that feel?
>
> (Silence) The Holy Spirit is able to connect with us. We all are so different, but he finds a way. I feel comforted during prayer times, but not *only* then. I have been indoors for the last few months, more so than usual, and I don't have a garden—only a few plants on my balcony. But these plants are full of life, like we are. So, through little observations like these I felt at peace to invite the Holy Spirit more often and ask God to fill my old body with his Spirit, so that I don't lose contact with him and that I can live with his joy and promises. It was something new [being in lockdown]; I am so used to being active, I have been all my life, but to pray that in my ordinary life I can welcome the Holy Spirit more, that is something I haven't been practicing before.

---

3. In Switzerland the first lockdown to prevent the spread of COVID-19 was between March and the end of May 2020. People were told to avoid all "unnecessary" contacts and to stay at home whenever possible. Older and more vulnerable people in particular were often forbidden, by their families or by those responsible for them, to leave their homes or to go shopping themselves. The churches were not allowed to hold meetings or services, and all cultural institutions and schools were closed.

> Lockdown changed my awareness of God's presence and I had the feeling that time was different too.
>
> I reflected on time and eternity. I realize that time as I know it will end in His presence. Have you ever thought about that? I read in a book by X. about this: eternity is not endless time; it will be God's time, and he created time for us.

I have quoted at length here because I think Alice's words express well how she was able, in the terms of her own Christian spirituality and prayer life, to discover new aspects of the working of the Holy Spirit.

The transforming power of prayer

The feeling of being connected with God in prayer my interviewees also experienced as a time and space of reorientation. Frank, for instance, talks of the "productive silence for prayer . . . where the contradictions are silenced for a moment and I reorient myself." The interviewees also experienced the times of prayer as a new opportunity to be connected with others.

> I am literally being carried by a net of prayer. It is a real power. It is not just a feeling! That is something special, this connection in prayer and this standing up for each other, I experience it as very real, and that gives me strength. (Lydia)

> To pray for others, to come before God in silence for others, being part of God's consoling love—it is something great. We can only do that because Jesus himself lives and prays for us. First Jesus for us, then we through him for others. (Daniela)

> Sometimes, when I wake up, a spiritual word comes to my mind and then I pray that this comforting word also reaches to the right address [or person]. (Marion)

Notice that some of the interviewees described the transforming dimensions of prayer in terms of their care for others: because of the experience of the love of God, we feel loved and can love others in prayer.

Prayer and creation

Some of the participants emphasized that creation gave them space to pray and to gain strength in illness and suffering. Ruth, for instance, described the forest as a place where she felt free to pray; it was the place where she felt most close to God. Others similarly were comforted and experienced joy at seeing plants and flowers growing and regarding them as a way of seeing God's presence in creation. Sally says, "I can see the leaves, the rays of light, yes, the movements through the branches of the tree, and [that prompts me] first [to] thank my creator for living and being able to experience a new day with him." Lydia also felt comforted by creation and its divinely appointed rhythm of becoming and passing away when she felt her thoughts going in circles.

Prayer and thanksgiving

Some of the interviewees mentioned that praying with prayers from Christian tradition or the Bible was helpful to get into a rhythm of thanksgiving and praise. Others meditated on Bible verses, which helped them to give thanks.

> The Lord's Prayer I pray very often [and] in different languages! And while praying, I like to imagine what it means! . . . I reflect while praying on what Jesus did for us. (Richard)

> He will also keep you firm to the end, so that you will be blameless on the day of our Lord Jesus Christ (1 Cor 1:8). That is such a comforting meditative Scripture: everything doesn't just depend on me! (Alice)

> Jesus Christ today, yesterday, and the same also in eternity (Heb 13:8). It is really a consolation if one has this verse in oneself and lives with it. (Daniela)

> I can bring everything before God and I remember thankfully in prayer that "the Lord is my shepherd." (Margarete)

The interviewees were all affiliated with the Swiss Reformed Church, which as a Protestant church has historically laid weight on teaching its members to read the Bible for themselves. These quotations show the participants' familiarity with the Bible and biblical language and their trust that God speaks to them through the Bible.

Prayer and suffering

In this section I quote longer interview responses to show the reader the particular intensity of the suffering which the interviewees described during the interviews. It is interesting that the interviewees described suffering not primarily as a medical state, even though they have and have had various and severe health problems. Especially noteworthy is that as they described it suffering always had to do with their life stories and with the different kinds of pain (physical pain, emotional pain, mental pain, social pain, spiritual pain) they had experienced.[4] Experiences of suffering, even when the interviewees reflected on them years later from a different perspective, remain crucial markers in their lives and are sometimes still reflected in the way they pray at the end of their lives. Thus, suffering experiences from past and present prayer praxis often seem to be connected somehow.

The following example shows how an interviewee remembered being excluded from prayer in her youth. She was working for a Christian family and was not allowed to be part of the prayer meeting which the family and a church community had organized because the wife was seriously ill.

> The husband organized a prayer for healing and when it was all arranged, they told me that I was not invited. They told me that I am not one of them and that I was not allowed to be in the house that day. That hit me so hard that I thought that if I weren't myself a Christian, I would throw myself off the nearest bridge. Being excluded from prayer went very deep. . . . Everyone says that we have Jesus Christ and his resurrection is valid and true, but somehow, we humans can't seem to live out this great message (pause). Maybe it is too difficult for us as humans to live this love of God. (Marion)

The experience of being left out or of being deemed somehow inadequate to be part of the praying community left a lasting impression on Marion's prayer life. She was always concerned to pray for everyone with whom she came into contact and to let them know that she was praying for them.

In this context of prayer and suffering, a number of other stories are of interest, stories that illustrate how life-changing some suffering

---

4. Saunders's observations of pain experiences, known as the "total pain" concept, is helpful here. See: Holder-Franz, ". . .dass du bis zuletzt leben kannst," 78.

experiences are and how they affect people's spiritual lives and their attitudes and habits of prayer.

The first one is that of one man who had a near death experience as a young scientist when he was working in Greenland. He had never prayed before and at the time had no interest in religion. But this experience changed everything for him.

> It was very emotional. I couldn't talk about it for more than a year! It was on an expedition in Greenland. I worked there and finished my thesis as a researcher there. I felt secure.... There were two of us. And we had our assistants. I was leading the expedition. One day the others went ahead. I was still taking photographs on a large mountain, I expected a big view, like the Rigi in Switzerland. Something really beautiful and also useful for my work.... And then I just changed my position, perhaps two meters or so, and while I changed my position in the middle of snow, I slipped because I hadn't noticed that there was only a small layer of snow and there was ice underneath. And I fell a few meters, there was a rock there, I tried to catch the rock, I missed it and I fell down—400 meters! It was a terrible moment. During this time, I had so many experiences, very fast! My whole life!... I saw my family, I saw my parents, my girlfriend, and I knew that if there was just one rock in this ice channel and I hit it, it would be the end of me! I knew I would be cut up and dead. And if not that, I would be catapulted over the rocks into the valley. The chance of surviving [such a fall] was very small. And on my way down I started to think, and I was asking myself: "What can I do?" I couldn't see any longer, because I had snow in my eyes. I remembered my rucksack, I had metal in it. I used the rucksack to slow down, and it helped. But as soon as I moved, it started again. And I knew that the next time I would have to pull on the rucksack with all my might, and I did, and it stopped. I did indeed stop, but only after falling 400 meters. I had my measuring instruments with me and I could see that I was at about 1000 meters in altitude. I knew then that I wasn't far away from my tent. We had our tent at about 1000 meters altitude. It was only a few kilometers away; it wasn't very far! So, I walked there!... I was in shock! When I reached my tent, I pulled my shirt off, it was full of blood, everywhere! I went into the tent, I laid down and was "gone." I couldn't understand what had happened! After a time, my assistant came along, a few hours later! And he saw that everything was covered in blood. He was shocked as well! And somehow, I recovered.... In those

FINDING "PEARLS OF COMFORT" 81

> days we had no radio connection! We were fully on our own!
> For a month. . . . I was thinking of God a lot. I had a feeling that
> I saw the other side, a light, something that didn't frighten me,
> but that helped me. (pause) [It was a] power to calm down which
> helped me during this fall to think of what I could do! . . . This
> situation was very important for me! Up to this time religion
> had not been very important to me. It felt remote! I thought I
> could handle everything by myself. Through that experience I
> asked God who he was and started praying that I might find out
> more about him. (Richard)

This long quotation from the interview with Richard reveals how experiences of suffering can be the reason for a person to start praying at all. Richard's delivery from what he thought would be almost certain death, and his recovery, led him to an intensive prayer life which he continued for the rest of his life.

A different story of suffering and prayer is that of Ruth, who, in contrast to Richard, only found peace with God over the course of many years. She endured a tragic accident happening to her husband. When that happened, they already had two little girls and she was pregnant with twin boys. She lost the twins in the seventh month; they couldn't be saved. She had to be there for her daughters and for her husband who, all in all, spent three years in hospital. He was first in a coma, then had one leg amputated, and later suffered from cancer. He did come home in between but did not recover. In short, despite battling with ill health for years, he died of cancer. Only after several years did Ruth have the strength to pray again and found God in nature, in her work in the garden, and in the woods. Her suffering was so great that only after many years she was able to recover her faith through prayer.

> More than 60 years ago, he had an accident. (Pause) We were
> both still very young. Our daughter M. was just five years old.
> He worked in B. at an iron foundry, they stocked large iron parts
> for construction companies. He was there and secured the big
> iron pipes as usual, but a chain [he used] was compromised
> and so the pipes fell on top of him before he could get to safety!
> (Pause) He was seriously injured and went to hospital. He was
> in a coma at that point, which was a very difficult time. He re-
> gained consciousness and after a good four months came back
> home. At home he developed a severe infection and had to go
> back to hospital. He was there for a full year. (Pause) They then
> had to amputate one of his legs. That wasn't the worst, for he got

> a prosthesis. But then he got cancer. He wanted to live; he really did. (Pause) He died of cancer after such a long illness. . . . It was a hard time for everyone! . . . I had no complaints at that time, I loved him, he needed my help and everyone did the best they could. The questions came much later! . . . For years I shut down, had no joy anymore! I did not experience joy anymore. The only thing I continued to do was the garden. Just work in this garden, to do something. (break) Some people wanted to comfort me: "You have your children" [they'd say]. But that's not the same, the children are not like S.! Children cannot replace him! . . . I learnt over the years to accept the "stones." Sometimes you also have to run on the stony ground. (break) But I didn't go to the cemetery every day! . . . I went to the forest . . . I spent a lot of time reflecting on death. (break) I could go at any time! I have nothing to lose here! I often pray that it won't last that long. I am prepared for death. (Ruth)

Through many years of walking in the forest and gardening, she recuperated a little by observing nature, such as trees, plants, and stones, and gradually was able to find her trust in God again through prayer.

Alice gives us a different account of suffering and prayer. Hers is one of compassionate suffering and its effect on prayer. What prompted it was the suffering of one of her children. Of her four children, one of them has had multiple sclerosis from a young age. Alice remembered that they organized a group of Christians to pray for his healing.

> Then a Christian group immediately said: "We'll pray for N." And of course, we as a family also did that. But God said: "No." He must bear this illness. And when one reads in the Bible: "Ask and it shall be given to you" (Matt 7:7), then you start thinking, so what does this mean in this case? And then you start realizing that God gives things to you and carries you in ways more different than you can imagine. That wasn't easy. The fact that N. himself did not give up his faith and hope in God, that remains a special gift to us all. I always think he has message for those who are ill in this world; he is the voice that has to be heard. . . . Because of N.'s illness, all the siblings have a close relationship with each other, which has given the whole family a completely different view of life and also a great sense of care for each other. (Alice)

Alice's own prayer life has been both shaken and strengthened by her experience of her son's suffering. From her initial posture of hope and trust, together with the other members of her family, that through prayer he might be healed from multiple sclerosis, she has grown to accept and trust that God's ways may be different. Although she still prays for healing and for his health, she no longer feels threatened or adrift when her prayers are answered in ways other than she expected.

Prayer as crying to God—looking for help

David is a man who learnt to pray through suffering. He comes from a very poor family and his father died when he was seven. He consequently had to help his mother a great deal and was thankful to have an older brother. He found joy in being part of his local group of scouts in his childhood and youth. There he found company and friendship. One of the leaders, who was like a father figure for him, gave him a special knife. When he lost the knife in the woods during a scout training exercise, he was desperate but didn't want to talk to anybody about it. He was about ten years old.

> When I realized that my knife was no longer with me, I was very upset. I went home and started to pray: "God, dear father in heaven, you know what happened, help me!" Four days later, when I was out of school, I went into that forest again and after a while I saw the knife stuck in the ground, really in the ground! No leaves covering it, clearly visible! The joy that God can do something out of love for me and that he can hear my prayer as a child, that made such a strong impression on me. In fact, it was so strong that it continues to strengthen my faith even now! It was such a big forest, without any obvious paths and with so many leaves! That experience encourages me a lot. (David)

Looking back at the end of his life, David remains convinced that his experience of finding the knife and his understanding of this as answered prayer has given him comfort throughout his life and has encouraged him to bring everything to God in prayer. He also encourages his grandchildren to pray to God about things that are important to them, and he prays faithfully for them as well.

Another very dramatic childhood experience of crying out to God for help is told by Sally. Sally's mother was raped when she was a teenager and she became pregnant. Later, she married Sally's father but he was only willing to marry her if she gave the boy away. She did this and later gave birth to Sally and another boy. Sally's mother, however, didn't recover from the ordeal and started to drink alcohol. This became so bad that Sally had to look after her mother on a daily basis.

> I cried a lot and couldn't understand what was going on and why my mother had to go through all this. Where was God? Why didn't God protect her? (Sally)

Looking back, Sally is aware that she prayed a lot, and cried out often to God. Yet at the time she did not feel that she got any answers. She didn't give up, however, and persevered in looking to God for help. Although she experienced God in many ways over the course of her long life, at the end of her life she was very aware that there may be times when one experiences God as silent, and that one has to face that without giving up.

In a very different situation but also in the context of prayer as a cry for help to God, Lydia told me about having a difficult childhood and later going through a divorce. She was not sure if she should believe in God. She started searching for God in different places and travelled a lot. When she was forty years old, she tried crying to God for help and slowly built up a life of prayer with God. Looking back on that time, she said,

> You have to live with your questions before and with God! That doesn't have to mean that you are not desperately looking for an answer... It was important for me to tell God that I could wait. ... It was a cry for trust. Can I trust you, God? That was my question! (Lydia)

Lydia's cry for help had to do with her learning to trust that God was there and would answer her prayers, even if it took a while to get a response and she had to be patient in the meantime.

Prayer and lament

It was not easy for the interviewees to speak openly about experiences of lament. They experienced lament, but they were rarely willing to open up to me about those periods in their lives.

> It is hard that I am so old and have to see that my son's multiple sclerosis is getting worse and worse. I went through a lot of lament. The Psalms are still a great help. Lamenting is also a form of love. You only accuse someone of something if you have a relationship with that person. (Alice)

Later in this chapter and in the theological response section, I shall address the use the participants made of the psalms. Here, Alice describes lament as a process that lasts for a long period of time, and that it was almost paradoxically bound up with a relationship of love and trust in God. Part of that relationship has to do with speaking frankly to the other, and this stance assumes that the relationship will be able to bear such truth telling.

Aaron, who is married to Bethli, gives us another example of lament which is brought to God in prayer. Bethli suffers from dementia. His wish was to care for her until she died. Aaron has become very weak himself and can no longer care for Bethli. He suffered greatly during the first COVID lockdown because shortly beforehand he had to put Bethli into a specialist nursing home.

> I miss my wife every day and I pray that she can die soon. Before lockdown, I visited her three to four times a week and she knew my name, she gave me a kiss and enjoyed being with me and her daughters. Then lockdown came. I tried to phone as often I could, but this was difficult. Often, she was too sad to speak; I felt she was missing me. It made me sad as well and I cried a lot. I started to wake up at night and prayed that this would change so that we might see and touch each other again soon. After ten weeks I was able to see her again, but she couldn't say my name anymore. I tried to sing with her; she used to be able to sing the church hymns by heart, but she didn't respond. . . . It was unbearable, and my daughters encouraged me not to go too often [because] it depressed me so much and I felt that I was losing my strength, I feel much weaker [now] than a few months ago. . . . I read my "Daily Light" [meditations] every day, but my only comfort is now that both our weakness lies in God hands and I hope that we can both die soon. It is a hard time. (Aaron, second visit)

Aaron still prays every day, and every day he brings his suffering for his wife and their relationship in lament before God. And although he prayed for a change and after a number of weeks a change did occur, his lamenting only became more intense when he realized that she no longer recognizes his name. His trust in God and his willingness to give himself and his wife into God's hands, however, remain even in a situation of desperate lament.

Prayer and mourning

Different interviewees described the suffering they felt of losing loved ones. Through their narratives, they gave deep insights into their mourning, and how it changed over time. Through their faith and especially through prayer they found a way to connect their mourning and remembering with God's presence.

Frank lost his wife a few years ago. He went to the grave every day after the funeral. He needed this time to sit on a bench next to the grave and to mourn in silence and in prayer with words from his wife's favorite psalm: Ps 139.

> She liked Ps 139. I always found it beautiful, but it was not as central [to me then] as it is now after her death. Only after her death did it really become mine. (Frank)

Frank describes how, through appropriating his wife's favorite psalm and using it as his prayer, it almost mystically brings him closer to her as he mourns her death before God.

Anne, similarly, lost her spouse and often feels alone. But for her, after different periods of mourning she found that a verse in the Bible—Isa 41:10—which formerly had no connection to her husband suddenly became especially helpful and like a guiding light to her in her mourning process: "So do not fear, for I am with you; do not be dismayed, for I am your God. I will strengthen you and help you; I will uphold you with my righteous right hand." This verse encouraged her to pray, to focus on her relationship with God, and not to give up hope. It reminds her that she isn't alone and doesn't need to fear because God is with her.

Regarding mourning and prayer, a further example is instructive. Aaron lost his son-in-law recently and the daughter who lost her husband is blind because of an illness she had. Mourning before God helps him to share these heavy burdens.

> I mourn often before God. The blindness of our daughter, then the death of my son-in-law, that often became too much for me. (Aaron)

Although coping with the death of his son-in-law along with his daughter's blindness often became too much for him, Aaron still managed to mourn his loss before God in prayer. And although his suffering remained, he experienced prayer and mourning as a form of comfort.

Scripture

During each interview I asked the interviewees if they could remember Bible texts of special relevance to them. Almost all of them could, after I had transcribed the interviews, I wrote all the different Bible texts down on a large paper by hand, and then wrote in my research diary:

> Through Jesus Christ, they discover and "see" something like a "red thread" and they can hold [on to] this "thread" through individual texts, passages, words, verses, pictures. It is like "seeing" the wider meaning of the divine story through a specific Bible text.[5]

The Bible as a book

For some of the interviewees, it was important to preserve a family Bible. Aaron, for instance, has such a family Bible (see, for instance, the picture below). It is far too big and too heavy to read on a daily basis, but this Bible is very special to him and his family and connects him to his family history, a history that was not easy for him and is part of his suffering still today in this time of illness and letting go.

> I have a big Bible in my office! Imagine, my Jewish relatives gave it to my parents at their wedding. They didn't survive the Holocaust. When we were children, the Bible was always visible in our living room. Each page has some pictures . . . as children we found that fascinating. . . . I always found it very special that the Jewish relatives gave my parents such a big and valuable Bible for a wedding ceremony. My father was a reformed Christian, my mother came from a Jewish background. Out of consideration for the differences, no religious wedding celebration was held. . . . My father died in Germany when I was seven. (Aaron)

The concrete presence of the Bible as a book which he can touch and hold has a comforting relevance for Aaron. Although he is reformed in his spirituality, the book acts in a similar way to a relic in other traditions, in that it somehow opens up a relationship with others who came before him, a relationship not bound by time. The Bible, given its large size and its prominent and highly visible place in Aaron's home, also embodies

---

5. Research note, 2019.

the unbelievable complexity of his Jewish and Christian background and heritage, something he doesn't feel a need to hide.

For Paul as a retired reformed minister, the different Bibles on his desk are also important as books which have been companions to him his entire life. He enjoys seeing them each day and reads in them, as he also does in his Greek New Testament, regularly. He has his favorite Bible, which is covered in a leather case. It looks well used and its pages are interspersed with various papers. He is preparing to move to a nursing home and has to give some of his Bibles away.

> I have my various Bibles . . . but now I am thinking of passing most of them on and giving them away to family members or people who are dear to me. (Paul)

He is comforted by the thought of his Bibles being in the possession of his family and those dear to him, and he wishes to pass these on personally to them with a blessing.

The Bible as "teacher"

Frank likes to read theological literature; he was a teacher himself and discovered over the years that the Bible can teach him a lot.

> The Bible tells me more than I can say, because I give the Bible the "right" to teach me. Not because the Bible is divinely inspired: it is not that simple. But I give it, I would almost say, power over me by listening to it and studying and trusting the Bible. The Bible is my teacher. Just as with a good teacher, so I listen to the Bible and trust that "this teacher" can say something important to me. (Frank)

Frank relates the teaching effect of the Bible to his trust in it, which is bound up with his faith in God and the Holy Spirit. The Holy Spirit as the "paraclete" is a teacher and admonisher, an encourager and a comforter. Through the word "paraclesis," comfort is very close to the empowerment of teaching.

In a different context, Daniela experienced that the Bible was and is like a good teacher to her. As a reformed deaconess, she hears Bible texts read every day during her community's prayer times. Although she worked as a nurse in different places, she has been part of a community for over sixty years and experienced "Bible teaching" as a hermeneutical circle or spiral. To allow the Bible to speak to one is like deepening the relationship with God and also experiencing that God can deepen his relationship to a person through different biblical texts. She told me that new perspectives can be given to her even through stories she has known for a long time and has read again and again over the years.

> I have come across Ps 121 again and again over the years . . . and suddenly in dark hours and when I am in need, these verses speak to me in a fresh way. (Daniela)

She recognizes the work of the Holy Spirit in such revelations, and knows that biblical texts can be experienced in a fresh and also in a comforting way.

The Bible texts or biblical stories which are part of one's life-story

Often the texts and stories which were mentioned also had a special meaning and a comfort dimension for the individual person. While some of the interviewees explained the deeper meaning to me, some of them just mentioned a verse or a name without explaining it in detail. Some told me that a special Bible verse had been given to them at their baptism or confirmation, on their wedding day, or at some other particularly special moment in their lives. It is striking that nearly all of the interviewees referred to the Psalms in a variety of ways, and that next to the gospels the letters of Paul had deep meaning for most of them.

To show the richness of the interviewees' Christian spirituality, I highlight different passages of their interviews. I am aware that the complete meaning cannot be surfaced, but by listening attentively to the different life-stories, one can discern a link between the biblical text and individual life experiences.[6]

Richard, who shared with me the near-death experience described earlier, was a geologist and told me that Ps 148, along with the Lord's Prayer, is very dear to him. Using Ps 148 he can praise God for creation, which was so dear to him as a scientist. That psalm reminds him of the day of his salvation on the snowy mountain in Greenland when for the first time he wondered about God and his existence.[7]

Frank, the theology teacher, has been engaged politically in "prayers for peace" for many years. For him, that the church is socially and politically engaged is vital. He describes being "at home" with some Bible texts, which to him is a form of comfort:

> There is the "Bible within the Bible" for everyone who reads it. There are, for example, the psalms, or the gospel texts, or certain epistles that you have made your own in a special way. One could say: that "one has built oneself a little house within the house." To me, Romans 8 and the Sermon on the Mount are very important. These are places of home, of comfort, because you let them come very close to you. (Frank)

---

6. In the process of interpreting the interviews, several times I thought about the words of Linda Finlay, that "phenomenology—when it is done well—discloses, transforms and inspires. . . . It is not just a research method. It offers a way of both being in and of seeing the world, from inside and out. It is not just an intellectual project; it is a life practice," Finlay, *Phenomenology for Therapists*, 26.

7. Psalm 148 (NIV): "Praise the Lord! Praise the Lord from the heavens; praise him in the heights! Praise him, all his angels; praise him, all his hosts! Praise him, sun and moon, praise him, all you shining stars! Praise him, you highest heavens, and you waters above the heavens! Let them praise the name of the Lord! For he commanded and they were created. And he established them forever and ever; he gave a decree, and it shall not pass away. Praise the Lord from the earth, you great sea creatures and all deeps, fire and hail, snow and mist, stormy wind fulfilling his word!"

The new life in Christ described by the apostle Paul in Romans 8 and the risky life of discipleship to which Jesus calls us in the Sermon on the Mount, give a form and structure to Frank's understanding of what it means to be at home. This encompasses the manifold meanings of comfort, which include admonishing and exhortation.

For Aaron, feeling at home in a Bible text has to do with his Jewish and Christian background and his search for meaning in his life story. All his Jewish relatives were killed by the Nazi regime in Germany during the Second World War, and he and his mother and sister survived by fleeing to Switzerland. He told me that he likes the stories of the Old Testament, especially the story of Daniel. Reading and valuing these stories as a child in a family in which he was brought up in the Christian faith was very important to him. It allowed him to read and experience that Jewish tradition is part of the Christian story. He heard through the story of Daniel that people are not always just lost and in danger, but that, as he did for Daniel, God is able also rescue us from harm.

> I read the Old Testament stories as a young boy. This was great, especially Daniel and David. But Daniel especially is close to me, also the way his very life was threatened. (Aaron)

Alongside its uplifting element, the story of Daniel also highlighted part of Aaron's struggle and lament: Why was the Daniel story so different from his story? Why did his Jewish relatives have to die? Why did his father, who was a Christian and a famous doctor, have to die in the last days of the war? Being there for people facing danger later became a major part of Aaron's life as he was employed as a social worker for over forty years.

The Bible and the "big story" of salvation

I described a further element of the way the interviewees include the Bible in their lives in terms of the "big story" of salvation. Here Lydia's interview is instructive. It occurred six weeks before she died. She had been suffering from cancer for more than three years and was preparing to let go. Her little granddaughter asked her a few days before I interviewed her which stories of the Bible were particularly important to her. When she talked about the "big story" of salvation in Christ to me, she was very alert and her voice was very intense: it was as if she wanted encapsulate what she considered to be especially relevant. Because it was like a testimony to me, I want to quote it here at length.

> What Bible texts are important to me? That's funny, my granddaughter asked me that too! She is not church minded at all, not even baptized. But she wanted to know which biblical stories were important to me. When I thought about it, I realized that the most important things for me are the "big stories," which hold things together! . . .
>
> Beginning with the one person who was placed in this world and was still very close to God, very close: at that point conversation with God was still effortless. But then the rift with God becomes worse and worse, and just when everyone is furthest from God, Christ comes. Christ closes the rift, the abyss! He makes it possible for people to come to the Father again: "No one comes to the Father except through me." (John 14:6)! Christ is on the one hand connected with the Father and on the other hand with people. He is God and human at the same time. Without him we would have fallen infinitely far in this downward movement, [and have become] unreachable! But with Jesus, this self-responsibility comes and the turning upside down of all the classic ways of thinking. . . . But we haven't got that far yet. We still think pretty much according to the image of the pyramid: the most important one is at the top, then the mass of people come are below. But Jesus states it differently: [he says that] the one who is the greatest must become the little one (Matt 18:4)! . . . Also, this abandonment of blood ties. When his family comes to Jesus and he rejects them, [he says]: Who are my brothers? Who is my family? Who are my sisters? (Matt 12:48) I don't think we can imagine that too starkly! Imagine, in a society where blood, heredity is important and counts, he cuts everything off; [he says:] that doesn't matter anymore! And then he says that those who are "united with me in Spirit are brother and sister to me"! (She is very animated; this seems to be very important to her). It is the turning around of everything! And then, at the end we will land in the heavenly Jerusalem, which is a city! It is a social entity, and humans are involved in the creation of this city. That is something other than a paradise. We must, I believe, keep that in mind and in our hearts, that we are on the way to becoming people who find their place in the heavenly Jerusalem, where God once again dwells completely in the middle of everything, and humans, creation, and God are again [indivisibly] together. . . . This heaven, this earth will pass away, but there is a new heaven and a new earth! And this new

earth no longer needs a sun from the outside: it shines from the inside! That is what fascinates me the most. Yes, one could also say that this comforts me, this view of life and of God and humans through the biblical lens. (Lydia)

In this rich narrative, questions arise. How does Lydia describe the biblical salvation story? Which biblical texts does she mention and how? Is the coming of Christ for her primarily a cosmic event for all time? How does she understand our human responsibility to become involved in the biblical path towards this promised shalom?

Lydia begins by remembering the communication between God and humankind before the fall, and then describes with excitement how things will be at the end of time, in the new Jerusalem. She loves the vision that humans can and will be creative in this new heavenly city of God and is clear that this is possible because communication is renewed and communion restored. At the end of life, she is no longer interested in the details of different biblical stories; now she prefers to concentrate on the "big story" of salvation, a story that culminates in the vision of the new Jerusalem where God dwells in the midst of everything and where peace will be a reality in a new way.

The Bible and the psalms

Praying the psalms was an integral part of their spiritual praxis for most of the interviewees. Remembering and praying a psalm at a certain time in their lives alone or in community was a strengthening experience.

God's guidance and help through the pilgrimage of life the interviewees identified foremost in Ps 23, but they also mentioned it in other psalms, such as 103 and 139. Through the psalms' poetic language and through the richness of their images and metaphors, the interviewees were able to connect their experiences of the past and present with some of the words in the psalms, which included rational and emotional dimensions. Walter Brueggemann, the Old Testament scholar, describes this well:

> The work of prayer is to bring these two realities together—the boldness of the Psalms and the extremity of our experience—to let them interact, play with each other, tease each other, and illuminate each other. . . . Metaphors are not packaged announcements; they are receptive vehicles waiting for a whole world of

experience that itself is waiting to come to expression. And if, in the praying of the Psalms, we do not bring the dynamic of our own experience, we shall have flat, empty prayers treating the language as one-dimensional description.[8]

Anne, for instance, brings this dynamic into how she thinks of Ps 23 when she feels lonely: "When I need encouragement, the first psalm I think of is the 23rd . . . it is like a treasure chest" (Anne). She connects the treasure chest of the psalm with the dynamic of her own experience, which can be enriched by the "treasures" in the text. Margaret similarly lives with the rich metaphors of the text. "'The Lord is my shepherd': this Psalm always comes to my aid" (Margaret).[9]

Both Margaret and Anne explained that through the metaphor of a shepherd they could imagine God as someone nearby and protective, but also as someone strong and powerful. They and other interviewees saw in the picture of the shepherd a deep connection of the two testaments of the Bible, and instantly connected this psalm with the words of Jesus in John 10:11 ("I am the good shepherd") and the parable in Luke 15 of the lost sheep.

For Marion, another of the interviewees, the "good shepherd" is *the* story in the Bible through which she interprets almost all the other parts of Scripture. Because she worked with children with severe handicaps in her youth and for years had to look after her sister who suffered from depression and suicidal ideation, she needed to focus on the "thick biblical story" of the "good shepherd." (She also collects sheep in her room; these I describe later under the "comfort of things.") What is special in her interpretation is that she likes to set up a dove, a symbol of the Holy Spirit, next to the shepherd.

> Can you see the shepherd? And the sheep? I have a lot of sheep. The shepherd takes care of the little ones. He does not leave them alone. . . . Here is a dove, next to the shepherd. The Holy Spirit tells the shepherd where to go and which sheep needs him. . . . That's the sheep that was lost and was found again. Do you see?

---

8. Brueggemann, *Praying the Psalms*, 17, 27.

9. Psalm 23 (NIV): "A psalm of David. The Lord is my shepherd, I lack nothing. He makes me lie down in green pastures, he leads me beside quiet waters, he refreshes my soul. He guides me along the right paths for his name's sake. Even though I walk through the darkest valley, I will fear no evil, for you are with me; your rod and your staff, they comfort me. You prepare a table before me in the presence of my enemies. You anoint my head with oil; my cup overflows. Surely your goodness and love will follow me all the days of my life, and I will dwell in the house of the Lord forever."

... That's the good thing about the story—that the shepherd kept searching and searching! How happy the shepherd was! He told the others: "I found my sheep again!" He also had great trust that God would look after the other sheep. He didn't have to take the whole flock with him! (Marion)

Marion emphasizes that it costs energy and a kind of passion to look for the lost. For her it is not a thing Jesus *has* to do, but something he *wants* to do—to bring home the lost and the suffering—and this is a comfort to her.

There are, however, also other ways in which the interviewees used the psalms. For Paul, comfort in the psalms is focused more on thanksgiving. He responded quickly when I asked for an example of a comfort text for him and told me that Ps 103 had a special meaning for him and his wife. The psalm was read to them at their golden wedding anniversary service. Right then and there, he quoted the first five verses to me, and smiled the whole time he recited them. It was as if by repeating these words out loud to me he was "creating" joy and trust and that joy was felt bodily by him.[10]

But Ps 31 became more important to him over the course of the last year of illness in Paul's life. He was very thoughtful and concentrated hard on remembering the words of the psalm, particularly as he quoted the verse, "My times are in your hands."[11] Here the dynamic in Paul's thought moves from thanksgiving to trust in God, that God will hold him at the end of his life.

Commentaries and theological/Christian books

For many of the interviewees, the comfort of the Bible is not something which is found only in solitary study. Anne and Margaret, for instance, liked to read the Bible with other people. Because of health reasons, this is not possible any more, but they find consolation using a commentary

---

10. Psalm 103:1–5 (NIV): "Praise the Lord, my soul; all my inmost being, praise his holy name. Praise the Lord, my soul, and forget not all his benefits—who forgives all your sins and heals all your diseases, who redeems your life from the pit and crowns you with love and compassion, who satisfies your desires with good things so that your youth is renewed like the eagle's."

11. Psalm 31:14–15a (NIV): "But I trust in you, Lord; I say, 'You are my God.' My times are in your hands."

for a specific biblical book and both have spiritual friends who read the same commentary on a daily Scripture reading.

> My Bible is always ready to hand and I read it with my commentary every morning. I know that some of my friends do the same, and this is a great comfort [to me] every day. . . . I have just finished Isaiah. (Margaret)

Through this praxis they feel connected with friends every day, though some of those friends live far away. Sharing in this praxis is like feeling a spiritual connection to friends.

Some of the interviewees shared a common practice of using the "Losungen," which in protestant circles refers to a daily word of Scripture with a prayer or a hymn verse chosen by the "Herrnhuter Brüdergemeine."[12] This is a very popular practice in Protestant circles because the Swiss Reformed Church does not follow the lectionary.

David, for instance, has the "Losungen" on his mobile phone, but most of the interviewees have it as a little printed book and read it in the morning or in the evening. Aaron prefers not to read the Bible so much anymore, but he keeps up with a little bit of Scripture reading through the "Losungen." It was also a ritual that he kept up with his wife when she still lived with him at home, and it helped both of them to start the day together and to do so with a moment of prayer.

Worship services and the Lord's table

The following subchapters refer to how the interviewees described their experiences regarding participation in worship services at the Lord's table.

---

12. The practice of having a biblical text as a shared daily "Scripture word" among the inhabitants at Herrnhut began in 1722. At that time, the Scripture was taken house to house by word of mouth, to serve as a common guide to meditation and conduct. This is how it was for eight years until, in 1731, a series of texts was printed for the full year, with the texts supplemented by hymn verses. So began the tradition which has continued ever since. The Old Testament texts are chosen by lot and a New Testament text is then added. This process takes place annually in Herrnhut (former East Germany), on behalf of the worldwide *Unitas Fratrum*, and from there the texts are distributed to each province, to be reproduced in a form suited to local needs. They are translated into more than fifty languages.

Church services

Many interviewees mentioned that going to church to pray, sing, and hear the Word of God together is or was very important for their spiritual life. Because of severe illnesses and weakness, however, going to church had become more difficult or even impossible for most of them. Nonetheless, they all had or have special comforting memories of services they had attended, which I would like to highlight with a few examples.

Frank finds it comforting to go to church with his children, especially after his wife died. Because he has experienced many different churches and church traditions over his lifetime, he is willing to accept that he can't feel at home with every part or kind of liturgy. For him, "going to church" means getting involved, being engaged in the service and with the people.

> There are certain services that are close to me because I celebrated them with loving people, for example, when I go to church with my children. . . . I don't expect every service to be my home. "We are only guests on earth," so why not be guests at a service? A worship service is also work. You go there and do something: you pray, you sing, you listen. (Frank)

Frank is no longer very fit and is encouraged when his children make the effort to take him to church. They know that he is comforted by going to church with them and that it does him good. He finds making the effort to go to the service strenuous but worthwhile.

Similarly, it is an effort for Marion to go to church, but she does so with the help of church friends. To be connected in the community means a lot to her. After a period of illness and being in hospital, she was sad that the people from church did not seem to show much interest in how she was and what she was experiencing. She described how important it was for her to be together with others in a service and afterwards to enjoy the hospitality, friendliness, and awareness of others.

> It was irritating when I came back to the Sunday services again with my walking frame after a long period of illness. Hardly anyone approached me or showed interest. I felt really strange. It is so difficult for me now because I live in the nursing home, and because we have to eat lunch so early, I can't go to church coffee anymore after the service. That means I automatically have less contact. I appreciated very much that L and M and also D were

friendly and asked how I am. That felt so good, even though I know that everyone has their [own] needs and a lot to do.

Here my awareness was heightened that comfort is experienced very differently by people in the context of the Sunday service. For some the service alone, and being there—perhaps with friends or family—is comfort enough, and they don't need other forms of community. For others, though, the service is part of a more comprehensive community experience; they want to be noticed and they want to talk to others as well.

Richard is an example of someone who needs such a comprehensive community experience around the church service. He enjoys being brought to the Sunday service by friends every Sunday. He himself, like Marion, lives in a nursing home and doesn't like it there. He remembers being active in the past in Singapore and Australia in churches where he experienced church growth.

> I need a lot of friendships! (he laughs) Often friends from church get me to join the Service on a Sunday morning. I like the singing and the preaching . . . and being together after the service. (Richard)

For Richard, church, including drinking coffee and chatting afterwards, has been one of the main places in his life where he has found and maintained friendships, and thus it is comforting for him still to be able to be part of such a network.

David, in contrast, doesn't have a need to meet people for coffee after the service. The service and being there with his spiritual friends is enough for him. Those elements, however, are vital to him. He found the experience of not being able to go to the service during the first COVID lockdown very distressing.

> I only have my cell phone and I like to send smileys to people or receive these little signs of encouragement. But I am not a technical person. I watched some of the services on TV but I missed going to church so much that it wasn't really very helpful to me. It was such a relief for me when we were allowed to gather as a church congregation again. Now Sunday is a joyful day again, being before God in community: this is the greatest gift for me—although I know that I am very old now and every Sunday could be the last. (David, second visit)

Listening to David, I realized that for him participating in the weekly service before God and in fellowship with others was a way of preparing for death, a type of *ars moriendi*, which however was also an *ars vivendi* as it comforted and strengthened him for the coming week. The detrimental effect of lockdowns on people who in the past had remained fairly stable and healthy thanks to the structure and rhythm of attending weekly worship and being part of a fellowship can only be imagined.

During the lockdown Daniela likewise greatly missed the fellowship in her community, although she is connected with the daily prayers of her community through an audio system. She prayed in her room, but realized as a spiritual person that being isolated from one's community was very hard. After four months at the end of the first lockdown she was allowed to enter the community chapel again. One specific element of the service was very important to her.

> Three weeks ago, I was allowed to attend a church service in our community for the first time after lockdown. This was so edifying! We sang so much; it was so wonderful after all this time! Singing in community is comforting! (Daniela, second visit)

Although Daniela is reformed in her spirituality, communal singing was for her the most comforting element of the service after the distressing time of isolation during the lockdown.

Finally, Ruth embodies a different type of person and experience of comfort in the context of church services. She finds God's presence in the woods and prays there alone. She has contact with the local minister and enjoys talking to her when she is passing by. She is very thankful that the minister is such a friendly person and has a great understanding for her personal situation. For her it is important that the minister knows her life story and that she is free and feels no pressure to be a visible part of a churchgoing group.

> I do not have high expectations. I like a clear message in the service, and I am happy that I have a conversation with our local minister from time to time. (Ruth)

The Lord's Table

In this paragraph, I refer to different aspects of the Lord's Supper and how the interviewees experienced comfort in its celebration. Before I do this, it is helpful to describe briefly the Protestant church context in which I work and am doing my research. In Reformed Theology, the Lord's

Supper is understood as a sacrament that spiritually and bodily nourishes Christians and strengthens their union with Christ. The outward or physical action of the sacrament is eating bread and drinking wine or grape juice. Reformed confessions, which are official statements of the beliefs of Reformed Churches, teach that Christ's body and blood are understood to be in the sacrament, but that this presence is communicated in a spiritual manner ("sign"). The Reformed doctrine of real presence is therefore sometimes called "mystical real presence" or "spiritual real presence." Over time, there have been and continue to be different Reformed discussions and beliefs around the Lord's Supper and its meaning.[13]

I asked all the interviewees if they experienced taking part in the Lord's Supper as comforting and helpful. Some of the interviewees had noticeable difficulties talking about such experiences. I wondered if that was because for the interviewees, all coming from a Reformed background, taking part in the Lord's Supper is also often bound up with self-reflection and an awareness of sin. But for those who did relate their experience, the aspect of Communion was the most evident in the interviews, whereas the Lord's Supper is understood as being with Jesus, as a foretaste of his promises and love for humankind.

Anne, for instance, experiences the Lord's Supper as a gift from God in time and space.

> For me, the Lord's Supper means the presence of Jesus. (pause)
> It has always meant meeting Jesus to me. (pause) It is directly from him. A gift! It is a foretaste—taste and see that the Lord is good—and the best is yet to come. (Anne)

The concrete elements of eating and drinking are important here as the foretaste is something embodied and not just virtually perceived. For Anne it is something she enjoys and to which she looks forward. Likewise for Frank the visible and concrete aspects of faith are particularly welcome. "I am not fixated on the Lord's Supper but I like it, especially the visibility of faith, the sensuality" (Frank).

In a similar way to Anne, Alice enjoys taking part in the Lord's Supper, and for her at the end of her life it is also a kind of *ars moriendi*, a preparation for eternity. Alice has a special comforting picture in her heart and mind which is connected with a sculpture in her flat, which depicts the Lord's Supper with his disciples, and is made in Africa.

---

13. See for instance Riggs, *Lord's Supper*.

> Yes I have my Lord's supper scene from Africa still here in my living room, so I can remember it.... It was not easy not being able to go to church and not taking part in the Lord's supper. I missed that. (Alice, second visit)

At those times when she could not take actually part in the Lord's Supper, Alice was comforted by looking at the Lord's Supper scene in her living room. It is situated in a central place there, and she can look at it while sitting in her armchair. She relates to me then what meaning the Lord's Supper has for her.

> I got a comforting picture from Prof. D. He said once that when you die, you move up a place at Jesus' Communion table (she laughs). I am comforted by this idea of sitting at the table with Jesus along with so many others. Even if it is only a picture. When we have completed our course here, then we will find a new place in his presence. (Alice)

This eschatological vision is something that Daniela also talks about. She remembers a friend who spoke to her years ago about the Lord's Supper and from that point on she reflected on it herself. For Daniela, word and sacrament belong together and meet in Jesus Christ, so that the Lord's Supper means communion with God. This communion is like a big table and an open invitation to everyone. It is an event that is beyond time and that defies understanding:

> In eternity we will be amazed that we have lived from Lord's Supper to Lord's Supper. This is the Lord's Supper: His word, as we read it, "Your word became my food." If we are so hungry for Him, then we live again and again by His word. One would like to shout this to everyone: "Come, everything is ready." There is a big table, everyone is invited! Taste and see how good the Lord is. (Daniela)

Finally, for David, the Lord's Supper is a Christian spiritual praxis which cannot be adequately explained in words, but experiencing that praxis in community and with spiritual friends has a comforting and strengthening quality to it. He describes this in terms of closeness and faithfulness, saying that "It helps me to stay close to Jesus" (David).

RELATIONSHIPS

Having in the previous section given some preliminary insights into the richness of comfort experiences in the interviewees' relationships with God and their individual spirituality, I will now present what I learned about my interviewees' comfort experiences which focus on the human aspect and different relationships. I do this because both divine and human aspects of comfort belong together. Through the central Christian doctrine of the Incarnation, it is possible to hold both aspects together. "The Incarnation overcomes the chasm between consolation from God and consolation of humanity."[14] Through and in Jesus Christ we can acknowledge that God lets his voice be heard in, with, and among human voices, and that Christ himself was in need of divine and human comfort in suffering. Recall that in the garden of Gethsemane Jesus said to his friends: "My soul is deeply grieved, to the point of death; remain here and keep watch with me" (Matt 26:38). Jesus asked his friends to comfort him with their presence and with their prayers.[15]

Along with the theological relevance of human comfort, the anthropologist Daniel Miller gives insights into aspects of the relevance of "comfort of people" through his research.[16] As would be expected, he shows that friendships, community activities, and churches play an important role in supporting people during illness, experiences of suffering, and old age. He was surprised to find that friendships can change during illnesses at the end of life. "A common finding is that those who are the most present when one becomes a terminal patient are not necessarily those one might expect."[17] Often those who are close to one have difficulties knowing how to respond to experiences of suffering, illness, grief, and dying.

Family

The following subchapters take up the findings in regards to the interviewees relationship with a spouse and to their wider family.

---

14. Hummel, *Clothed in Nothingness*, 45.

15. For the palliative pioneer Cicely Saunders this biblical story and the connection between human and divine comfort in suffering was one of her "foundation stones." See Saunders, *Watch with Me*, 1.

16. Miller, *Comfort of People*.

17. Miller, *Comfort of People*, 198.

Relationship with a spouse

Just before the first COVID-19 lockdown began, Aaron had to have his wife admitted to a special nursing home for people with dementia. During my first visit she was still living with Aaron in their flat. We organized the time for the interview to be when she typically had her afternoon nap so that he could concentrate better. After we had spoken for half an hour, his wife came and joined us. As a researcher, I experienced how respectfully and with how much care Aaron treated his wife. Similarly, his wife was able to comfort him in different ways despite her dementia. I quote at length from this interview as it becomes obvious in this unplanned and unique interaction how their comforting one another towards the end of both of their lives is tightly interwoven.

> I don't know how to carry on anymore. She forgets everything, we can hardly talk anymore. Then it helps when I listen to the hymns again or we listen to them together. Bethli knew a lot of music by heart. She still remembers part of the "St. John's Passion" by Johann Sebastian Bach and a lot of church hymns. She enjoys music so much! (Aaron)
> *Bethli comes into the living room.*
> (Aaron) "What do you want, darling?"
> (Bethli) "I want something to drink."
> *Aaron pours her some water into a glass. Bethli sits with us. It takes a while until Aaron is able to concentrate again and to talk with Bethli in the room. She sits next to me and I look at her and talk with her a bit so that she feels she is part of the conversation. At the end of the interview, I noticed Aaron looking at Bethli, his eyes filling with tears.*
> (Aaron) "Yes, there are a lot of positive things. We both (looking at her) have always had a good marriage. It hasn't always been easy with me, Bethli!" (He looks at Bethli)
> (Bethli) "Yes, it wasn't always easy with him." (Bethli answers and laughs)
> (Aaron) "Bethli looked after me so lovingly. She cared so much for me. Yes, we have a good marriage!"

I visited Aaron a second time after the first COVID lockdown and the situation had changed dramatically for both of them. Aaron's caring relationship with his wife had increasingly become an almost unbearable experience of suffering. In this second visit, returning to his occasional feelings of despair during the first visit, that there are now more times and situations in which he can no longer find any comfort or strength. Aaron spoke of suffering that can be so demanding and terrifying that there the only response can be lament and despair. Aaron expressed his wish to die, not only because of his own weakness but also because he can't bear not being with Bethli anymore. That only a few weeks of lockdown worsened her dementia so dramatically that he no longer even experienced the comforting aspects of music anymore was an unbearable realization for Aaron. That suffering was compounded by having experienced comfort in being near to her and having had bodily contact with her ("she gave me a kiss") and experiencing her expressions of tenderness toward him—then realizing that this also no longer possible. He felt that during those few months he had lost what he regarded as quality of life: having to have Bethli admitted into a nursing home, having no more intimacy with the one he loves so dearly, and experiencing that his own physical strength was ebbing.

For many years their experiences of comfort were bound up with each other. For this they were thankful and they could look back and express that gratitude to each other. But this very closeness, trust, and shared comfort made it all the more difficult for them when they could no longer be with each other.

> I miss my wife every day, and I pray that she can die soon. Before lockdown I visited her three to four times a week and she knew my name, she gave me a kiss and enjoyed being with me and her daughters. Then lockdown came, I tried to phone as often I could, but this was difficult. Often she was too sad to speak, I felt she is missing me. It made me sad as well and I cried a lot, I started to wake up at night and prayed that this would change and that we might see and feel each other again soon. After ten weeks I was able to see her again, but she couldn't say my name anymore. I tried to sing with her, she used to be able to sing the church hymns by heart, but [this time] she didn't respond. . . . It was unbearable and my daughters encouraged me not to go too often, it depressed me so much and I felt that I was losing my strength, I feel much weaker than a few months ago. . . . I read my "Daily Light" every day, but my only comfort is now that both our weakness lies in God's hands and I hope that we can both die soon. It is a hard time. (Aaron, second visit)

Family bonds and comforting one another

All interviewees mentioned strong relationships to different family members, primarily to children or grandchildren but also to a sister or to a brother, sometimes to other relatives. Frank, for instance, mentioned that after the death of his wife, going to a church service with his children was comforting to him.

I have chosen to reflect more deeply on only two examples because the interviewees described them with different details which are instructive in the context of my study.

The first is Alice, who has strong family bonds. She has regular contact with all her children and grandchildren through a WhatsApp chat. To know what they are doing and to participate in this WhatsApp group means a lot to her. Although she is getting weaker and, as she told me during my second visit, had to go through the lockdown without seeing much of her family at all, she decided, despite all the risks of the pandemic situation, to go and see her son who suffers from multiple sclerosis and who was lonely too.

> Of course, my family was a great source of comfort. We have a WhatsApp family group and I can read what they discuss and often they send pictures, which I enjoy very much. I am thankful that they taught me how to use social media. I feel connected with my dear ones and don't have to write back all the time. . . . After a few weeks during lockdown of not seeing my ill son we all decided that I as his mother was allowed to see him. So, I went and read to him every week for two hours. He is not able to read anymore but enjoys his audible books and of course when others have time to read a book or the newspapers to him. It makes a difference when you hear a text through a person's voice and someone is there with you. So usually I sat next to him; there was no "social distance." He is my son who needs me and I love him. That's all that matters. (Alice, second visit)

Clearly, Alice experiences the mutuality of comfort very strongly. Because she can visit her son and comfort him in his suffering by sitting next to him and reading a book to him, she also is comforted through being connected to him and spending time with him. She is aware that she isn't sure how long she will be able to this for him. Her son also comforts his mother through showing her that he is enjoying this time with her and through appreciating her coming to see him despite her age and health difficulties and the COVID crisis. In this narrative, the mutuality of comfort is not only described but can be seen and felt through Alice's words. She describes some important aspects of the beauty of mutual comfort experiences in suffering and how this renews each one's strength for their own journey.

Another example is David and his book. David wrote a little book describing his personal experiences of comfort to give to his children and grandchildren at the end of life. I heard him read from this book, but he never gave it to me to look at because he truly regarded it as a family treasure. Until I interviewed him, he hadn't actually shown this book to family members; they only knew it existed because he had talked about it. Lockdown and loneliness changed David's attitude towards his personal "book of comfort." He experienced his family and especially his grandchildren going through a difficult time during the COVID crisis and had a hard time finding meaning in all that had changed. After several weeks, two granddaughters came from another part of Switzerland to see him. During that visit, they asked him if they were allowed to read from his "comfort book." This was a special moment for David because these granddaughters were the first in his family to hold it and to read from it. Thanks to that interaction, he was able to talk to them about the spiritual comfort he experiences and how he is finding comfort at the end of his life.

> All those little stories played an interesting role after lockdown, when two of my granddaughters were allowed to visit me again. They came from C. It is a long way from here, but they came a few times to visit me. And guess what? They knew about my book and asked if they were allowed to read it. So I gave them the book and this was very special. They asked me about my childhood experiences, how difficult it was to lose my father when I was seven. Then they also asked me how my mother had lived out her faith and what had given her strength to carry on as a widow, being poor and taking in work to do at home for only a small amount of money. So, I had long conversations and I was so thankful that I could share these stories and my conviction that God was guiding my life in so many ways. . . . They mentioned a few times how important and comforting it has been to see me after lockdown and to hear me tell them about how I had gone through so many difficulties in life with God, and why I was not afraid of COVID. I had the feeling that they needed to hear that it is possible to overcome fear and anxiety through faith and hope in God. Through our meetings I became

quite aware that this time was very hard for young people too and that I could comfort them by sharing my little "God stories" with them. I miss seeing them. (David, second visit)

David was missing his family and was aware that they missed seeing him as well. His personal comfort book gave him the opportunity to combine divine and human comfort at the same time. This recalls what the apostle Paul wrote in the second letter to the Corinthians:

> Praise be to the God and Father of our Lord Jesus Christ, the Father of compassion and the God of all comfort, who comforts us in all our troubles, so that we can comfort those in any trouble with the comfort we ourselves receive from God. (2 Cor 1:3-4)

David was happy to be able to communicate this type of comfort to his grandchildren. And for his grandchildren it was comforting to hear their grandfather recount at the end of his life how he had walked with God for so many years in difficult circumstances, and to experience him as a grandfather who was open to their questions and anxieties.

Friends

Before we delve into the findings of the interviews, it is helpful to ask what a friend is and what effect friendship might have on people. It can be said that the experience of friendship is part of being human and can be seen as a universal phenomenon. According to Lillian B. Rubin, in a reference to Aristotle, friendship is like "a single soul dwelling in two bodies."[18] Friendship can also be understood as a "context for care for the other quite apart from a calculated response."[19]

Regarding the effect friendship has, John Swinton writes instructively for the context of this study that:

> Friendship enables human beings to experience themselves as they are, that is, as their "true selves," equal, relational beings loved by a relational God and fundamentally connected to an open and accepting community which manifests that love in a tangible form within its own relationships.[20]

---

18. Rubin, *Just Friends*, 15.
19. Hunter, et al., *Dictionary of Pastoral Care*, 447.
20. Swinton, *From Bedlam to Shalom*, 82.

The interviewees referred to their friends and the importance of their friendships in various ways. Especially at the end of life there are experiences of loss through the death of friends or through debilitating illness, and these make nurturing friendship more difficult.

At almost one hundred years old, Sally, for instance, talks about the loss of friends. She survived the Second World War in Germany and experienced a lot of distress in her childhood. However, throughout her life she has been connected with numerous friends. In her living room she has many photographs of family members and friends. Although she has a daughter, she misses her husband and a lot of her friends, most of whom have died, and sometimes she describes the loneliness as being almost unbearable. Nonetheless, she is able to connect her faith with the comfort of understanding Jesus as a friend.

> Most of my friends have died already. This is not easy.... So I have to remember that my Saviour is there. He is my best friend, my great consolation! (Sally)

With respect to the effects of illness and old age on friendship, Marion talks of her experience with her best friend. She lived in the same flat with her best friend for nearly twenty-nine years. Neither has children or is married. They knew each other through different church projects abroad and in Switzerland. They had a common daily rhythm and supported each other for a long period of time. Because of different illnesses and old age, they had to go into a nursing home. Marion was able to accept this step, but her friend couldn't. Her friend became depressed, and it was hard for Marion that she was not able to help. Both also had longer periods of very bad health and were in hospital for a number of months. The experience of friendship becoming strained and of being ill and in hospital for a long time was an experience of suffering.

> Yes, after twenty-nine years of living together, it's not easy that we now have to let go in a different way. She can't accept old age and doesn't want to live in a house like that, where a lot of the people suffer from dementia. That bothers her.... I had to learn to distance myself from her, but it is not easy. We are still friends and meet and read our Bibles together. (Marion)

Although the relationship has become strained and difficult, they still both regard each other as friends and search for ways to connect with each other, especially in a spiritual way.

The death of a spouse and experiencing friends as comforters

Another experience of loss is that of Frank, who lost his wife through death, but who also describes how his friends stepped in to help and comfort him. Frank lost his wife and found that his friends were able to comfort him during the mourning process in a special way. His children weren't at home anymore and when he talked to me about that period of life, he was almost transported back into the experience, and seemed to lose all sense of his current time and space.

> My children had all left home when my wife died. But I had some friends left. I have some close friendships. My friends came every evening, almost every evening, and always wanted to eat with me (he laughs). They didn't actually comfort me, but their comfort was that they didn't notice my desolation. They showed me that life goes on, and that I am not the only "desolate one." I didn't find it particularly pleasant at the time. I had the feeling that it was necessary to talk about my deceased wife. Certainly, they also did that—they weren't blind—but that was not the main subject of their conversation. And they refused to "deify" my situation as the only and truly bad thing. There is something else other than you and your feelings, they have always clearly shown me that, not just with words, but in how they behaved and always ate with me (he laughs again). This group was really important to me (long silence). When I was with them, I could also show myself as being in need of comfort. It is not only about the *need* to be comforted, but also about one's *willingness* to be comforted. That is almost as difficult as doing the comforting! (Frank)

In this situation, comfort happened through seeing each other and eating together, but not always talking about the loss and the actual theme of comfort, although every now and again his friends were happy to give him the space to do this. After telling me about his friends and experiencing them as "strange but beloved comforters," he also began to reflect on another friend who was not able to open himself up to be comforted after losing his wife. By remembering his own story and his own mourning process, Frank recognized how essential it was for him at times to share his sadness and grief with his friends and how they helped him to go through a period of lament and disorientation.

> I know a man whose wife died early, at the age of forty. They had a young son. After the death of his wife, he immediately

organized everything so that the child would not notice that anything was different. He organized a children's birthday party. He never showed himself to be in need of comfort or consolation, but instead locked everything up in himself. He didn't want to "impose" on anyone. And I find that a problem! (he becomes energetic) It is problematic for me to refuse to show myself as needy, to [refuse to] show myself as small. When such a misfortune hits you, you *are* small. You *are* weak, and confused (pause). There's a temporary insanity. When someone is terribly in love, when someone is filled with hatred, or if you lose someone, then it is difficult to access reality (pause). Real people, who were not fixated on me, were important during my time of mourning. (Frank)

Frank couldn't understand his friend's behavior (or that of the younger man whose wife died at the age of forty) and saw a danger in not being able to share one's weakness, suffering, and mourning with others. He found it difficult to accept the limits his friend set around human comfort and of feeling helpless in that situation.

When reflecting on this, I thought it would have been interesting to ask if perhaps at that time the friend was more attuned to and concerned about his child's suffering than his own. This child was much younger than Frank's own children when his wife died. Perhaps, I thought, the friend was thankful that life could go on and that he could prepare something "normal" like a birthday party for his child. I have discovered that people find their own ways to survive in situations of trauma and loss, and it is difficult to generalize how they "should" act or speak at particular times. This means that although there will be better and worse ways to comfort people, experiences of comfort are very much bound up with the individual and their unique personality and situation.

Church friends

Regarding friendships, the interviewees often described them as connected to their church community. Anne, for instance, has a lot of friends she knows from church. During my first visit, she was living still in her flat to which she could invite her house group for Bible study and tea. She was aware that for one lady her hospitality and friendship was especially important because this friend needed to arrive a bit earlier than the others and to have a rest after the meeting.

> We all love each other; we have now been meeting for forty-four years! First, we [typically] read a passage from the "Losungen," or a psalm, and then we pray. At the moment we are reading from the prophet Daniel! We read [the text] together and talk about it. We also collect prayer requests; everyone can be involved. One woman gets brought to the meeting; she no longer lives in D.: she is very ill. But it is so important for her to take part. Some time ago she had a stroke, but she didn't want to stop coming to the house group. When she comes, she sits up there (she points to a place at the table). She is a clever woman, but since the stroke she can't talk anymore. So she sits with us, looks at us happily and, when the meeting is over, we eat together and then she has a nap here in my flat before she gets picked up again. So, we are there for each other. The youngest in the house group is sixty, the oldest is ninety-three! (Anne)

Anne understood what she did as a kind of comfort ministry which was inclusive of friends who were disabled or very weak. Every week for many years she opened up her home and was glad to be able to offer hospitality to her friends.

I visited Anne again in September 2020 and she had moved into a nursing home to which she could not invite people. I couldn't have a long conversation with her because the nurse and the doctor had to see her after I'd been there for a few minutes. But one of the first things she said to me was: "I can't invite my house group anymore; M. must be very lonely." And she asked me for advice, whether it would be possible to meet in the nursing home with her house group. I was not able to discuss that with her because I had to leave, but I made a research note:

> It must be very hard not being able to gather with her spiritual friends. I had no time to ask whether some of them have been able to visit her. I was struck by her remark that M. was lonely, remembering how special that relationship was and how she cared for her every week.[21]

The first COVID lockdown had an effect on the living circumstances of a number of the interviewees who were still alive at that point. During that time, Anne had to move into a nursing home. For David, who loves going to church, lockdown was hard because no church services or gatherings were allowed. He has numerous good friendships through his church community. One of these friendships developed significantly

---

21. Research note 2020.

and became especially close during the COVID crisis. He himself sees this friendship as a mutually comforting relationship. To admit to the other person that life was not easy and to be open to hearing that from that friend too made a difference for David, and he valued the depth of friendship they had developed during lockdown.

> During lockdown and afterwards I tried to keep in contact with one church lady, R. She rings me once a day, and because we have a similar Christian background, we can share prayer thoughts and we were very open to each other, so that we could also admit when life felt miserable and when we had had bad nights or days. We also exchanged our prayer lists, for the world, for family issues, and for other people with whom we were in contact. . . . It was something which we both experienced as strengthening and we knew that every day we could share good and difficult things with each other. To talk to someone who can understand the need to keep in contact with our God through prayer helped me very much. (David, second visit)

David discovered the possibility of developing and enjoying a new quality of friendship, which he found comforting during a time of crisis. Spirituality and friendship are interwoven here and both parties experienced growth even though David is in the process of letting go of life.

Daniela's experience of spiritual friendship is also instructive for my study. She has a special friend who is not part of the community in which she lives. For her this is a spiritual Christian friendship.

> I think of my dear friend, who also lives in a community, but in Germany. We both went on holiday together a lot. She is very sick and we haven't been able to communicate for some time now. Unfortunately, this is no longer possible. It is a letting go, for both of us. But we hope to see each other again. In Jesus we are connected. . . . So, we are on the road together towards heaven. We are both suffering but we can carry each other. (Daniela)

They are both preparing for dying, but she can envision her friend through this trust that they are connected through Jesus. She believes that death is not the final thing they can expect, and that they are on the road to heaven together. She finds comforting this hope of a future with Jesus, beyond death and dying.

A further aspect of the context around church friends is that of the relationship to one's pastor. Richard talks about this.

> I need a lot of friendships (he laughs)! . . . Friends from church are very important [to me] (pause). And the pastor is a very good friend too. He led one of the Bible groups to which I went for so many years. In this Bible study group we really had "cosmic times," big moments! . . . He was with me when my wife died and also at the funeral. (Richard)

Because Richard had had a breakdown after his wife died, he had had to go into a nursing home a few kilometers from his former home. Not to be in the same village any more was not easy for him. He sees the pastor as his friend and is comforted when he comes to visit him. The friendship grew through their regular meetings at Bible study and their intellectual exchange around spiritual subjects.

Similarly, Aaron remembers a pastor during the interview and described him as a friend:

> You might be interested to know that I have a good memory of Rev. S.! He had a sober nature and was able to preach well. That suited me. But then there was an incident, and I decided not to go to church anymore. Pious people are sometimes not easy, and a certain kind of narrowness was difficult for me. . . . The pastor understood why it was difficult for me to come, and that was a good experience for me! . . . Later, I had to support a person after a bad accident, and I went to him and asked him what I should do and how to react. He took me aside like a friend and said: Just be there and listen! (Aaron)

The pastor to whom Aaron is referring died a number of years ago. He was able to give Aaron the freedom he needed and to be there for him at a special time when he was in trouble. This relationship gave Aaron comfort.

My dog as friend

One further element of interest in the context of friendships is the relationship between humans and animals. Heidi loves nature and lives in a little flat with her dog. To have her dog with her was very important to her. A few weeks after my interview, she was diagnosed with cancer and had to move first into a hospital and then into a nursing home. Because her relationship with her dog was so strong, she chose to find a nursing home where the dog was allowed to visit her and sometimes even stay overnight. She was part of my church congregation, but unfortunately the only nursing home where dogs were allowed to visit was not near where I lived. I was only able to visit her twice in the nursing home and phoned her about two weeks before she died. That was when I heard that her dog had died and that she was very upset about it.

At that time of the interview, she didn't know that she would have to go into hospital soon and was suffering from an aggressive form of leukaemia. The interview was just about to start when Heidi started looking for her dog in her apartment with me. After she found her dog, she showed me the small garden and explained the different plants to me in detail. She had a lot of flowers on the garden table. After we took a seat in her dining room, her dog came and sat next to her feet. Heidi stroked her a lot and I noticed there was a lot of bodily contact between Heidi and the dog during the conversation. At the end of the interview, she verbalized this special relationship and became nervous because the dog was no longer sitting next to her, saying: "She is such a quiet animal, she's a little bit like a friend!" I noted in my research diary at the time that Heidi only seems to feel well and happy when her dog is nearby. This is instructive in showing how intense the interaction between a person and an animal can be. The comfort dimension of the relationship seemed to have to do with presence but also with touch, as she was constantly in contact with her dog, which she subsequently described as being "a little bit like a friend."

APPRECIATION OF BEAUTY AND BROKENNESS IN CREATION, MUSIC, THINGS, AND ART

Having discovered how relationships with family, friends and, in one case, with an animal have a comforting or consoling effect on the interviewees, I now turn to the third level of comfort dimensions that my respondents described. The interviewees shared what kind of beauty had a consoling power for them. Often creation was a topic, but music and art were also frequently mentioned. Some of the interviewees could see beauty in things and enjoyed touching them, looking at them, or listening to them. I realized that these phenomena must be attended to and interpreted in different ways.

Creation

Regarding the comfort dimension of creation, Richard, who quoted Ps 148 in his interview, which I mentioned earlier, underlined that praying the psalms was essential for him. In this particular case the psalm was bound to an important experience in his life. Richard was a scientist and found comfort in the spiritual dimension of praising God for creation. Richard quoted Ps 8 alongside Ps 148:

> O Lord, our Lord, how majestic is your name in all the earth! You have set your glory above the heavens. . . . When I look at your heavens, the work of your fingers, the moon and the stars, which you have set in place, what is man that you are mindful of him, and the son of man that you care for him? (Ps 8:1, 3–4 NIV)

Richard was aware of God's care through creation, and his observation and learning from creation deepened his faith as a scientist. He himself never mentioned Teilhard de Chardin, but as he spoke about his sense of wonder and his eagerness to find out more about creation and on the other hand of his reading and reflecting on the biblical narrative, I remembered words by Teilhard de Chardin:

> We may, perhaps, imagine that the creation was finished long ago. But that would be quite wrong. It continues still more magnificently, and at the highest levels of the world.[22]

The idea of God being engaged and present in an ongoing creation was a strong element of comfort in Richard's spirituality. He understands himself as part of this marvellous creation and of the mystery of life.

Marion, similarly, is fascinated by the mystery of God's creation. She experienced nature in the weeks of the first COVID lockdown in a particularly intensive way. At first she could only observe creation from her balcony in the nursing home, but after a few weeks the nursing home allowed her to go for little walks outside around the house.

> I am so thankful that lockdown was in spring. I like spring, and I was comforted by observing how things are growing and blossoming despite the virus. . . . I can enjoy every little flower, the colours, the forms. This helps me so much. God's creation is a mystery, a source of comfort. (Marion, second visit)

---

22. Teilhard de Chardin, *Divine Milieu*, 20.

To experience spring during dangerous times, to notice the plants growing and blossoming, and to be able to see and touch things was a strong sign for Marion and gave her strength not to give up but to continue to trust and enjoy life. Alice and Daniela also had similar experiences of their awareness of beauty in creation expanding during lockdown and the comfort quality of such observations being higher than usual. Daniela, for instance, said: "When I think of how much comfort and joy I have just sitting in our garden, this joy just to watch things grow and develop!" (Daniela, second visit)

Frank, interestingly, described experiencing creation as "objective consolation" when he was mourning following his wife's death. He tried to explain how he experienced a change in his process of mourning through different experiences in creation:

> There is the dimension of objective consolation: for example, that spring returns after winter, that the sun rises after the night and that darkness disappears again. For me there is something like an objective consolation of life. I can remember when my wife died. There was first of all the absence of all consolation. And then, I very often went to the cemetery, [to] a bench next to [her] grave. There was also a tree. And after many walks in the cemetery, I suddenly noticed a bird in that tree and then heard the bird singing. For me, that was also a level of what I call objective consolation or consolation through time—namely, that mourning gradually changes, that mourning may turn into something like melancholy after a while. Mourners often have a dangerous attitude: they don't want to let go of their sadness, thinking that would signal their betrayal of the dead. As a feeling it is very strong, but it is also very hostile to life. . . . It was good that I saw the tree and heard that bird singing next to the grave. (Frank)

Frank remembered a special moment in his experience of creation. Although he referred to the term "objective consolation," he could combine that with a subjective experience he himself had, as of "being in creation" and "being part of creation," something which changed his understanding and his feelings of suffering and grief. After a process of deep depression and mourning, through his perception of the singing bird next to his wife's grave, Frank was able, to open himself up to new experiences of hope.

Ruth describes another element of comfort through creation, a day on which she found an unusual blue stone in the woods.

FINDING "PEARLS OF COMFORT"

I walked in the woods, when my husband died. . . . Often, I picked up stones on the way and took them with me, smaller and bigger stones, which I would then keep in my room. Once, I discovered a big blue stone.[23] My niece was with me that day. During the walk we put it back down and then forgot about it. I regretted that very much [when we got back] home and we went back to the forest and we found it again! (she smiles at me). Since then, I look at this blue stone often every day and I like to touch it. It has a lime crust on one side, making it not just beautiful, but also interesting. It has beautiful and a very ugly side. (pause) One has to learn to accept difficult times, . . . also to accept the stones. Sometimes you also have to walk on stones. (Ruth)

Ruth here has a special awareness of nature. I noticed in the interview that she can describe in detail the beauty of a leaf of lettuce or of a special flower, for instance. For her, walking in the woods had been a comforting activity for years, and all the more so after the accident and death of her husband. Yet the way she is in touch with her blue stone is different, for she has to look at it and touch it and turn it over to see the different sides of it. It is like seeing in the "blue stone" part of her life experiences; for both include aspects of beauty, but also strange and even ugly aspects, yet all the facets are part of the same stone or life. Ruth once

23. See the image of the blue stone. Ruth's daughter sent me the photograph after the interview but photographed only the "beautiful" side of the blue stone.

said in the interview that she was thankful to God that she is accepted by God and that God has gone through all her suffering with her. "I thank God every day for wanting me like that."

For my interviewees, part of the comfort of creation was that there, as in life, there are different aspects to experiences, some beautiful and others ugly and broken, and yet they are all somehow connected in the framework of God's presence and care.

Music

The interviewees often mentioned music or songs that they liked and which gave them comfort or consolation. Some of them had a special focus on religious music, while others found music in general to be a source of comfort. Ruth, for instance, enjoyed folk music a lot, and hearing radio programs with that type of music in Swiss German pleased her. Heidi liked to go to concerts, and part of the enjoyment for her was dressing up for the occasion and then having good company. Sitting in a concert hall and enjoying the music was an experience which signified quality of life to her. She liked beautiful things and also beautiful music. At the end of her life, she could not go out anymore, but she was still interested in hearing Wagner.

> Wagner is always an experience for me. When I was young, I was in Sweden for two years, I saw all the operas there. I had the feeling that all the dramas of life were in that music. (Heidi)

Heidi, I think, was fascinated by that music because in Wagner's operas, the music and story express the different dimensions of life such as birth, falling in love, experiencing friendship, suffering, betrayal, and then grief or consolation. To live through a story which is not my own but into which I feel I am plunged with all my emotions, and then to resonate with different parts of that story, all this is a powerful experience for her.

Aaron spoke of a different element of the power of music as comforting. Music plays a big role in his life and that of his wife. When they were younger, they went to the opera, attended classical music concerts, and collected recordings of different composers' music. In their old age, they often enjoyed Christian music together at home, especially that by Bach, Mozart, and Händel. They also loved different church hymns, and Bethli knew some of the hymns and some of Bach's Cantatas by heart. However, dementia and the strain of the first COVID lockdown took those memories away. Aaron found this very hard and was pained that this comfort dimension was no longer accessible to her or to them as a couple. When I asked him during the first interview to name a song or a piece of music piece that brought him comfort, he immediately mentioned a church hymn which is part of our Reformed hymn book in Switzerland.[24] I quote it at length here as it seems important to me that a large part of his life story and his understanding of comfort is bound up in the experience he relates.

> "So nimm denn meine Hände" ("So take my hands"), that's it! You wouldn't have thought that. I can tell you exactly where this hymn first played a role in my life. It was as if God had knocked on my door (pause).
>
> It was 1945, and at the time there were heavy bomb attacks on the town of R. My father was still there, but I was in Switzerland with my mother and my sister. I still remember we were in G. at the time, and we were called to the telephone by some other children. The telephone was in a house which produced war material. When mother came back to us—I can still see it clearly even now—she walked very slowly I knew something very bad had happened. She only said: "Father is no longer alive." (pause) The funeral was some days later. My father always wanted to be buried in R., but we were in G., which was almost 200 km away. At the time, it was 1945, the trains were not running normally anymore, and we didn't have a car. Then we learned that there were regional trains from time to time, but because of the air bombing they only ran at night. It was January, there was snow. . . . My sister and mother took a sled with them and so we attempted our journey to get to my father's funeral. The funeral service was in a church, a large one in R. We all knew that with the bombings happening all the time, it could be over with us any time. We managed to get there. So, we stood there, my mother, my sister, and my uncle who had also come with us. Then the hymn was sung: "Though I may feel nothing of you/ and Thy might, still to my goal You guide me/e'en through the night." That moment . . . the melody and the lyrics . . . I could never forget it again (pause).
>
> Nowadays I can't sing very well anymore, but I often remember the melody and the lyrics. I hum it to myself, sometimes several times a day. It is important for me to hold onto it. "Though I may feel nothing of you/and Thy might, still to my goal You guide me!" I also want the hymn to be sung at my funeral, and

---

24. See picture below.

my daughters know that! . . . The hymn has given me consolation! When I hear it, I feel like there's ground beneath my feet. Of course, there are other hymns that are good and beautiful. But this song has to do with my life, and it still touches and calms me even today. (Aaron)

To understand Aaron better, it is helpful to show the text of the German original and an English translation.

So nimm denn meine Hände, by Julie K. Hausmann[25]

So nimm denn meine Hände/ Und führe mich	Lord, take my hand and guide me/upon my way.
Bis an mein selig Ende/ Und ewiglich.	I know You are beside me/till my last day.
Ich mag allein nicht gehen/Nicht einen Schritt;	I dare not take without Thee/one single stride,
Wo du wirst gehn und stehen,/Da nimm mich mit.	You are concerned about me/both day and night.
In dein Erbarmen hülle/Mein schwaches Herz	Lord, cover in Thy mercy/my erring heart.
Und mach es gänzlich stille/In Freud und Schmerz;	Of heaven make me worthy,/when I depart.
Lass ruhn zu deinen Füssen/Dein armes Kind;	Let at Thy feet abide me,/Thy will to know.
Es will die Augen schliessen/Und glauben blind.	Thy hand will ever guide me/in weal and woe.
Wenn ich auch gleich nichts fühle / von deiner Macht,	Though I may feel nothing of you/and Thy might,
du führst mich doch zum Ziele / auch durch die Nacht:	still to my goal You guide me/e'en through the night.
so nimm denn meine Hände / und führe mich	So nothing can impede me/upon my way,
bis an mein selig Ende / und ewiglich.	as Thy dear hand will lead me/till my last day.

I know from my own experience as a pastor that this hymn with its lyrics is still a comforting melody for many people. Aaron always refers to the third verse and can resonate with this experience of despair and emptiness: that there was nothing he could feel of God's presence, only sadness and disorientation at losing his father at the age of seven at the

---

25. Hausmann (born 1826 in Riga; died 1901 in Estonia). Julie K. Hausmann was a Baltic German poet who wrote this poem after losing her fiancé.

end of the war. Like in the psalms, the hymn admits to this strong feeling of lament in despair. But it also takes the worshiper further, showing a way not to remain in despair, but to hear a voice of trust that can be for them like a light in the darkness, like hope in the midst of suffering. It tells of a God who can't always be felt but is still there, a God who leads the individual towards a goal which is good and meaningful. Although the suffering or grieving person can't see and experience this yet, the hymn also nudges one to surrender oneself to God in times of trouble. The hymn asks God to take the person's hand, not only to guide them but also to care for them. This "other" hand is necessary in utter weakness and in times of longing for help. Aaron says: "It was as if God had knocked on my door." This hymn with the words and its melody helped him to regain trust in a God whose paths he often can't understand and helped him to lament before God and to find his bearings again amidst the trials of life.

For Frank, church hymns are a special source of comfort. He is especially at home with hymns by Paul Gerhardt.[26] He takes Gerhardt's hymns as source of comfort because of the situation in which they were written. The time in which Paul Gerhardt lived was the period of the Thirty Years War. His wife died relatively young, a few of his children died of different diseases, and he lost his job as a pastor in Berlin because of a theological debate. Says Frank,

> The hymns by Paul Gerhardt are important to me. In his hymns the word consolation appears very often, although in his life he experienced so much suffering. "But the limbs, they grow weary, but now I stand, am lively and happy"[27]—he wrote this song while his wife was depressed. So, his comfort songs offer not some kind of general comfort, but comfort in a particular situation: poverty, the aftermath of the Thirty Years War, his failure in Berlin, etc.! For me, this is also a piece which makes me "feel at home." When I think of a beautiful church hymn, I inevitably think that it must have been written by Paul Gerhardt and I am always quite surprised if it isn't. I trust Paul Gerhardt's hymns so much that I have settled down with them and his consolation songs or they have settled in me. . . . These are songs that I can

---

26. Paul Gerhardt (1607–76) was a German Lutheran theologian, minister, and hymnodist. Over twenty hymns of his are in the Swiss Reformed Hymn Book.

27. This is a quotation from the hymn "Die güldne Sonne," specifically from the first verse: "Mein Haupt und Glieder, die lagen darnieder; aber nun steh ich, bin munter und fröhlich."

only sing because I know they come from an experience of being comforted amidst in suffering. (Frank)

Frank describes in a similar way why he likes the famous German Christmas hymn "O du fröhliche" written by Johann Daniel Falk:[28]

> For example, the Christmas hymn "O du fröhliche." A somewhat cheesy song. But I know that the one who wrote it lost four children and then opened a home for orphaned children. It was originally an all-year round hymn; he wrote it for Easter and Pentecost too. Because I know that, I can "forgive" the cheesiness of the song and can accept it for myself. Because it contains the experience of consolation (pause). A heart always belongs to an appropriation of something. Not only the mind, a heart that is either raging or angry or sad or downhearted or happy. These moments of the heart are always part of bringing something "home" to oneself. Whether it's music or something completely different. (Frank)

Frank expresses that music is a way to reach the heart and that is has an effect on our emotions. Interestingly, for Frank reflecting on a situation or a time in which a text or a song was written was very important. To him, it is like being in a conversation with a song and the song writer's biography. When he decides to trust the person who wrote the song or text, then he is free to "settle down" with a melody or words and is able to receive the song with his heart. Like Martin Luther said: "My heart, which is so full to overflowing, has often been solaced and refreshed by music when sick and weary."[29] Music has been used throughout human history to express and affect human emotion. People also receive health benefits from listening to music which are explained in music therapy and through research in other disciplines.[30] Music therapy has developed interesting methods to support people in distress or suffering through

---

28. Johannes Daniel Falk (1768–1826). Falk studied theology but he did not become a minister. He went to Weimar where he frequented the literary circles of Schiller and Goethe. Falk and his wife were the founders of the Falk'sche Institute, a public place of education for orphans. In late 1815 or early 1816, he wrote the German text "O du fröhliche, O du selige gnadenbringende Weihnachtszeit, Welt ging verloren, Christ ist geboren, freue Dich, freue Dich O Christenheit," that became a popular Christmas carol sung to the melody of the Catholic hymn "O Sanctissima."

29. *Evangelisches Gesangbuch*, 594: "Die Musik ist die beste Gottesgabe. Durch sie werden viele und große Anfechtungen verjagt. Musik ist der beste Trost für einen verstörten Menschen, auch wenn er nur ein wenig zu singen vermag. Sie ist eine Lehrmeisterin, die die Leute gelinder, sanftmütiger und vernünftiger macht."

30. For example, Feld and Brenneis, "Doing Anthropology."

music.[31] The Christian tradition is rich in music and I am convinced this can be comforting during suffering and at the end of life.

Daniela similarly is comforted by hymns and Christian songs, which she has learnt and sung regularly over many years. As part of a protestant community of religious sisters, she sings biblical texts and prays the psalms daily. The music in her community is diverse; they sing psalm melodies from the old church, church hymns, and modern worship music. In the two different meetings I had with her, Daniela was able to give me numerous examples of Bible texts with a melody, and she admitted that she can remember the Bible texts better with the help of melodies. She described to me that through singing she had more joy, that this emotional engagement in music meant quality of life to her. She spoke about being engaged in music or singing or singing inwardly, and that she finds strength in this "inward singing." "It's very strange, sometimes it seems to me as if God speaks directly to me through songs" (Daniela, second visit).

Daniela found that some of the melodies she knows through practicing over the years and using them in devotion and at worship came to her more often during the crisis of the first COVID lockdown. Because she was much weaker when I visited her the second time than the first, she had to trust more that God would guide her in the way she needs it. She experiences a kind of surrender in prayer, and is surprised how intense her spiritual life has been although she is feeling so fragile and is losing strength. Clearly, spiritual growth is not only a question of physical strength or of engaging in a variety of activities; it can develop right up until the end of life.[32]

Sally describes another way in which music is experienced as comforting. She had a special way of enjoying music. Because she has difficulties sleeping and severe pain in her back, she is used to listening to a lot of music at night. She still lives in a house, and she told me that she plays loud music and often moves to the music. This freedom gives her emotions space and comforts her. At the end of the interview, she said,

> Finally, I have to tell you how I got into dancing. For a few years at high school, I had a teacher who was responsible for music. One day she asked me to listen to a piece of music with my eyes closed. That's what I did. (Pause) I see myself sitting there today.

31. Powell, *How Music Works*.

32. Saunders observed this with her patients at the St. Christopher Hospice in London. *Watch with Me*, 19–30.

Then she asked me to listen to the piece again and dance with it, using movements that it inspired in me. Then I began to dance. After playing that, she came up to me, embraced me and said: "You have such a feeling for music." This was my first encounter with dancing, I still love doing it today. Dancing and moving to music gives me consolation and joy. (Sally)

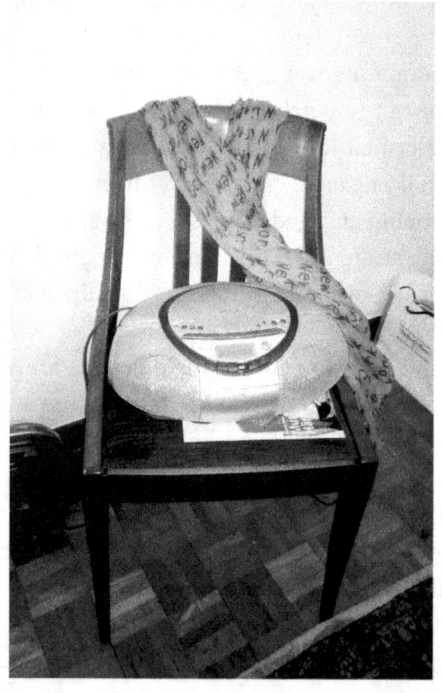

After the interview, Sally showed me how she dances. She didn't feel at all embarrassed. She also showed me her music collection, which was very diverse and extensive and included ballads and love songs from the nineteen twenties and thirties. Because she had such a difficult childhood and little or no encouragement at home, this music teacher, who spent time with her and encouraged Sally to feel music through movement and so to express herself, encouraged her enormously and gave her self-confidence. Sally kept up her dancing, especially at night, when pain and traumatic memories robbed her of sleep (her scarf and CD player can be seen in the picture above).

The comfort of "things"

In the interviews and the described experience of the participants, I was surprised to find how important "things" were to them and how willing they were to talk about and show me them. The anthropologist Daniel Miller in his book *Comfort of Things* writes about his observations in a hundred different households in London that possessions often had a profound meaning to people.[33] Often these things were not expensive artifacts, like paintings or sculptures, but ordinary things like a mirror, a piece of furniture, or decoration in a room. A year before Miller's research was published, the theologian Stephen Pattison developed a way to acknowledge the visible and various artifacts of pastoral care. He began his book with a quotation from Oscar Wilde: "The true mystery of the world is the visible, not the invisible."[34] Because of our "ordinary blindness," humans ignore most of what is visible, he writes, and thus he tries to broaden our understanding of how humans engage with the visual dimension of material existence, meaning for example with images and with artifacts of all kinds. He writes,

> The visual dimension is fundamentally important in structuring human thinking and experience.... Not having a critical awareness of relationships with the visible artefacts does not mean that these relationships do not exist.[35]

Sensual perception, or one could say whole-body perception, is vital for the examples that follow from the findings in the interviews. Some of the interviewees can describe how the visible touches them, so that through a figure, a sculpture, or a mug they can experience spiritual longing or feel the presence of someone dear to them.

Frank, for instance, reflects on the subject of the "comfort of things" and gives me examples of how important this visual haptic dimension of comfort is to him. To understand the connection between the things and the people, I think it is helpful to quote at length from the interviews.

> But one is not only familiar with people, but also with things, and things can also be a piece of home. For example, I have an old pullover. My wife wanted to throw it away, but that was not a good idea. I have worn it for such a long time during my life.

33. Miller, *Comfort of Things*.
34. Pattison, *Seeing Things*, 1.
35. Pattison, *Seeing Things*, 2.

> That is one thing. But there is also a candlestick that my now deceased wife gave me. Things remind us for example of people. Things warm us. They can also be books. There are books that are important to me beyond their scientific value. With me, it is like "nesting" with an author: I settle down with them and they can tell me more than I can tell myself, because I trust them to tell me something. I have questioned these books for a long time, and they are familiar to me.... I have a cup made of clay on my desk. I have glued it back together several times when it broke. Many decades ago, a dear person gave it to me, and it somehow belongs to me. It has already survived many moves. (pause) But buildings also warm me up, they comfort, if you want to use the word here. For example, a romantic church. I know one nearby, and I went their again and again, and it was becoming more and more precious to me. (Frank)

For me, what is striking here is that he uses the phrase: "Things warm us." This phrase can be connected with the wider use of comfort: it is comfortable, it gives us a kind of connectedness and security. If he wears the pullover, he can feel the fibre, see its color and form. When he touches the broken and repaired mug on his desk, he is reminded of different periods of his lifetime and recall that decades ago there was this dear friend at a special occasion who gave him this personal gift. Books have a special meaning too. On his bookshelf he has a collection of books he can touch and read. He can see his notes and remember the content from when he was using them during his years spent teaching. What is remarkable is that the things "warm" him, but that they don't become idols. He likes it if they are close by, but he doesn't build a shrine for them. They remain objects, things, albeit beloved things, but for him they do not have the same connotations as relationships or his Christian spirituality.

Alice also has a connection to things. She likes to treasure furniture from the past. It is not only a question of elegance and beauty, although her flat is undoubtedly beautiful. It is more that she appreciates being connected to her ancestors through paintings and furniture. She also has a collection of photographs showing those she loves, and a lot of religious symbols which have a meaningful past for her or for her deceased husband.

> I furnished the apartment together with my husband. The cross over the door, he hung it up there. And I have a lot of furniture. I got it from my great-grandparents, then my grandparents had

it, then my parents, and now I can enjoy it. It gives me a strong connection with those who went before me. (pause) I also have a cupboard in the dining room, which is from my grandmother in Holland, and when I see it I always think of her too. She had it in her bedroom. It's actually quite astounding how things like that can perpetuate relationships (she smiles)! The sofa comes from East Prussia, from my grandparents-in-law. It was a different world then! To keep these things is not a burden for me. But it is very enlightening for me if you ask me about my things which I have around me (she points to different things). I got this from friends and the desk was from my husband. I've never really thought about it this way, but it is true: things and what they stand for have meaning for me! (Alice)

Alice comes from a large international family with connections to different countries. For her it was a new thought that treasuring these different pieces of furniture, some of which have been in the family for over 150 years and are still in use, should have such meaning for her. Her ancestors are not present through portraits or photographs, just through furniture. I had the impression that it was a significant family ritual to pass furniture on, and perhaps the death of someone beloved was the time to ask the next generation to treasure these pieces again.

During her experience of suffering, Marion felt she needed specific things to comfort her. She has a collection of sheep, a shepherd, a dove, and a wooden crib. Next to that she has different pictures and paintings on her wall. She values spiritual books and photographs. Because she moved from a flat into a much smaller nursing home room, she took with her only pieces with special meaning. The numerous sheep on her shelves are striking, so much so that the first impression one has on entering her room is of this collection, as well as of a separate sheep on her bed.[36] I wrote in a previous chapter that as a result of her experiences of suffering and her search for comfort, she puts the "good shepherd" at the center of her spirituality.

> I like the story of the shepherd and the lost sheep. I have a whole collection of sheep (stands up slowly and gets some of the sheep, all made of different materials). They are all different. For example, this was made by a mentally handicapped child. And that is quite a woolly one. They don't fit into the herd. If you look around, they are all different but yet belong to the same shepherd. Look, there is the shepherd. There are two very small

36. See image below.

sheep next to him. He has to take special care of the little ones. He cannot leave them alone.... I also got a dove from a friend. It symbolizes the Holy Spirit. The Holy Spirit watches over everything. The Holy Spirit tells the shepherd where to go and which sheep need him.... Look, there are more sheep (she goes and gets some more). Take it into your hands! You may stroke it! These sheep are beautiful.... One is on my bed; I like to have that one at night to be reminded of the good shepherd. (Marion)

From her time caring for children with disabilities, Marion learnt that a whole-body experience can help one to feel comforted. I assume that is the reason why she has such a relaxed way of combining complex biblical knowledge and personal comfort experiences with the way she can enjoy things, especially sheep. When she asked me to hold and stroke a sheep, I felt as if I was entering into her story with all my senses. I touched the sheep and also stroked it, but I didn't feel like the same kind of comfort she experienced from it. I realized at that moment how difficult it is to appreciate things together which only have deeper meaning for one of the persons involved.

Art

Besides such ordinary objects or things, my interviewees also spoke about various kinds of comfort they derived from art. Returning to Marion: she doesn't only collect sheep; she also has an eye for art and the artistic. It's a bit of a roundabout story, but let me tell it. Marion has a very intense relationship with her brother. He was a teacher and is deeply interested in theological literature. Marion and her brother suffer from Parkinson's and both shared the time of suffering with their sister, who suffered from manic depression. Her brother is not someone who talks a lot but he, like Marion, writes letters to comfort other people, including his sisters. He has always had an interest in art and always searched for good material to include in his letters. Sometimes he would send photocopies of paintings or sculptures to Marion. One of the pictures he gave to her years ago is now hanging in a frame in Marion's little room in the nursing home.

> Can you see the cross in that frame? My brother sent it to me, many moons ago! It is a resurrection cross. It is Christ on the cross, but above you can already see the Father's hand pulling him up. My brother reads a lot and found it and then cut it out and sent it to me. (I get it from the wall and we look at it) You see, Christ is the one who is suffering, and yet he is also the one who will be drawn to heaven by the Father, do you see? It is only a picture; the actual cross [depicted here] is a sculpture in a monastery in Dissentis. It's called "Resurrection cross." (Longer silence, quiet contemplation) Suffering is not the final thing. It is as if the image of the cross is saying: "I am already there. You are not alone." (Marion)

Marion knew that the picture of the resurrection cross was hanging there, but taking it from the wall and looking at it and meditating on it together with her was also a profound experience for me as a researcher. Only by taking time to look at it carefully could I see what she meant and appreciate the big hands behind the cross. For her, resurrection and suffering were visible together in this picture, and this was important to her. At the end of the interview, she came back to a very personal spiritual question concerning the cross and what it meant. Marion struggled again and again with the question of why the suffering of Jesus was necessary.

> For many years I wondered why Jesus' death on the cross was needed at all. Couldn't God have found another way to free us from guilt? No: again and again I received the answer that it is love, [it is about] surrendering one's self. Especially in difficult times, which others also have to go through, the cross and also the necessity of the cross became something like a consolation to me, something I could trust and hold on to. (Marion)

This resonates to a degree with something Paul showed me. He went to Britain as student and discovered in Glasgow one of the Crucifixion paintings by Salvador Dalí. At the time, he was very touched to see it and be able to appreciate it. He took a postcard of it back home, kept it during all the years he spent in Africa and Switzerland, and later bought a poster of it, which hangs right over his desk where he has his different Bibles and the books he is reading.[37] Besides this painting, there are other artifacts in the flat too, many of them from Africa, also photographs, sculptures, and a colorful tapestry:

> This one picture is important to me. It's by the Spanish painter Dalí. I find it very provocative. His crucifixion painting has been unforgettable for me since I was young. I saw it in Glasgow. It immediately appealed to me, and I had to buy a postcard of it. I had the strong impression that this [perspective on the crucifixion illuminates] the burden Christ carried for us, for the whole world. This touched me deeply. It was always a helpful picture for me.... Seeing Christ's suffering and the whole world together. (Paul)

37. See image below (author's photograph).

Paul had always wanted to go to different countries and he told me in the interview that his greatest childhood fear was that he would only get to see Switzerland in his lifetime. Not much traveling was possible while he was studying theology, but he was able to go to Britain for a while, and there he decided to get involved in a Christian school in Africa. He was able to live in Africa with his wife and their two children for more than thirteen years. Through this picture of the cross Paul could see a variety of aspects of the Christian faith and hope. He recognized that the art conveyed a message not restricted to Europe or some small corner of Switzerland, but that it has meaning and impact for all humans, or, as he said twice, meaning "for the whole world." He also mentioned the provocative side of this painting. Paul wanted to understand the Christian message as a message which can free people from bondage and change people's lives. He saw his Christian social engagement in Africa from this perspective.

Lydia gives another perspective on art as comfort. Artistic expression was important to her, and Lydia did a lot of painting before she got cancer. When I visited her, she was not interested in creative activities anymore; she was far too weak and had to sleep a lot. Because I knew that her paintings were well known and that she had had an exhibition a few years ago, I asked her about her paintings.

> Yes, people feel addressed by some of my paintings. . . . I didn't think much about painting, I just liked it. But one day while I was praying it became clear to me that I should do that more often. . . . I am not an artist. . . . But the more I have forgotten myself in the painting process, the more I have understood the sentence which came to me: "You should learn to hear with your hands." I never had any idea of what a painting should look like at the end. Most of the time I started with white. It sounds a bit strange, but with my pictures I don't have the feeling that I painted them, do you know what I mean? The pictures were created only by my being the instrument for them! . . . The pictures that should go out into the world, they are out there now. And what happens to the paintings after my death, I have no idea, but God will see that the right thing is done. (Lydia)

Lydia gave me an insight into how a painting can come into existence. Like the people who devote themselves to painting icons, she sees herself as an instrument of God. She experienced that people respond to her paintings and that they experience them as helpful or comforting.

She does not paint landscapes or people; what she creates are more like "soul paintings," kind of a "love dance" of colors and forms. Through her painting she expressed what was in her and emphasized that the time spent painting was a time of devotion, prayer, and meditation.

CONCLUSIONS FROM THE FINDINGS

In the conclusions to these findings, I want to highlight the main observations that have emerged in reference to the three main themes of the interviews:

- being carried through the relationship with God (Christian spirituality: prayer, Scripture; worship services and the Lord's supper);
- being carried through relationships with others (family, friends, community, church);
- being carried through the appreciation of creation, music, "things" (or objects), and art.

To do this I have decided to use the metaphor "pearls of comfort" again:[38]

- "pearls of divine comfort";
- "pearls of human comfort"; and
- "pearls of comfort through creation, music, and artifacts."

Although I have ordered them in this way, they should not be understood as being entirely distinct from each other. The pearls are each interwoven, one with the other.

"Divine comfort pearls"

The following subchapters take up the dimensions which have emerged from the findings and put them into relation with the three main themes.

Prayer

The interviewees described the transformative power of prayer in different ways. Frank, for instance, said: "I believe that prayer is a place and a certain time, where the contradictions are silenced for a moment, and I reorient myself." Most interviewees see the connectedness in prayer not only as an individual act but emphasise that through prayer they are also connected with God and sometimes also with others. Christian prayer is thus described as "more than a feeling" or a coping strategy and can be described as part of "living or breathing in relation" with God. Aaron and Frank were adamant about this, that their comfort in faith was that God cares even when one sees or feels nothing oneself. The findings show that Christian spirituality is more than simply a habit or act, although it can be that sometimes. They understand prayer primarily as a connectedness with God, a sign of a lively relationship. One could also describe it as a fruit of "being on the path of discipleship." "We can only do that because Jesus himself lives and prays for us. First Jesus for us, then we through him for others," as Daniela put it. Or as Barth wrote in regard to prayer: "This is what we do when we trust; and in so doing we do all

---

38. See the introduction to this chapter where Lydia speaks about pearls and the New Jerusalem.

that is required of us."[39] But the interviewees see prayer not only as an act or praxis to help the individual, but also as a ministry through which to reach others in their suffering and need. Christian prayer is therefore also a call to God, one which includes the human cry for a change of circumstances and for transformation.

I was surprised that despite their suffering and at the end of life, the interview partners had often kept up a daily prayer praxis to pray for others and for the world.[40] Prayer they understood as an ongoing dynamic between God and humans and between humans through God's Spirit. For some of the interviewees it was a great help to pray with prayers from Scripture (psalms, the Lord's Prayer) or tradition. To borrow the words of other believers they regarded as helpful; it gave them a feeling of connectedness within the Christian prayer tradition.

One of the results of the research was establishing that prayer praxis, form, and content, had a connection with the experiences of suffering and comfort over the course of one's lifetime. Interviewees often established a kind of prayer praxis which proved itself to be helpful. Some of the interviewees recalled that in a particular instance of suffering a special prayer, a psalm, or hymn had been comforting and that for that reason they returned to this experience later in life and remembered the power of this comfort. It seems that strong experiences of comfort become imprinted physically, so that they resurface later or at the end of life. Recall, for instance, that Aaron testified that some of his comfort experiences created a strong memory of comfort, a feeling he could retrieve years later and that had an impact on him concerning how to let go at the end of life.

In this regard the interviewees also understood lament to be a form of prayer that enables the person to verbalize anger, pain, and brokenness towards God.[41] Alice sees that lamenting is also and perhaps foremost a

---

39. Barth, *Call to Discipleship*, 14.

40. A prayer in Cicely Saunders book *Beyond the Horizon* is by George Appleton and is an example of how Christian prayer includes the suffering of others and praying for the transforming power of God: "O Lord we pray thee for all weighed down with the mystery of suffering. Reveal thyself to them as the God of love who thyself doest bear all sufferings. Grant that they may know that suffering borne in fellowship with thee is not waste or frustration, but can be turned to goodness and blessings greater that if they had never suffered, through him who on the cross suffered rejection and hatred, loneliness and despair, agonizing pain and physical death, and rose victorious from the dead, conquering and to conquer, even Jesus Christ, our Lord." Saunders, *Beyond the Horizon*, 28.

41. "Lamentation is first and foremost a mode of communication with God; it is a

form of prayer through which one can bring contradictions before God. Suffering can be so great that comfort is not easily found. Ruth's story tells of the darkness, loneliness, and pain she experienced. To lament in the woods, to bring God the pain again and again allowed her to be with the one she could not see or feel anymore. When she collected stones, and then many years later found the "blue stone" in the woods, aspects of comfort began to emerge through creation. The suffering demanded a long time of lamenting, and at the end of her life when she was reflecting on comfort, she realized that it had taught her that "It is important to listen and to wait" (Ruth).

Prayer includes not only the further dimension of lamentation but also of thankfulness. The interview with Lydia, for example, which occurred only a few days before her death, gave an insight into what it means for a Christian to accept death as the completion of life and to let go in gratitude after battling with cancer for three years.

Scripture

Next to prayer, what also emerged was the importance of Scripture as a divine pearl of comfort. Frank describes "nesting" with a text and "feeling close or at home with certain texts or verses." He also talks about building "a little house within the house." And, as Lydia said, "I trust in the 'big story' of salvation in the Bible." Several of the interviewees described their deep trust in God, their emphasis being not only on God or Jesus Christ but also on the Holy Spirit working among and in us as the Comforter and Advocate. That Marion placed a dove made out of clay next to the shepherd Jesus, and that Alice described that "being in touch" with God's Spirit during the first COVID lockdown gave her another understanding of God's Spirit present in her life are reminders that "The Holy Spirit is able to connect with us. We all are so different, yet he finds a way" (Alice, second visit).

With regard to Christ, it was not only the compassionate, wounded, and dying Christ, but also the risen and victorious Christ whom interviewees mentioned and named in the context of Scripture and different biblical quotes and stories.

---

form of prayer.... Lament expresses rage, anger, hurt, and disappointment about situations and about God, but it does so within a context that is bounded by trust and a hope that, despite the apparent lack of any evidence, God is active in the world." Swinton, *Raging with Compassion*, 111.

I noticed as a researcher that for a lot of the interviewees the presence of God through Christ and of the Holy Spirit was simply a "normal" part of faithful living. Paul's so-called "Trinitarian" blessing speaks about this mystery and normality in Christian spirituality: "The grace of the Lord Jesus Christ and the love of God *and the fellowship of the Holy Spirit be with you all*" (2 Cor 13:14).

The worship service and the Lord's Supper

For many of the interviewees, especially for David, Richard, and Alice, church and especially the worship service were important. However, people experienced comfort differently in the context of the Sunday service. For some, the service alone, and being there, was comfort enough, and they didn't need other forms of community. For others, the service was part of a broader feeling and context of community with God and with others, a context in which they wish to be noticed and where they also want to talk to and discuss things with others.

Especially in light of the dramatic changes caused by the first COVID lockdown in 2020, some of the interviewees who were still alive had to reorient their spiritual lives. Then, and afterwards for some of them, they were no longer able to attend worship services very often or to take part in the Lord's Supper, a ritual which a number of them understood as a foretaste of the eschaton. Although many of them missed this, they realized that at the end of life, prayer, music, and a few words of Scripture which they hold onto even when they were alone could have a rich comfort dimension.

"Human pearls of comfort"

The interviewees spoke of experiencing different levels of comfort not only through divine connectedness but also and especially through human comfort. Lydia said: "I am connected with Christ and the Holy Spirit on the one hand and connected on the other hand to humans and creation—I have experienced this during my present time of dying."

Family

The findings show that experiences of benevolence and love in human relationships have a comforting quality when one is suffering. Here, the relationship some of the interviewees have or had with their spouses was particularly significant. Much of the comfort they needed was the result of having lost their spouse. For some of them, family relations with their children or grandchildren were a special source of comfort, but also of worry. Having a big family with four children, Alice appreciated the care of her family. They helped her feel part of a wider community and they encouraged her through little messages and phone calls. Alice also found comfort in reading books to her son who suffers from multiple sclerosis. It was important to her to stay in relationship with him, even during the lockdown, and for them both to experience the mutual comfort of being with someone they loved and who loves them.

Mutuality and comfort are likewise topics which emerged from David's second interview. He told me about his two granddaughters who visited him a few times after lockdown. They knew that David was writing 'a book with comfort stories of his life' to pass on to the next generation when he died. He was able to react in a helpful way to ease their anxiety because of the COVID situation, and they were able to empower and encourage him through the interest they showed in his life and his stories of faith.

Finally, touching and sharing other expressions of intimacy and tenderness was essential for Aaron and his wife. Part of his need for comfort arose from his extreme suffering at not being able to be close to his wife anymore when she had to go to a nursing home and he couldn't visit her.

Friends

Contacts with friends and, for some, with "spiritual friends," was comforting and important. For instance, Alice said, "I experienced how precious it is to have Christian friends. It is as if there is a way of understanding at a deep level yet without using words." These special relationships comforted the interviewees in different ways. To share time together and realize that life goes on was a key experience in Frank's life when friends visited him and ate with him frequently after his wife died. Though not immediately, it became comforting to him that they were there but were not only focusing on his grief and loss. Upon moving to a nursing home,

Richard described that friendship is a source of comfort when nothing is the same anymore and one loses family members and no longer has access to one's home and church. That friendship can change and still be developed in old age was something David spoke about. He spoke also of his need for a close spiritual friendship during long periods of loneliness.

For Marion and for others, listening attentively and trying to understand the other person were central qualities of a good friendship. She emphasized how she had learnt through many experiences of suffering how important it is to take time to listen carefully, and that often "explaining suffering" can be counterproductive. Despite many possible interpretations or explanations, they all realized that listening involves not only understanding that the friend/other person needs time to be or to speak, but also being empathetic. A variety of research work in palliative care studies underlines this thought. The anthropologist Daniel Miller writes in his book *Comfort of People* about how essential it is for people who are mourning or have severe illnesses to have "people with whom they feel able to talk directly about what is happening to themselves without embarrassment or explanation."[42]

"Pearls of comfort through creation, music, and artifacts"

The following subchapters involved in this third main theme take up reflection around the three dimensions of experiences in creation, through music and artifacts.

Creation

As I described earlier, Marion and others regained strength and hope during the first COVID lockdown with the help of little observations in creation. Lydia referred to the experience of being in touch with nature and creation during her final days of life. At the time of the interview, she often lay on her bed and observed different trees through her window. "I admire creation. When I notice that my thoughts are going in circles and suffering hits me, then it helps me a lot to concentrate on how wonderful everything is that is created by God" (Lydia). Sally likewise describes how important it is for her to "greet" a new day, waking up by a big window facing her garden. "I wake up every day in my bed right by the window,

---

42. Miller, *Comfort of People*, 198.

and I can see the leaves of some trees. I can see the rays of light, and I can see the movements through the branches, and first I thank my creator that I am alive." (Sally). Heidi similarly told me that every day she walked in her small garden with her dog and thanked God for the beauty, the colors, and all the growth in creation.[43] It became clear through these different descriptions that experiencing creation at the end of life is a whole-body experience which has comforting elements.

Music

All the interviewees referred to being comforted by music. They described how in different situations they found comfort in special music or hymns, some of which reminded them of very powerful moments in their lives. One example of this was Sally. Singing and dancing had become a comfort strategy for her in her life. As a young girl, through the encouragement of one of her teachers, she had learnt to express herself in dance and found it comforting to dance alone by herself at night when she found it difficult to sleep. She loves music, love songs, and ballads. In listening to music and in dancing she finds connection and strength and acceptance thanks to her strong emotional life.

Artifacts

As I described earlier, all the interviewees responded to the theme "appreciation of things," and some of them described to me how they had

---

43. See image with plants and flowers.

experienced comfort through objects. It was sometimes difficult to describe what made an artifact meaningful. But it was clear that it was a specific and individual subjective reading of an object that made a difference in how to understand it and why it was important to keep it. Often the objects were not apparently of great value, nor were they artistically distinctive. For something to become important to someone, it did not simply depend on the objective beauty of that thing. Frank, for instance, described his oft-broken and repaired mug like this: "Things warm us up. Things also mean a piece of home. . . . For example, I have a ceramic cup on my desk, which I have glued back together several times. Many decades ago, someone dear to me gave it to me and it somehow belongs to me" (Frank).

Yet some of the artifacts also had value as beautiful objects. These include pieces of art or print of original art. Paintings had a special meaning to some of the interviewees. Heidi, for instance, had oil paintings by her father-in-law all over her flat. Though these paintings were well done, this was not the main reason she cherished them. To see the Swiss mountains that she and her deceased husband loved so much, and to remember the different places in creation they had experienced together was the key point.[44]

For Paul to have a copy of Dalí's painting of the crucifixion nearby and to be able to meditate on it every now and then had a special meaning for his Christian spirituality. Because it was "only" a copy of the painting, it was not essential for it to be kept in the family when he died. For him, the painting was a comforting means to stay connected with his spiritual roots and to feel and remember his theological reflection as a Reformed theologian and teacher.

Aaron's big Bible in his flat was, as a book, a symbol or metaphor for his life story. It was very important to him that this book would be passed on because through it would enable a future generation to remember his life and those who came before him.

Alice was surprised how many things were important for her to feel comfortable. By reflecting in the interview about the significance of "things," she became suddenly aware that not so much the things but the people and the relationships she had with them were important.

Daniela was aware that she did have only days or weeks on this earth and started to give "things" away to people she loved. As a way to express

---

44. See image with Alps.

her affection to people, things helped her to let go and pass them on to others. Daniela realized that another person would not experience the same comfort she had through a particular object because that item was connected to her specific life story. Nonetheless she trusted that the other person would understand that this object had been of great personal value for her. To let go and prepare for dying also meant letting go of a lot of "stuff" and things, and to be open to preparing for what was essential, namely making space for the divine.

4

Reflecting theologically around comfort and consolation in areas such as prayer, trust, peace, the body, and "things"

GOING THROUGH THE INTERVIEW material again and again, visiting some of the interviewees a second time after the first COVID lockdown, returning again and again to numerous books on comfort and consolation and finding a way to write about comfort and consolation in the chapter to follow, it became clear to me that a theological response in this research has to be strongly connected with the material of the interviewees and at the same time open up a certain freedom to connect what is "in front of me" (aware that I cannot capture it fully) with insights from theology and other disciplines.

    The starting point of this chapter is the human experience of comfort and the human experiences of being in need of comfort and consolation and of being able to comfort others. I am aware that different dimensions of comfort came up in the interviews, and that I had to decide which findings and theological *topoi* I should explore in more detail to be helpful and to deepen the understanding of comfort. I decided to start with the anthropological, philosophical concept, which describes the common human need for comfort and which develops comfort as a human category. From there I delved into the interviews again and made notes. Through the conclusions from the findings which highlighted what I have called "divine pearls of comfort"—prayer, Scripture, and the worship service with the Lord's Supper; "human pearls of comfort"—chiefly family and friends; and "pearls of comfort through creation, music, and artifacts," in this theological response I want to discuss the question of how the various pearls of comfort and Christian faith are related.

As I wrote in the introduction, I understand practical theology as being in critical dialogue with other disciplines as well as with Scripture, church tradition, and experience. In my research around a phenomenological approach to human experience and existence, I found instructive for the context of this study the work of the German philosopher Hans Blumenberg, who has written at length about the universal human need for comfort and consolation. At the beginning of this study, I started with biblical insights, as I wanted to prepare myself for people at the end of life who value scriptural words or texts from the Christian tradition. Coming from the individual experiences of consolation, I would now like to look first at Blumenberg and his thoughts around the constitution of human beings and then consciously return to the Bible. In turning back to Scripture there I will look at the writings of the apostle Paul, especially as found in the second epistle to the Corinthians, where he refers to God as "the God of all comfort."[1] Within the context of the data analysis, I take up the theme of lament, as that is vitally related to the way the interviewees share their experiences of suffering.

Within church tradition and experience, first I found the concept of *fiducia* as taken up by the Reformers and then later mainly by Protestant theologians to be helpful in discussing my theme. Second, I then address the focus on Christian comfort at the end of life by studying Bonhoeffer's letters and writings from prison, but also his reflections on the comfort dimensions of discipleship, and then John Swinton's work around shalom and living and dying as a Christian. Third and finally, I reflect theologically on the awareness which emerged from the findings that the Christians' experiences of comfort at the end of life are necessarily embodied experiences and often include an appreciation for creation, music, and artifacts.

A DISCUSSION OF HANS BLUMENBERG'S PHILOSOPHICAL WORK ON COMFORT

I have previously mentioned that studying the work of the phenomenologist and philosopher Hans Blumenberg was helpful in reflecting

---

1. 2 Cor 1:3.

the phenomenon of "experiencing comfort and consolation" as a human experience in general. Blumenberg comes from a Judeo-Christian family background and experienced the Second World War in Germany. He writes extensively on Augustine and the scholastic philosophical discussions of the Middle Ages in his dissertation, but he wanted his philosophy not to be bound to one particular religious narrative or faith tradition. Rather, he felt the need to describe certain phenomena philosophically and anthropologically, and thus understood himself as a phenomenological anthropologist and philosopher. Among others, he studied Husserl, Gadamer, and Heidegger in his book *Beschreibung des Menschen* ("Description of a Human").[2] Blumenberg criticized Husserl because he was sceptical that anthropology was a sufficient form of epistemology in philosophy.

> For Husserl, philosophical anthropology is a philosophical understatement. His premise is that philosophy as phenomenology can do more. It must be able to give a theory of every possible kind of consciousness and reason, of the object of the world, even of intersubjectivity.[3]

Blumenberg argues that Heidegger followed Husserl in this prejudice towards anthropology. Blumenberg says that Heidegger preferred the question of subjective "being" to anthropological insights. Blumenberg clearly opposes a fundamental ontological instrumentalization of the "Daseinsanalytik" in *Being and Time*.[4] For Blumenberg, anthropology must be a sceptical discipline that concentrates on describing phenomena and avoids premature determinations ("Bestimmungen"). "Description" rather than "determination" is important for Blumenberg, an approach he shares with other philosophers, such as Helmut Plessner.[5] Blumenberg emphasizes reflection and interpretation. For him, "seeing" is always the "seeing" of the individual, who is necessarily temporally and locally situated and cannot unite all perspectives at the same time and certainly never everyone's perspectives.

---

2. Blumenberg, *Beschreibung des Menschen*, 2014. The English translation of the book title is the author's own translation.

3. Blumenberg, *Beschreibung des Menschen*, 30. The English translation is the author's own translation.

4. Explained in more detail in: Dober, *Ethik des Trostes*, 40–44.

5. Plessner, *Philosophische Anthropologie*; Plessner, "Die Stufen des Organischen und der Mensch."

As I mentioned above, although Blumenberg had no interest in describing humankind in relation to God, he had a deep interest in examining the phenomena of "comfort and consolation" as vital human experiences throughout history. For Blumenberg, a human being is the being whose ground can never be completely transparent. "A human person is always faced with the possibility of tipping over and tipping back."[6] In short, human life is precarious. Through his phenomenological observations, he thus determines humans to be in need of comfort, of something to hold onto. Because of his preference not to try to describe comfort in terms of the transcendent, he feels able to explore the dialogical elements of comfort between humans.

> That you comfort me and are comforted by me, therein lies a deep meaning of our humanity. Without the others we would not be comforted ("bei Trost"), and not close to ourselves. . . . We are opaque to ourselves, but by the possibility of "delegation" we are more likely to trust the other to have an image of us that could be sufficient.[7]

According to Blumenberg, the need for comfort and consolation becomes visible when we show our pain and suffering to the other person. As human beings we are in need of comfort and consolation because we are aware of contingency. This awareness of contingency, of being thrown about and of being overwhelmed by circumstances not under our own control, is something that theologians have also written about, and which we also find in the psalms, for instance.[8] The theologian Sybille Rolf, who wrote her dissertation on the topic of meaning and comfort ("Vom Sinn zum Trost") writes,

> Loss of a person, loss of a home, but also of life prospects, loss of health, loss of security and the experience of the hidden God can give a person the feeling of no longer being "comforted," but urgently in need of comfort, so that the term of loss as a crisis experience is best suited to adequately describe human need for

---

6. "Immer steht der Mensch vor der Möglichkeit umzukippen und zurückzukippen," Blumenberg, *Beschreibung des Menschen*, 70.

7. "Ohne die anderen wären wir nicht 'bei Trost,' geschweige denn bei uns. . . . Wir sind uns selbst undurchsichtig, aber kraft einer Delegation von Zuständigkeiten trauen wir dem anderen eher zu, ein Bild von uns zu haben, dass uns genügen könnte," Blumenberg, *Beschreibung des Menschen*, 629. (The English translation above is the author's own translation.)

8. Ps 69:2 (NIV): "I sink in the miry depths, where there is no foothold."

consolation. The experience of desolate insecurity seems to be one of the constitutive elements of human existence.[9]

Such experiences are reflected in certain of the interviews, especially those of Aaron, Heidi, and Alice. Based on their physical and conscious constitution, people ask questions like: "Why me? Why us? Why not me too? Why not us? Why me at all?"[10] etc. Humans are in need of comfort and consolation because they cannot escape their peculiar constituted consciousness, their body, or the time in which they live, or the people with whom they suffer and whom they lose. Blumenberg develops from what he describes as an anthropological deficiency not only the need for consolation as such, he also examines the small and larger consolations of which a person is capable. According to Blumenberg, the constitutive need for comfort is rooted in the challenge of having to endure the big questions of life.

Humans are beings who have developed a way of life that is capable of distancing itself from itself. This is both a reason why they are in need of comfort and consolation but also helpful in allowing themselves to find themselves again as it allows them to delegate.

While Blumenberg describes human existence as one "in need of comfort and consolation," he also discusses ways to experience different modes of comfort. There is a whole arsenal of tools to provide consolation to hold and help a person. But there are also those which are "false ways of comfort" and can lead a person into danger. Here it is necessary to find ways to determine constructive forms of comfort as opposed to those which are destructive. Thus for Blumenberg it is vital to show through philosophy and phenomenology that comfort experiences can be seen within an ethical investigation. He examines different rules by which humans can decide rationally what kind of comfort experiences are good or useful and which ones can be described as "false comforters."

Blumenberg's philosophy of comfort and consolation can be seen as elaborated through three "modi": Thoughtfulness or reasoning; memory or the practice of remembering; and humor and a form of modesty which

9. Rolf, *Vom Sinn zum Trost*, 176. (This quote is the authors own translation.) The strengths of her research and theological reflection lies in the argumentative process that consolation, in its Christian understanding, is not the same as "finding meaning." "Finding meaning" is not that which suffering believers are able to finally hold on to, or as Falque in his book *Guide to Gethsemane* discusses in the context of anxiety, suffering and death that through the lens of the narrative of Gethsemane we have to think about "the suspension of meaning," 27–28.

10. See Blumenberg, *Beschreibung des Menschen*, 639.

doesn't take itself too seriously.[11] All three modes are seen in different discussions and disciplines and also have a long tradition in theology. Thoughtfulness contains for Blumenberg: freedom, God's existence and immortality. For him, the character trait of thoughtfulness has an enlightening and critical potential; it helps us not be seduced by false consolation but to reflect on the meaning and effects of comfort dimensions for oneself and for others.

In studying Blumenberg, I saw potential for Christian theology in thoughtfulness: the need in our time to reflect cautiously and prudently before judging. It resonates with Christian virtue ethics and the contemporary discussion around "phronesis" but also from philosophical traditions in the past.[12] Blumenberg develops the category of "comfort and consolation" as a *conditio humana* out of the observation that all humans are anthropologically speaking "beings in deficiency" ("Mängelwesen").[13] Arnold Gehlen already described the human being as "a being in deficiency" that has fallen out of its natural balance.[14] Blumenberg would identify comfort and consolation as the "compensation of a structure of deficiencies" that goes beyond the limits of the real capacity of such compensation.

Especially in the experience of memory, which for Blumenberg is a principal mode of comfort and consolation, he writes that the act of remembering is a formative or transformative force. As humans, he says, we can experience change through remembering. Memory is for him an incomparable power of resistance against nothingness and suffering. Memory is not just the action or experience of a single person, it can also happen in community, where others are contributors to the memory act.[15]

---

11. Dober, *Ethik des Trostes*, 229–96.

12. Phronesis is explained and discussed by Hughes, *Aristotle on Ethics*, and MacIntyre, *After Virtue*.

13. "Comfort is a category whose peculiarities are closely related to the characteristics of the human species." "Trost ist eine Kategorie, deren Eigentümlichkeiten aufs engste mit den Merkmalen der Spezies Mensch zusammenhängen," Blumenberg, *Beschreibung des Menschen*, 623.

14. Gehlen, *Der Mensch*.

15. That memory is likewise vital for theological reflection. "At the heart of God's intimate knowing of human beings lies God's remembering of us. In Psalm 8:4 the psalmist asks wistfully what it is to be a human being: 'What is man that you are mindful of him, the son of man that you care for him?' The adjective 'mindful' derives from the verb 'remember' (Hebrew: *zkr*). While the psalmist may not be totally clear in his mind about what a human being is, he is very clear about one thing: God is mindful of human beings. To be human is to be held in the memory of God. God watches

Blumenberg's readings of the passion story of Christ and his hearing of the music of the "St. Matthew's Passion" by Johann Sebastian Bach reveals to him that in the Christian story God has abandoned being at a distance from human suffering and has instead with his son entered into human life in need of consolation and comfort. God's son Jesus gets involved with the risks and the hardships of a finite and vulnerable existence, with a temporal consciousness ("Bewusstsein"), in order to remain a God of comfort. Blumenberg recognizes that the biblical story of Jesus Christ has the strength to comfort humans in living, suffering, and dying. "Anyone who knows about mortality is in need of consolation—but also capable of consolation."[16] Blumenberg reflects on the culture of remembrance coming from the Judeo-Christian tradition as a legitimate form of comfort, which enables people to delegate and to comfort others. In the language of Christian theology, we might call this the comfort of discipleship.

Blumenberg wants to understand pain and suffering, comfort and consolation in all their complexity:

> The possibility of comfort and consolation is difficult to understand when observing the phenomenon of pain and its opportunities to relieve itself of consciousness through expressions.... The one who feels pain turns to certain addressees. Why? Can we assume that a person expects sympathy, encouragement, or comfort? In fact, this is where the response of consolation comes in, which mostly if not always occurs to the extent that the person in need of consolation reveals himself as such, as it were opens up the realm of consolation.[17]

In his reflections, Blumenberg refers to the German philosopher and sociologist Georg Simmel, whose work is central to his own studies on comfort and consolation:

> The concept of consolation has a much deeper meaning than we consciously tend to ascribe to it. Mankind is a creature seeking consolation.... Consolation is the strange experience which, while allowing suffering to exist, cancels out, as it were, the suffering of suffering; the evil itself is not its concern, but its reflex in the deepest instance of the soul.[18]

---

over human beings, knows them intimately, and remembers them," writes Swinton in *Dementia*, 211.

16. Dober, *Ethik des Trostes*, 273.
17. Blumenberg, *Beschreibung des Menschen*, 624.
18. Simmel: "Der Begriff des Trostes hat eine viel weitere tiefere Bedeutung, als man

How can it be that the "reflex in the soul," as Simmel describes it, can be touched and changed in an experience like comfort or consolation although the suffering and pain themselves do not simply go away? That this is part of human experience also emerges from the different interviews in this study. When she describes her loving and caring relationship to her son who suffers from an incurable progressive illness, Alice, for instance, fragile herself, finds comfort in caring for him, although her son's and her own suffering doesn't simply disappear. Or when one thinks of Aaron, who is somehow comforted in the midst of the final period of dementia of his dear wife and despite his suffering manages to hold on to his faith.

Blumenberg tries to describe this experience in the following way:

> It seems that suffering is not only to be influenced by others in real terms by providing help, but also through a peculiar act of fictive diffusion, by taking part in something in which they cannot participate in real terms. By simulating the others' suffering, a kind of delegation of suffering, the sum of pain, to these others takes place. And it is not indifferent to how many there are and to what extent they appear credible in wanting to take on their share or having taken on their share. The sufferer gives up his pain; he delegates the function that he, as the bearer of the pain, must initially exercise himself and alone. Consolation is based on human general ability to delegate, not to have to do and bear everything that is incumbent upon him and that falls to him alone.[19]

---

ihm bewusst zuzuschreiben pflegt. Der Mensch ist ein trostsuchendes Wesen. Trost ist etwas anderes als Hilfe—sie sucht auch das Tier; aber der Trost ist das merkwürdige Erlebnis, das zwar das Leiden bestehen lässt, aber sozusagen das Leiden am Leiden aufhebt, er betrifft nicht das Uebel selbst, sondern dessen Reflex in der tiefsten Instanz der Seele." *Fragmente und Aufsätze*, 17.

19. "Es scheint, dass das Leid nicht nur reell von anderen zu beeinflussen ist, indem sie Hilfe leisten, sondern auch durch einen eigentümlichen Akt der fiktiven Diffusion, indem sie Anteil an etwas nehmen, woran sie doch nicht reell teilnehmen können. Indem die anderen zu leiden simulieren, vollzieht sich eine Art Delegation des Leidens, der Summe des Schmerzes, auf diese anderen. Und es ist nicht gleichgültig, wie viele es sind und in welchem Masse sie darin glaubwürdig erscheinen, ihren Anteil übernehmen zu wollen oder übernommen zu haben. Der Leidende gibt von seinem Schmerz ab, er delegiert die Funktion, die er als Träger des Schmerzes zunächst selbst und allein auszuüben hat. Der Trost beruht auf der allgemeinen Fähigkeit des Menschen zu delegieren, nicht selbst und allein alles tun und tragen zu müssen, was ihm obliegt und zufällt." Blumenberg, *Beschreibung des Menschen*, 625. (The English translation above is the author's own translation.)

For Blumenberg, it is impossible to describe pain or suffering in an objective way, with the result that in such experiences the other is called to be respectful in the face of pain and vulnerability. For him, just as the experience of a person is unique, so also is their experience of pain or suffering.

> The peculiarity of consolation is related to the fact that the condition to which it refers—pain, suffering—is by its nature incommunicable. The sensory expressions we have for these states are of such a subjective nature that no one can assume that they can convey to another an impression of the state of pain or suffering in which they find themselves. But the impossibility of objectification also means that everyone must tolerate the other's expression of feeling. . . . Respect is the first thing that is required and through which the protective function of the subjectivity of the expressions of sensation testifies to itself. As paradoxical as it sounds, even pain makes one vulnerable. Vulnerable to the possible attempt of others to distrust its expression, to reinterpret the choice of the protective function as an escape under its protection. Any form of psychologism increases the vulnerability of the one who claims the protective need of the subjectivity of expressing pain. Now it can be said that the need for consolation is still an increase in this vulnerability. The one who lets his need for consolation be known places himself under the protection at least of the respect of others, even if they do not give him the consolation he seeks.[20]

---

20. "Die Eigentümlichkeit des Trostes steht in Zusammenhang damit, dass die Befindlichkeit, auf die er sich bezieht—der Schmerz, das Leid—ihrer Natur nach nicht mitteilbar ist. Die Empfindungsausdrücke, die wir für diese Zustände haben, sind derart subjektiver Natur, dass niemand davon ausgehen kann, er könne einem anderen einen Eindruck davon vermitteln, in welchem Zustand des Schmerzes oder des Leidens er sich selbst befindet. Aber die Unmöglichkeit der Objektivierung bedeutet auch, dass jeder den Empfindungsausdruck des anderen tolerieren muss. . . . Respekt ist das erste, was geboten ist und worin sich die Schutzfunktion der Subjektivität der Empfindungsausdrücke bezeugt. Schon der Schmerz, so paradox es klingt, macht verwundbar. Verwundbar gegenüber dem möglichen Versuch der anderen, seinen Ausdruck zu misstrauen, die Wahl der Schutzfunktion als Flucht unter ihrem Schutz umzudeuten. Jede Form von Psychologismus erhöht die Verwundbarkeit dessen, der das Schutzbedürfnis der Subjektivität des Schmerzausdrucks in Anspruch nimmt. Nun kann man sagen, dass das Trostbedürfnis noch eine Steigerung dieser Verwundbarkeit ist. Wer seine Trostbedürftigkeit erkennen lässt, begibt sich unter den Schutz zumindest des Respekts der anderen, auch wenn sie ihm den gesuchten Trost nicht spenden." Blumenberg, *Beschreibung des Menschen*, 629. (The English translation above is the author's own translation.)

The important insights of Blumenberg's phenomenological observations of comfort and consolation resonate well with the findings described in the interviews. The three areas in which the interviewees described comfort and consolation (being carried thanks to their relationship with God; being carried thanks to relationships with others; and being carried thanks to the appreciation of creation, music, art, and "things") can be seen as a fruit of different experiences which Blumenberg's three comfort "modi" try to describe: *thoughtfulness, memory,* and *humor.*

At different levels, thoughtfulness and memory are very present in the interviews as even the formulation of the interviewees' experiences and feelings of comfort and consolation involve reasoning and remembering. Humor too, highlighted in some quotes where the interviewees laughed or smiled, is also part of their experience. Alice, for instance, laughed about her idea of what comfort is, that after one has died one can sit at a big table with Jesus. By laughing, she could achieve a healthy distance from herself and mentioned that this was "only a quote from a professor" she had heard. Nonetheless, this "inner imagination" had a strong quality of comfort for her, which she felt she could share with others and with me, while enjoying its humorous quality. Another example can be seen in Sally's description of dancing alone at night, even in her old age and severe heart problems. She could laugh about her inner desire to do this and her way of expressing joy and life through movement, realizing that it gave her comfort to do it and yet that it was in some ways a bit unusual for someone almost a hundred years old.

Blumenberg's understanding of a person as a "being in deficiency," "Mängelwesen," is a presupposition for his description of comfort and consolation as a phenomenon and *conditio humana*, a category of what it means to be human.[21] To take his insights into a critical, fruitful dialogue within theology it is helpful, next to the Incarnation and passion of Christ, to look at the biblical story of the beginning of creation and humankind. From that faithful perspective, one can remember that humans are understood as part of creation and are created in relationship to one another and foremost for relationship with God. That we alone are not sufficient does not mean, in a biblical sense (contrary to Blumenberg's vocabulary) that we are "deficient"—"Mängelwesen." Rather it underpins the importance of God having created us for community with him and with others. This communion and community is one to which

---

21. Blumenberg, *Beschreibung des Menschen*, 623.

humans are called but also one into which vulnerability and brokenness have come, described in the Bible through the narratives of disobedience before God, mistrust, sin, and shame.

The biblical narrative gives witness that humans and the whole universe are waiting for God's shalom. This perspective of waiting is not just some illusory and naïve thought but is grounded in the life, death, and resurrection of Jesus Christ. Lydia, for instance, in the actual process of dying, describes the quality of her comfort as faith in the "big story of salvation," which includes the confidence of salvation in Christ even in the midst of suffering and the longing for the fulfilment of shalom. Although Lydia trusts in the "big story of salvation" she feels the very real tension involved when the promise of shalom seems to be so far away in the actual brokenness and suffering of existence. In his work on comfort, the theologian Volker Weyman takes this tension into account when he writes about the problem of false consolation:

> The tension between appeasement and false consolation ("Vertröstung") on the one hand and encouragement and comfort on the other seems inevitable. That is why the question remains acute about consolation that does not deceive, but carries one.[22]

Comfort has a lot to do with trust, with allowing oneself to be carried. And yet the thoughtfulness, which is so important for Blumenberg, is also vital if one is not to be deceived. Faithful, practical theology has the task of bringing this thoughtfulness into the practice of entrusting oneself to Christ.

To discuss Blumenberg's work in more detail here is beyond the scope of this project. But his insights first, that humans are categorically in the need of comfort and consolation, and second, that the ethical investigation of such comfort, which is necessary to allow differentiation between true and false comfort, can fruitfully be approached through the "modi" of thoughtfulness, a practice of remembering, and humor, are useful for my further discussion within this theological response to the

---

22. Weymann, *Trost?*, 9: "Die Spannung zwischen Besänftigung und Vertröstung einerseits sowie Ermutigung und Getrostwerden andererseits unumgänglich. Deshalb bleibt die Frage akut nach Trost, der nicht trügt, sondern trägt." (The English translation of the quote is the author's own translation.)

In 2024 the University of Zürich edited a collections of articles on Comfort and Consolation to discuss the phenomenon of comfort: Pfenninger and Koch, "Trost und Vertröstung."

Eschmann and Roser, "Vom Trost, der trägt" (Of the consolation that sustains), 1.

findings from the data analysis. In taking up the topics of thoughtfulness and remembering for the better understanding of comfort and consolation for a Christian (which Lydia referred to as the "big story"), I now turn again to Paul's witness to comfort in his descriptions of his own experience of being in need of comfort and then comforting others in the context of his faith in Christ.

Reflections on experiences of comfort and the writings of the apostle Paul

As described in the first chapter, in the New Testament "παρακάλεω/parakaleo" appears as *calling for help, calling near*, and its noun form as *admonition, encouragement, consolation*, and *comfort*. In the interview material of faithful Christians at the end of life, they describe comfort experiences which come from being comforted by God and sharing this experience with others, with family members, friends, in their Christian community, and in the relationships they have built up over time. Although I repeat various insights from the introduction, I want to return to Paul's understanding of comfort and look at it more deeply. His texts around comfort and the "God of comfort" are the main sources for theological reflection concerning comfort and consolation in the New Testament within Protestant theology and they resonate well with the described experiences of the interviewees.

Marion, for instance, when she herself cannot sleep because of her physical condition, writes letter of encouragement to others and prays for them. This, as she tells me in the interview, is comforting for her as she realizes that for her the comfort of Christ includes her engagement towards others, through which she herself is then comforted again.

The interviewee Paul, in a different way, feels comfort while meditating on his picture of Dalí's portrayal of the crucified Christ hanging over the entire world, because it shows him the immense power of consolation in Christ for the whole world, and because it allows him to delegate part of his own suffering and to start praying for others around the world. This is what Simmel writes about in the quotation above, when he says that real consolation has a mysterious power in that, while allowing suffering to exist, it "cancels out, as it were, the suffering of suffering."

Through the apostle Paul's use of the word "παρακάλεω/parakaleo" one is brought to the realization that consolation and experiences of comfort create a community in which the ones in need of consolation do not remain alone but themselves also become part of a ministry of comfort to others.

The suffering of the apostle with and for his suffering community becomes what we might call a "mutual or reciprocal consolation community." The message of Christ, which obviously does not simply make life conflict free or even necessarily easier, but which opens up the possibility of true and reliable life, is what Paul calls "παράκλησις/parakleisis" (1 Thess 2:3). Because of his separation from the church community and the tribulation in which it lived, Paul had sent Timothy from Athens to them, saying of him: "He should strengthen you and comfort you in your faith, so that no one should waver in these tribulations" (1 Thess 3:2).

Consolation brings strength in weakness, resilience in distress, encouragement and stability when life is under attack and uncertain. Consolation here is by no means a "false consolation" for better times or a distraction from what is afflicting the community, but rather a strengthening and encouragement that allows this community (and by extension, all of us) to perceive and withstand an oppressive situation differently. And in this Paul is at the same time a giver and also a recipient. Thus, he writes to the Corinthians what Timothy told him after his return from the congregation in Thessaloniki: ". . . we were comforted over you in all our affliction and distress by your faith." (1 Thess 3:7).

Consolation and comfort in this biblical, Pauline sense leads to a multi-layered and reciprocal understanding of consolation. As mentioned before, the interviewees gave rich accounts of such experiences. We see further examples, for instance, in Daniela, Alice, and Richard. I remember Daniela and how she felt connected and called to a ministry of comfort towards her old and fragile friend in Germany, and I recall her conviction that that friend also, although no longer able to speak to her on the phone, was praying for Daniela's strength as well. There was also that conversation with Alice after the first COVID lockdown in which she describes the immense comfort she experienced at seeing her chronically ill son again and reading a book to him. She described the effect of mutual comfort and specifically its spiritual aspect.[23] Or I remember Richard experiencing care and friendship when he was feeling weak and lonely in the old people's home and someone regularly brought him to Sunday service for worship and to spend time together in fellowship with

---

23. Alice, see under: "Family bonds and comforting one another."

other Christians. These examples express something of that mutual comfort dimension to which Christians are called. Whether one is in need of consolation or is the one doing the comforting: both individuals remain dependent on the giver of life, who gives them strength in weakness and courage to comfort.

It is astonishing that the second letter to the Corinthians, which is like no other in depicting Paul in distress and tribulation, begins with such praise of comfort and consolation. Comfort and consolation are situational events. Consolation comes to Paul in his distress and to others in their suffering and can thus be understood as a relational word, perhaps even a relational event, according to which the person is not left to their own devices, but finds a comforter in their distress. This comforter stays with people, holds them, and does not give up on them in their distress and suffering. This comforter has a name: It is God, the father of Jesus Christ, who shows himself to be the "father of mercy and God of all consolation."

Consolation is also relational, because in it God maintains his relationship with humankind, even if humankind has lost or destroyed this relationship and sees itself as abandoned. This divine consolation also creates relationships between people: Although Paul himself is in need of consolation, he takes seriously others' distress. Paul can write at the beginning of his letter that only those who are familiar with struggle and who are themselves dependent on consolation are apparently able to comfort; only those who do not regard themselves as superior or strong, but find themselves in need of consolation can discover the wisdom of the Gospel. God's foolishness is wiser than that of humans and God's weakness is stronger than that of humans (see: 1 Cor 1:25). Through the event of the cross—a sign that God sticks to the world and to us humans at all costs—God shows himself to be the "father of mercy and God of all consolation." Such consolation comes closer to the afflicted than all the well-intentioned encouragement of others and all one's own attempts to escape suffering. Comfort notably often comes during suffering itself, not after the situation has changed. Like in other biblical narratives and prayers, there is a change of situation associated with comfort and consolation. But it happens in such a way that the change is not a prerequisite, but rather is opened up through the consolation. "For just as we share abundantly in the sufferings of Christ, so also our comfort abounds through Christ" (2 Cor 1:5).

It is remarkable that suffering and consolation come from Christ together. Christ does not avoid suffering. Hence, in his own suffering Paul perceives the suffering of Christ with us and for our sake as an event of his unconditional devotion to us. That is why the affliction which he experiences and with which he is troubled, the affliction of which his opponents accuse him, can become the place where the power of the Gospel comes into effect:

> If we are distressed, it is for your comfort and salvation; if we are comforted, it is for your comfort, which produces in you patient endurance of the same sufferings we suffer. (2 Cor 1:6)

Consolation and comfort, which are granted through Christ's devotion to us, therefore resist an understandable wishful thinking for a life without suffering or pain, realizing that this is merely false consolation. Such comfort and consolation is thus able to encourage people to endure suffering and to support those who are suffering, while in no way glorifying or ignoring that suffering.

Consolation could be seen to come only from a position of strength. But Paul does not share comfort with the church community from a position of strength. When he speaks of comfort and consolation, he reveals himself as someone who himself is in the need of such comfort, something about which, as I noted above, Blumenberg writes. Paul emphasizes that he and the church community together remain dependent on the care of Jesus Christ. In 2 Corinthians, the fact that affliction and consolation coincide for Paul leads him to express this paradox in words:

> In everything we are oppressed, but not cornered; in doubt but not in despair; pursued but not abandoned; thrown to the ground, but not destroyed. (2 Cor 4:8)

Paul's language here is different to "everyday wisdom language." Some forms of everyday wisdom or "false comfort" attempt to console by trying to keep a distance and are therefore unable to come close to the sufferer in their situation. On the other hand, Paul's dialectical twists and turns are about conflicting and intertwined experiences, that though "we are thrown to the ground, we are not destroyed." Though this cannot be established as a general rule of experience, it does reflect the almost mysterious experiences of opposites which are opened up through faith.

Some interviewees were able to speak about this. On account of her extreme suffering when her husband died and she soon thereafter lost their unborn twin children, Ruth could say at the end of her life that she was thankful to God for her life; even though she felt that she had been thrown to the ground, she acknowledged that she had not been destroyed and was able once again to experience joy and comfort with others and also with God. How this is possible remains a mystery, and yet the gospel talks about this in the context of the cross. God's care for people often takes place hidden under the opposite of what people like to imagine and desire as salvation: namely, on the cross. The crucified Christ in whom God turns to everyone at all costs, says Paul in his letters, this crucified Christ is the light of the world. Through Christ light can shine in wounded and suffering hearts. This reality prompts Paul to speak of a treasure that is entrusted to us, a treasure that we can carry only in earthen, fragile vessels.

> Now we have this treasure in jars of clay to show that this surpassingly great power is from God and not from us. (2 Cor 4:7)

Such surprising and illuminating experiences of opposites are often revealed by Paul's language and dialectical expressions:

> Unknown, yet well-known; dying, and yet we live on; punished, yet not killed; sorrowful, yet always rejoicing; poor, yet making many rich; having nothing, and yet possessing everything. (2 Cor 6:9)

This is not about demonstrating superiority despite adverse living conditions. Here, the experience of a lack of life and of suffering becomes a place where, paradoxically, life, joy and peace appear. If one is to experience encouragement in suffering and consolation in distress, a language is required that does not describe what is being negotiated, but opens up reality. Such a reality does not respond by granting understandable wishes, but prompts one to listen carefully to the sustaining consolation of faith. In being consoled and comforting at the same time, Paul is united with the church community, connected with his sisters and brothers, with his friends in Christ. It is Paul's experience and faith that the God of all comfort does not leave one to despair. That doesn't preclude times of doubt and of suffering, but allows trust to penetrate those dark times.

Prayer, lament, and comfort in the experience of Christians through the lens of theological thinkers

The aforementioned dialectic which the apostle Paul describes, resonating as it does with the experience of the interviewees, is also one we find in theological literature. The question guiding us in this chapter of theological reflection is how to relate the pearls of comfort found in the interview data analyses with the Christian faith. Part of the movement of faith includes coming honestly before God, and allowing one's suffering, pain, and the questions surrounding them to be formulated in lament. Lament is the formulation of the one side of Paul's dialectic around comfort. In Aaron's interviews, for instance,[24] he allowed himself to formulate his lament in my presence, describing his feeling of emptiness and of being overwhelmed by his experiences with phrases like "it is unbearable," "I am depressed," "I am losing my strength," and "I pray to God that we can both die soon." Aaron continues to pray, but his prayer is mainly one of lament as his relationship to God is being challenged.

Reflecting on such experiences of extreme suffering, the German theologian Dorothee Sölle writes,

> All extreme suffering evokes the experience of being forsaken by God. In the depth of suffering people see themselves as abandoned and forsaken by everyone. That which gave life its meaning has become empty and void.... Every suffering that is experienced as a threat to one's own life touches our relationship to God.[25]

Regarding this touching of our relationship with God, Alice, for instance, said to me in the interview that "lament is a form of prayer." This implies the experience of strong emotions and deep feelings. "The verb 'to lament' can be used in English as equivalent to the verbs 'to wail,' 'to mourn,' 'to cry,' 'to groan,' 'to yell,' 'to whine,' 'to scream,' 'to howl' and 'to weep.'"[26] Often it is the case that one of the fundamental experiences of suffering is precisely the lack of the possibility of verbal communication. To experience suffering often also means becoming more and more isolated.

---

24. See "Prayer and lament."
25. Sölle, *Suffering*, 85–86.
26. Klein, "Phenomenology of Lament."

Being in communication with others, praying, or having someone to talk to is a basic human need, especially in times of suffering and also for the process of lamentation. Having spent time with dying people for more than half a century, Cicely Saunders, wrote about the Christian approach to suffering and lament by referring to Jesus Christ in the garden of Gethsemane:

> I am sure the most important foundation stone we could have (for the care of the dying) comes from the summing up of all the needs of the dying which was made for us in the Garden of Gethsemane in the simple words "Watch with me." I think the one word "watch" says many things on many different levels, all of importance to us.[27]

Although Saunders opens up the narrative of Gethsemane to a wide range of interpretations, she writes not only of Jesus' request to the disciples to watch with him, but also of his lamenting before God in extreme suffering as he asks his father to let the cup of suffering pass him by. For Christians, the passion of Christ is unique, and thus the scene at Gethsemane of Jesus expressing his need for comfort is of immense importance. Here, because he has become human, even the Son of God experiences what Blumenberg called the *conditio humana* of being in need of comfort. Christ's cry for help and his loneliness, his obedience to his mission, and his fear of being forsaken by God shows astonishing solidarity with alienated humanity.

Some of the mystical texts, like those written by Julian of Norwich,[28] Tauler,[29] and John of the Cross,[30] take this up and express experiences of darkness before God

The Swiss Catholic theologian Hans Urs von Balthasar in his book *Mysterium Paschale* emphasizes in a different way the uniqueness of Christ's suffering. The incident at Gethsemane shows that his disciples and friends were removed from Jesus by distance and sleep, and that "Jesus enters an 'aloneness' whose suffering seems to cut off all access to its own inwardness: at the most a silent 'assisting' from a distance, is all that is possible."[31] The horrible isolation of Christ, says von Balthasar,

---

27. Saunders, *Watch with Me*, 12.

28. Julian of Norwich wrote the best known surviving book in the English language written by a mystic, namely, *Relevations of Divine Love*.

29. Johannes Tauler (1300–61) was a German mystic, a disciple of Meister Eckhardt, who belonged to the Dominican order. He is known as one of the most important Rhineland mystics.

30. John of the Cross (1542–91) was a Spanish mystic and a Carmelite.

31. Von Balthasar, *Mysterium Paschale*, 72.

was necessary in the sense that Jesus goes on loving alone, for the world is so in need of redemption and healing that he had to abandon himself in faithfulness to God, his father. At the same time, Gethsemane reminds Christians of a grievous loss to the world, "to be so cut off from the most momentous, heart-breaking, cosmos shaking moments in the life of Jesus Christ. What we have left in the gospels is only barely a glimpse of the inner drama. And yet, for Christian faith, in this inner space all the world's salvation lies enclosed."[32] For von Balthasar, this "safeguard" protects the uniqueness of the passion of the Redeemer and the consolatory Christ from invasion or misunderstanding, and makes space for forms of lament with and before Christ.

Whereas von Balthasar tries to capture the uniqueness of the inner drama of Christ's path to the cross, for Saunders the garden of Gethsemane, though unique, is also a symbolic narrative for the suffering that people can endure, a metaphor for human anxiety and lamentation, which Jesus himself shares with us: "My soul is very sorrowful even to death; remain here and watch with me" (Matt 26:38).

These words recall for us that even his friends failed to pray and lament with him. His closest disciples, with whom he shared acceptance and persecution and so much more during his life time, did not have the strength to be with him in the way he needed it. A further perspective on this is given in a poem by Rainer Maria Rilke, who reflects the question of how to approach the Gethsemane narrative by using poetic language with new questions. His poem "The Garden of Olives" defends against what he sees as the misunderstanding that Jesus saw himself as consoled, but rather emphasizes his unspeakable despair and fear of suffering and dying:

> Later it was said: an angel came -.
> Why an angel? Alas it was the night
> Leafing indifferently among the trees.
> The disciples stirred in their dreams.
> Why an angel? Alas it was the night.
> The night that came was no uncommon night;
> Hundreds like it go by.
> Then dogs sleep, and the stones lie.
> Alas a sad night, alas any night
> That waits till it be morning once again.[33]

---

32. Von Balthasar, *Mysterium Paschale*, 72.

33. Rilke, from "The Garden of Olives," translation from *The Poetry of Rainer Maria Rilke* quoted in Sölle, *Suffering*, 80. See also Falque, *Guide to Gethsemane*, 54–55. Falque combines Rilke's poem with the general human experience of isolation and despair.

Though the mystics, von Balthasar, Saunders, and Rilke each approach the darkness Jesus experiences in Gethsemane in different ways, each of those ways can offer comfort. Von Balthasar emphasizes the unique and cosmic dimension of Christ's experience and through that the possibility of comfort. The mystics and Saunders, although not questioning the uniqueness of Christ's suffering, concentrate on the human experience of suffering shared by Christ, which is then perceived as comfort. Here, Rilke primarily sees comfort in Christ's solidarity with all who suffer.

In the realm of lament and comfort, poetic language has a special quality. This is seen in Scripture, especially through the Psalms, which have a canny ability to touch the heart. In this poetic and emotional language, the interviewees, after having travelled through life, found that praying the psalms allowed them to be part of an experience which wasn't theirs but connected to their lives which were sometimes full of uncertainty and often also painful.

The interviewees were clear about lament for suffering not being forbidden anywhere in the Scriptures. Far from it: they know and knew that to lament is an essential part of human and Christian expression in suffering, and that in many strange and harsh life situations it is a "normal" way of expressing fear, need, loss, and pain to God.

> The articulation of negative feelings can help to distance oneself from them. Once those feelings can be communicated, they can also be transformed, if they are voiced in a shared space of experience, they are taken beyond one's own control (at least to a certain degree) and thus become open to change. If they remain locked in, they poison the soul. Hence, the prayer of lamentation in hope for God's help is as indispensable as the air we breathe. It keeps the self alive and protests the vitality of relations in which alone it can thrive.[34]

It is vital that with the example of biblical openness to lament in mind, Christians can be encouraged not to hide lament or suppress it. Consolation does not suffocate lamentation, but refreshes people in the midst of their affliction, as we see, for example, in the language of Ps 94:19: "If the multitude of worries oppress my heart, your consolation refreshes my soul." Psalm 23 expresses a similar sentiment: "Even though I walk through the valley of the shadow of death, I will fear no evil, for you are with me; your rod and your staff, they comfort me." In different

---

34. Welz, "Trust and Lament," 127.

parts of the psalms, one can recognize that people in desolate situations find a language of trust in the midst of suffering and fear.

In his writings, the Swiss theologian Rudolf Bohren described his experience of suffering, of losing his wife tragically and unexpectedly, and his need for lamentation. For Bohren, the act of receiving a psalm from his friend that day was pivotal, and he experienced it also as a guiding word for his children at that time:

> I was not able to read the Bible; but there I felt lifted up . . . the Psalm gave me language: "O Lord, listen to my prayer, hear my supplication, in your faithfulness, in your mercy hear me. . . . My spirit within me wants to despair, my heart freezes in my breast." (Ps 143:1, 4). . . . Of course, I don't remember what Walter Wolff said about it, but when the children came and we sat in misery in the evening, I was able to pass the psalm on to my children, as it were. . . . My friend also gave me a verse from an old hymn. . . . I can say that God's comfort came through these two texts.[35]

Consolation and comfort often cannot be given if lament is excluded. Because that which gives consolation and comfort has to do with painful and sometimes dreadful life situations in which the experience of the *deus absconditus* is oppressive. This resonates with what the German systematic theologian Volker Weymann writes,

> The worst cannot and must not be withheld from God, the evil should not be glossed over in order for praise to become possible. Rather, as in Psalm 22, one can even realize that the inevitable steep gradient of lamentation opens up the way to praise.[36]

Lament can become a first step in entering and continuing upon a path of experiencing real comfort and consolation. Time and the process

---

35. "Ich war nicht in der Lage, in der Bibel zu lesen; aber da fühlte ich mich aufgehoben . . . der Psalm gab mir Sprache: 'O Herr, höre auf mein Gebet, vernimm mein Flehen, in deiner Treue, in Deiner Gnade höre mich. . . . Mein Geist in mir will verzagen, mein Herz erstarrt in der Brust.' (Ps 143, 1,4) . . . Natürlich weiss ich nicht mehr was Walter Wolff dazu sagte, aber als dann die Kinder kamen und wir abends im Elend sassen, konnte ich den Psalm meinen Kindern gleichsam weitergeben. . . . Eine Strophe aus dem Gesangbuch gab er mir auch. . . . Ich darf wohl sagen, dass Gottes Trost mit diesen beiden Texten kam." Bohren, *Sterben und Tod*, 313–15. (The English translation is the author's own translation.)

36. Weymann, *Trost?*, 22, "Vor Gott muss und kann das Schlimmste nicht zurückgehalten, das Böse nicht beschönigt werden, damit Loben möglich wird. Vielmehr kann einem wie an Psalm 22 gar aufgehen, dass im unausweichlichem Gefälle der Klage der Weg ins Loben sich öffnet." (The English translation is the author's own translation.)

of lamenting are important. Waiting for God's presence in time and for God to come is part of the process of comfort in lamentation. Theologically speaking, such waiting has the power to overcome meaninglessness, despair, and death. Lamentation is thus also part of the expression of God's bestowal of grace and promise to save human life. It can help to free the suffering person from the traumatizing effects of evil and can open them up to life and community once more.

Here, I want to mention a text within the protestant tradition, which can be seen as connected with that bestowal of grace, and to connect it with Sally's interview. Sally, who in her childhood and young adulthood had experienced extreme suffering in the Second World War, was only able to open up to others with her lament about what had happened to her and her family towards the end of her life. She spent a large part of her life in inward lament and prayer, and was able to see over time how God had formed in her pearls of comfort, to which she now witnesses with gratitude and praise. Her way of understanding how God has worked in her life resonates with words from the Heidelberger Catechism. The first question and answer of the Heidelberger Catechism is: *"What is your only consolation in life and in death?"*[37] Consolation here is connected with the question of what I can rely on in life and in death. The Heidelberger Catechism answers that question with the words: "that I am not my own, but belong to my faithful Saviour Jesus Christ, with body and soul, in life and in death." The catechism, published in 1563, formulates the doctrine of the Reformed church tradition developed by the reformers Zwingli, Bullinger, and Calvin. The interviewees come from this Reformed tradition, and thus it will be helpful now to look in more detail at some of the main Protestant interpretations of the correlation between consolation and faith.

---

37. "The Heidelberg Catechism" (1563) was composed in the city of Heidelberg, Germany, at the request of Elector Frederick III, who ruled the province of the Palatinate from 1559 to 1576. The new catechism was intended as a tool for teaching young people, a guide for preaching in the provincial churches, and a form of confessional unity among the several Protestant factions in the Palatinate. An old tradition credits Zacharias Ursinus and Caspar Olevianus with being the co-authors of the catechism, but the project was actually the work of a team of ministers and university theologians under the watchful eye of Frederick himself. Ursinus probably served as the primary writer on the team, and Olevianus had a lesser role. The catechism was approved by a synod in Heidelberg in January 1563.

Comfort and *fiducia*

At the beginning of my theological response, I discussed the relevance of Blumenberg's anthropological phenomenological insights. Now I ask how it can be that the "reflex in the soul" (as the philosopher Simmel describes it) can be touched and changed in an experience like comfort or consolation although the suffering and pain themselves do not simply go away? How is it possible that the one who is in the need of consolation and comfort can delegate life and death to a God who is described by Scripture? How is it possible that interviewees lamenting their suffering nonetheless describe their faith experiences as very real?

One possible answer mentioned above comes from the Heidelberg Catechism: "*I am not my own, but belong to my faithful Saviour Jesus Christ, with body and soul, in life and in death.*" To discuss "comfort and faith" further, it is essential to show that the ability to have trust or to trust in God can enrich the discussion of comfort and consolation in a crucial way. The discussion on "faith" or "trust" can be explained in different ways. In the following discourse, I try to show how the terms *fiducia* or *fides* can help to deepen our reflection on comfort and consolation and take the interview material seriously.

I begin by reflecting on the term "faith" as "trust." The subject of trust in God has always been a central component of theological discussion. Furthermore, the personal experience of trust in God is described in different ways by thinkers from the early church (such as Augustine) and later by mystics (such as Julian of Norwich or Theresa of Avila) and others. The Reformation, however, brought a new emphasis on the experience of faith as trust and the correlation of that trust with Scripture. Martin Luther, for instance, paraphrased faith in his translation of Hebrews 11:1 in the September Testament of 1522 as "a certain trust in that which we can hope for."[38] In particular, he reminds us that, "Faith means trusting and building on mercy"[39] and "*Fidem (. . .) est fiduciam necessariam in gratiam Dei.*"[40] Here, Luther describes faith as a kind of trust, as "being confident in" or being able to rely on. In the Latin quotation, in addition to the term *fides*, Luther also mentions the term *fiducia*

---

38. "Eyn gewisse zuuorsicht des, das zu hoffen ist."

39. "Glauben heist auff die barmherzigkeit gewiss trauen und bauen," Martin Luther, *Martin Luthers Werke*, 17.2:577.

40. "Faith . . . is a necessary confidence in the grace of God," *Martin Luthers Werke*, 1:361 ll. 7–8 (no. 759).

for confidence or trusting faith, a word which has played a role in theological debates for centuries. Martin Luther himself did not have a closed systematic concept of the words. For Luther, fides can refer to both the carrying out of and the content of faith. And the use of *fiducia* is also an open term for Luther that focuses on justifying trust or confidence in Jesus Christ. Over the course of the development of Protestant dogmatics people often spoke of *fides qua creditur* ("the act of faith") and *fides quae creditur* ("the content of faith").[41]

These two terms, however, describe not only a life-promoting trust in God but also a trust that can lead astray. Luther refers to this as "*stulta fiducia*" and he sees it at work in a trust in earthly means of power or in a trust in justification by works. For Luther, faith and trust always have to do with the promises of God, which are described to us in the Bible. *Fides* or *fiducia* are thus linked to the promises of God. *Fiducia*, which responds to the divine promise and appropriates the salvation promised in Christ, suggests that *fiducia* and trust are interchangeable terms in Luther's thought. Luther emphasizes that on the one hand this "appropriation" takes place in the power of the Holy Spirit and on the other hand is an event that applies to me personally and is for me (*pro me*) or for us (*pro nobis*). It is this understanding of trust, in which both the act of faith as well as the content of faith is made possible and given by the work of the Holy Spirit, which some of the interviewees repeatedly expressed. They testify that, for instance, through prayer, through spiritual songs or melodies, through meditating on Bible texts or a picture, they experience this sense of being taking up into faith, but note that it eludes a purely rational understanding. Thus, the power of the Holy Spirit, who enables and helps to shape faith and trust, is always only partially comprehensible.

The Luther researcher Wolf-Friedrich Schäufele writes concerning this: "The '*fiducia*' that makes up the essence of faith is an effect of the heart and a movement of the Spirit."[42] Thus, for Luther, faith is not the work of humans, but rather the work of God and the gift of the Holy Spirit, which does not abandon people to their passivity, but rather allows them to be open to a trusting relationship.

Trust in God can thus, in one sense, be described as friendship with God in the Holy Spirit towards Christ. This pneumatological orientation

---

41. Schäufele, "*Fiducia* bei Martin Luther."

42. "Die das Wesen des Glaubens ausmachende *fiducia* ist ein Affekt des Herzens und eine Bewegung des Geistes." Schäufele, "*Fiducia* bei Martin Luther," 175. (The English translation above is the author's translation.)

of the concept of faith also points to the New Testament concept of *paraclete* and *paraclesis*, which combines the Holy Spirit and the act and movement of consolation in faith. The Swiss reformer Huldrych Zwingli, amongst others, makes this clear in saying that we "feel" (experience) faith "through the Spirit of God in our hearts."[43] "Faith is the true thing existing from the Godhead, which alone is rightly hoped for, which is given to humans, through which they trust surely and firmly in the invisible God."[44] The fact that Zwingli always has the human need for consolation in mind is expressed, among other things, in the fact that he had a verse of consolation and promise from Scripture printed on his publications as a biblical motto: "Come unto me, all of you who are burdened and heavy-laden, and I will give you rest" (Matt 11:28). In Zwingli's thought this is a Christologically justified "abandonment." In his commentary on Matt 11:18 Zwingli says,

> He who was pinned to the cross calls to him all who are haunted by the fear of sin and damnation, and says: "Come unto me. . . ." For it is Christ alone, the one who lifts up and comforts desperate and anxious consciences, who calms the restlessness of the soul and gives peace and quiet.[45]

Like Martin Luther, Zwingli connects this event of peace and comfort with the work of the Holy Spirit: "God's spirit, I say, deigns to draw the poor spirit of humans to himself, to connect and link them with himself, to transform them completely unto himself. This nourishes the soul, and makes [one] joyful and certain of salvation."[46]

For both Luther and Zwingli, consolation, hope, and peace are rooted in their understanding of *fiducia*, this trust in God, which includes both the experience and content of the Gospel. This trust concept of *fiducia* applies to the whole life of Christians and is not limited to times of suffering and dying. Zwingli describes trusting faith as "surrendering"

---

43. Zwingli, *Zwinglis Schriften*, 3:272, ll. 12-14 (= *Huldreich Zwinglis Sämtliche Werke*, 3:786, ll. 12-14).

44. "Der Glaube ist die wahre und von der Gottheit bestehende Sache, auf die allein zu Recht gehofft wird, die dem Menschen gegeben ist, durch die er gewiss und fest auf den unsichtbaren Gott vertraut," *Zwinglis Schriften*, 4:228 ll. 19-21.

45. Zwingli, *In Evangelium Matthaei* 11 (*Huldreich Zwinglis Sämtliche Werke*, 6.1:282; the English translation above is the author's own translation).

46. "Gottes Geist, sage ich, geruht, den armen Geist des Menschen zu sich zu ziehen, ihn mit sich zu verbinden und zu verknüpfen, ihn ganz in sich umzuwandeln. Das nährt die Seele, macht sie fröhlich und des Heils gewiss," Zwingli, *Zwinglis Schriften*, 3:266 l. 9.

to the salutary promises of God, which can be believed and hoped for in God's devotion to people, especially people who are suffering and in need of consolation. Both Luther and Zwingli made it clear that faith and thus trust are always endangered and challenged. Zwingli researcher Peter Opitz writes: "With Zwingli 'trust' always [includes] the moment of the 'nevertheless' of faith, not least against its constant endangerment by 'idolatry' in one's own heart."[47] Through the explanations described, both theologians want to make it clear that when people do indeed entrust themselves, when they "surrender" or "abandon" themselves to the Spirit of God and turn to God in faith in Jesus Christ, God sustains them and is comfortingly close, and thus peace can be experienced even in suffering or at the end of life. Trust can thus be understood as that moment in which activity and passivity not only alternate but coincide. As the interviewees also partially describe, the moment in which trust in God sets in is at that highly intimate act of turning to God in which they experience themselves as being held by God. From this there can develop a constant trust and faith in God. In my research, this was particularly evident in prayer experiences.

Prayer in such a setting can therefore be described as that act of trusting devotion to God in which a human enters into communion with God as a physical, spiritual, social, and emotional creature and reaches out trustingly, expectantly, or pleadingly for the mercy of God. In prayer, faith in God proves to be trust, because on the one hand it leaves itself to God and on the other hand it trusts God to act and hear. Faith as *fiducia* is therefore a prerequisite from which good and real consolation or peace comes. This is how Martin Luther explains it in his interpretation of Psalm 80.[48] Luther's *fiducia* characteristic of the believer's relationship with Christ, denotes the same relationship of trust as that between children and their mother. Faith in Christ can be compared with the trust with which chicks hide under the mother hen's wings. Experiences of consolation, among other things, flow from trust in God. Both Luther and Zwingli name them as affections worked through the Spirit by God. Trust in God or *fiducia* is therefore the basic requirement for these affections of the human heart.

---

47. "Stets besitzt bei Zwingli 'Vertrauen' das Moment des 'dennoch' des Glaubens, nicht zuletzt gegen dessen beständige Gefährdung durch den 'Götzendienst' im eigenen Herzen," Peter Opitz, "Evangelium als Befreiung," 207.

48. Martin Luther, *Martin Luthers Werke*, 3:617 ll. 34–36.

Such explanations are exciting and helpful because they overcome the dichotomy between *fides qua* and *fides quae*, and in the term *fiducia* they address the relationship between execution, experience, and content. It is evident that the interviewees approach their experiences of comfort by trying to describe trust phenomena in which they encounter the Christian faith in a comforting and strengthening way. At the same time, they experience this in a personal and emotional way (*pro me*). For instance, Lydia's reflection on the "big stories" of Christian faith and the way she is able to describe God's presence for her in her suffering is a helpful example to remember regarding how experiencing faith and the content of faith can come together.

In the twentieth century the Reformed theologian Karl Barth also approached the term of *fiducia* in Section 63 of his Church Dogmatics. There he describes in more detail the dimensions of trust as an act and as directed towards Jesus Christ as revealed in Scripture.

> But what is left then, what then really follows from the knowledge that the establishment of my rights and my life in the death of Jesus Christ happened once and for all and was revealed once and for all in his resurrection? This follows from the fact that for myself, without being able to evade the accusation of my injustice and the threat of my death sentence following it in any direction, I may have a whole, a certain and, because certain, therefore also comforting, strong and joyful confidence. I can rely on what has happened for me. I am allowed to keep myself safe in my heart. I am also allowed to think my few thoughts in peace, say my few words in peace, do my few works in peace. For I am allowed to look forward as I am and full of what is mine, as it is and as it happens. Where? Certainly not into the blue of any better future, but certainly to the fulfilment of the promise given to me in Jesus Christ, i.e. to the revelation of the judgment that was spoken in him about me, which recognizes my right and life. I can trust in this. On this positive side, faith is simple—and that is why our forebears talked about fiducia at this point—trust! Not an arbitrary one, but one that responds to the word spoken to me, not an indefinite one, but trust based on the knowledge of faith as the knowledge of Jesus Christ. And let's add to this right away: in this answering and well-founded trust, in that it is about myself, it will always also be about the community and the world.[49]

---

49. Barth, *Kirchliche Dogmatik*, 4/1:865–66: "Was bleibt dann aber übrig, was folgt dann aber wirklich aus der Erkenntnis, dass die Herstellung meines Rechtes und

That this trusting process also has an impact on interpersonal relationships, on others in the world in which I live, is also expressed in the various interviews. The areas of divine and human consolation are not opposites but are intrinsically intertwined. This also applies in particular to the experience of the Christian community, in which many of the interviewees participate and feel connected. This solidarity in trust in Christ then also creates the basis for mutual encouragement and consoling sympathy, which is ultimately based on God's Spirit and work.

Another aspect of faith and comfort can be found in the distinction of "trust" and "reliance" and the process of comfort in suffering. The German theologian Wilfried Härle in his *Dogmatics* emphasizes that reliance means "that a person moves away from himself and towards someone or something else, indeed gives himself to other(s)."[50] Here it is of interest that in contrast to a purely passive understanding of the word, "Vertrauen" ("trusting faith") shares its linguistic roots with "(sich) trauen" ("to dare") and "Treue" ("truth" in the sense of faithfulness or loyalty). Claudia Welz writes, "From this perspective, trust is the disposition to

---

meines Lebens im Tod Jesu Christi ein für allemal geschehen und in seiner Auferstehung ein für allemal offenbar gemacht ist? Das folgt daraus, dass ich für mich selbst, ohne dass ich mich der Anklage meines Unrechts und der Drohung meines ihm folgenden Todesgerichts in irgendeiner Richtung entziehen kann, eine ganze, eine gewisse und, weil gewisse, darum auch getroste, starke und freudige Zuversicht fassen darf. Ich darf mich auf das, was für mich geschehen ist, verlassen. Ich darf mich in meinem Herzen geborgen halten. Ich darf auch meine paar Gedanken im Frieden denken, meine paar Worte in Frieden sagen, meine paar Werke im Frieden tun. Ich darf nämlich von mir aus wie ich bin und voll all dem Meinigen her, wie es ist und geschieht, vorwärtsblicken. Wohin? Gewiss nicht ins Blaue irgendeiner besseren Zukunft, wohl aber auf die Erfüllung der mir in Jesus Christus doch gegebenen Zusage, d.h. auf die Offenbarung des in ihm doch gerade über mich gesprochenen Urteils, das gerade mir Recht und Leben zuerkennt. Ich darf vertrauen. Glauben ist nach dieser positiven Seite schlicht—und darum haben unsere Alten an dieser Stelle von *fiducia* geredet—Vertrauen! Kein willkürliches, sondern das auf das mir zugesprochenen Worte antwortende, kein unbestimmtes, sondern das in der Erkenntnis des Glaubens als der Erkenntnis Jesu Christi begründete Vertrauen. Und nehmen wir hier gleich dazu: es wird sich in diesem antwortenden und begründeten Vertrauen, indem es sich um mich selbst handelt, immer auch um die Gemeinde und die Welt handeln." (The English translation above is the author's own translation.)

50. "Dass jemand sich von selbst weg—und sich auf jemand oder etwas anderes hinbewegt, ja sich an andere(s) hingibt." Härle, *Dogmatik*, 57. (The English translation above is the author's own translation.)

act in a way that stays loyal to the other in the face of possible disappointment, which explains why it is appropriate to speak of the risk of trustfulness."[51]

One can see this in the book of Job, which is mentioned in the introduction in the previous paragraph on "comfort and lament." Recall that in lamenting he was also waiting, trying to rely on God. Job's trust is very much tested and his act of lamenting is in part a rebellion against God. But even in this rebellion, there are moments of trust and faith in God as well, when he confesses in suffering that "his redeemer lives" (Job 19:25). Saying and praying these words includes an experience that goes beyond understanding or cognition, an act of reliance at its limits. It is "the 'covenant structure' of trust as a joint venture, thereby further clarifying that trustful faith is by no means to be localized in the trusting person, but is expressed in the acts between him and God."[52] One of the key words of Scripture which bridges suffering, in waiting for God's help and experiencing God's comfort, appears in Rom 8:35-39:

> Who shall separate us from the love of Christ? shall tribulation, or distress, or persecution, or famine, or nakedness, or peril, or sword? As it is written, for thy sake we are killed all the day long; we are accounted as sheep for the slaughter. Nay, in all these things we are more than conquerors through him that loved us. For I am persuaded that neither death, nor life, nor angels, nor principalities, nor powers, nor things present, nor things to come, nor height, nor depth, nor any other creature, shall be able to separate us from the love of God, which is in Christ Jesus our Lord. (Rom 8:35-39 KJV)

That a serious reflection on comfort and trust must take critical thoughts into account is shown in a sentence by the German theologian Oswald Bayer: "The last word of Christian faith is surely [that] nothing can separate me from the love and mercy of God that is in Jesus Christ our Lord (Rom 8:38f.). But can the last word also be made the first?"[53] To find and experience trust in God there must also be time and room for expression of mourning and questions. Welz agrees with that and refers to a narrative from Copenhagen and to a church where Kierkegaard used to worship. Kierkegaard stands as a philosopher and theologian for the inner, emotional, and intellectual battle of faith and trust in God.

51. Welz, "Trust and Lament," 133.
52. Schulz, *Theorie des Glaubens*, 129.
53. Bayer, "Zur Theologie der Klage."

In Vor Frue Kirke, Copenhagen's cathedral, where Kierkegaard was a regular visitor, there is a corner dedicated to Job and to all mourners and grievers. Here, a remarkable creed encouraged lament. "We believe that God is great enough to harbour our little lives with all their grievances, and that he can lead us from the darkness through to the other side." Once the eyes have become accustomed to the dark, a picture with a cross becomes visible. Prayer notes can be pinned to the cross which is inscribed with the words from 1 Peter 5:7, "Cast all your anxiety on him because he cares for you."[54]

This trust and confidence that God does care and that it is a personal care for me and my situation is a core part of what constitutes comfort and consolation for the individual. Barth wrote about this in terms of the peace which it allows, even though it is not just "into the blue of any better future" but it is built on the promise of life in Jesus Christ. This leads me to a discussion of comfort and peace and what that means when put into relation with the described experiences of the interviewees.

Comfort and shalom

Having explored the significance of "faith" or *fiducia* and the central meaning of the passion story of Christ, I now address "peace" as mentioned above to consider the biblical concept of shalom together with comfort and consolation.[55]

Struggling at times with faith and trust in God at the end of life as Christians, all the interviewees also described a search and longing for peace. Lydia who was suffering from cancer and was prepared for death, said in the interview only a few weeks before she died:

> I remain faithful to God, and trust in his faithfulness . . . it is time to be more and more in his peace. . . . I abandon myself in suffering to God and place myself in His call for me. The more I learn that, the more I can feel that I am being carried by him. (Lydia)

Her words echo those of Dietrich Bonhoeffer's writing on suffering and comfort, where his emphasis is to see this movement of peace in the work of the Holy Spirit.

---

54. Welz, "Trust and Lament," 135.

55. Shalom is the Hebrew word for peace, which also covers a wide range of meanings such as health, well-being, completeness or happiness. Compare for instance "shalom" in Brown et al., *Hebrew and English Lexicon*.

> As bearers of suffering, they stand in communion with the Crucified. They stand as strangers in the power of him who was so alien to the world that it crucified him. This is their comfort, or rather, he is their comfort, their comforter (cf. Luke 2:25). This alien community is comforted by the cross. It is comforted in that it is thrust out to the place where the comforter of Israel is waiting. Thus, it finds its true home with the crucified Lord, here and in eternity.[56]

Bonhoeffer argues that through the Holy Spirit, the crucified and risen Christ exists as the church-community. The unity between Christ and his body is such that all members of the church—the young, the aged, the strong, the ill or dying—can recognize Christ's presence and his comfort, which is guiding humans towards God's eschatological promise.

> It is the Holy Spirit who brings Christ to the individual (Eph 3:17; 1 Cor 12:3). . . . The Holy Spirit creates the community (2 Cor 13:13) of the members of the body (Rom 15:30,; 5:5; Cor 1:8; Eph 4:3). The Lord is the Spirit (2 Cor 3:17). . . . In Christ we no longer live our own lives, but Christ lives in us. The life of believers in the church-community is truly the life of Jesus Christ in them (Gal. 2:20; Rom 8:10; 2 Cor 13:5; 1 John 4:15). In the community of the crucified and transfigured body of Christ we take part in Christ's suffering and glory.[57]

Similar to the interviewees, Bonhoeffer often refers to prayer, Scripture, music and poetry as a way to stay connected with God during suffering and isolation as a member of Christ's body and these practices comforted him and gave him peace. What he also wrote to his friend Eberhard Bethge at the end of his life and in isolation was how much he missed the other aspects of comfort, such as through community, confession, and the Lord's Supper. Not able to have many contacts, he emphasizes the power of Christian friendship as an inherent ministry of comfort. "And now today, be for me—after so many long months without worship, confession, and the Lord's Supper and without *consolatio fratrum*—my pastor once more, as you have so often been in the past, listen to me."[58]

Although isolation and being a prisoner are not the same as being ill or facing the end of life, some of Bonhoeffer's experiences resonate with the findings in the interviews. Noticing during my second visits that

---

56. Bonhoeffer, *Discipleship*, 73.
57. Bonhoeffer, *Discipleship*, 201–3.
58. Bonhoeffer, *Letters and Papers from Prison*, 161.

people felt like prisoners and were very much isolated, it struck me how important some of his insights are for my research. When human comfort and Christian community was hardly possible, Bonhoeffer described how much he could experience the power of praying the Psalms, meditating on chapters of the Bible, and remembering Paul Gerhardt's hymns. Frank, as discussed in chapter three, described how he saw Paul Gerhardt's hymns, formed and created in a particular experience of suffering, as having a special comfort and peace-giving quality for him. Gerhardt's hymns, according to Frank in the interview, have the power to give one a new orientation and peace and to overcome the fear of death with faith. Knowing that these hymns were written more than three hundred years earlier in circumstances of despair and loss, Bonhoeffer himself wrote to Bethge that his hymns were a source of comfort to him: "Paul Gerhardt proved of value in unimagined ways. . . . You are the only person who knows that '*acedia tristitia*' with its ominous consequences has often haunted me."[59] Out of a need for comfort, Bonhoeffer wrote prayers himself. I quote one here as an example of looking out for comfort in suffering, for help and God's shalom.

> Lord God,
> misery has come over me.
> My afflictions are about to crush me,
> I don't know which way to turn.
> God, be gracious and help me.
> Give me strength to bear what you send.
> Do not let fear rule over me. . . .
> I trust in your grace
> and commit my life entirely into your hand.
> Do with me
> as pleases you and as is good for me.
> Whether I live or die,
> I am with you and you are with me, my God.
> Lord, I await your salvation and your kingdom. Amen[60]

Only a short time before he wrote the prayer, Bonhoeffer described in his *Ethics* that only a community which has faith in the resurrection of

---

59. Bonhoeffer, *Letters and Papers from Prison*, 162; "acedia tristitia" is a reference to the "sloth of sadness" as one of the seven deadly sins, which can be described as a condition in which comfort and peace are missing.

60. Bonhoeffer, *Letters and Papers from Prison*, 180.

Christ and in God's future for humanity can find peace in the here and now as it awaits the fulfillment of what God has in store for it.

> The miracle of Christ's resurrection has overturned the idolization of death that rules among us. . . . Nothing betrays the idolization of death more clearly than when an era claims to build for eternity, and yet life in that era is worth nothing, when big words are spoken about a new humanity, a new world, a new society that will be created, and all this newness consists only in the annihilation of existing life. . . . Within the risen Christ the new humanity is borne, the final, sovereign Yes of God to the new human being. Humanity still lives, of course, in the old, but is already beyond the old. Humanity still lives, of course, in a world of death, but is already beyond death. Humanity still lives, of course, in a world of sin, but we are already beyond sin. The night is not yet over, but day is already dawning.[61]

Longing for a renewed and healed reality was also part of what was expressed in the different interviews. Alice was yearning to see her disabled and ill son in the new light of resurrection and everlasting shalom. Aaron was desperate to trust in God that his dear wife who suffered from dementia was not lost but continued to be carried in the memory of God and in God's new creation. Ruth was letting go with the trust that suffering was not the last word, but that despite dying her daughters and grandchildren could see how she experienced transformation in suffering and was experiencing a healing and peaceful relationship with God. To hold on to the promises of Scripture allowed the interviewees to see God's vision of shalom for them and for the world and also in God's peace experienced in their present circumstances. It allowed them to bear witness to their faith that death was not all, that faith and trust was enriching their imaginations so that they hoped and trusted that there is more to come in a future which is filled with God's shalom. This *vision*, this *fiducia* or confidence was like a "guiding light" (Brueggemann) which had the power to shine in illness and mourning, in difficult questions and in bodily and spiritual weakness. "Shalom is the substance of the biblical vision of one community embracing all creation."[62]

The Hebrew term for peace—shalom—has different meanings. The roots mean "wholeness, completeness, and wellbeing." Secondary meanings include "health, security, friendship, prosperity, justice, righteousness,

---

61. Bonhoeffer, *Ethics*, 39.
62. Brueggemann, *Living Toward a Vision*, 16.

and salvation." John Swinton describes it thus: "The meaning of the word shalom, is thus seen to express opposition to any disturbance in the well-being of a person, society, or nation."[63] And Brueggemann writes, "It is well-being that exists in the very midst of threats."[64] Taking up Swinton's and Brueggemann's words here, one can well see the experience of comfort and consolation, as described by the interviewees, as an outworking of shalom. Although the individual experience at the end of life is the focus of my research, it is helpful to show the wider dimension of longing for shalom and the biblical promise of shalom in order to understand its significance for Christian faith. One of the most important descriptions of shalom in the Bible is a word in the book of Judg 6:24: "Yahweh is Shalom." And the apostle also writes that Jesus is Shalom: "For he himself is our peace" (Eph 2:14). And in John's gospel Jesus promises that he will give his shalom to all who trust in him: "Peace I leave with you; my peace I give you. I do not give to you as the world gives. Do not let your hearts be troubled and do not be afraid" (John 14:27).

Shalom is therefore an "announcement that God has a vision of how the world shall be and is not yet."[65] Such shalom should not be seen as an abstract concept but rather as a personal gift from a relational God. Right before Jesus refers to the peace which he shares with his disciples in John 14, he speaks about the "paraclete," the comforter, admonisher, and advocate, the Holy Spirit, the one who will "teach you all things" and whom the Father will send.[66] Peace, thus, is put directly in relationship with the comfort which the comforter, the Holy Spirit, brings.

And because brokenness, illness, suffering, and dying are experienced as an integral part of our lives, humans are in the need of such comfort and peace. God's encouragement can be experienced in the power of the Holy Spirit. This comforting movement of God can be seen as a "shalomic redemptive movement" whose aim it is that the weak, the lonely, the suffering, and the dying experience that peace "which transcends all understanding."[67] As we read in various passages of Scripture, it touches not only the individual person but also communities. Because

---

63. Swinton, *From Bedlam to Shalom*, 57.
64. Brueggemann, *Living Toward a Vision*, 16.
65. Brueggemann, *Living Toward a Vision*, 39.
66. John 14:25.
67. Phil 4:7: "And the peace of God, which transcends all understanding, will guard your hearts and your minds in Christ Jesus" (NIV).

that "guiding light" of God's shalom is part of Christian hope, John Swinton writes,

> Because of the fall, human beings are unable to fully experience shalom, but to the extent that they are living consonantly with His design for human functions they experience ... it. The concept of shalom is therefore seen to be both a goal and a holistic process which is initiated and sustained by God as He seeks to deal with the relational alienation of creation through His ongoing movement in history, towards that goal.[68]

Swinton underlines that Christians are unable to experience God's shalom fully yet and that we stay in need of God's shalomic movement which, as I have written, could be described as a movement of comfort and consolation towards shalom. But he also emphasizes the communal aspect of shalom. "The person's suffering must be understood and embraced as a communal concern, and acknowledged, dealt with, and cared for within the context of the Christian community."[69]

The interviewees similarly emphasized that the restorative work of Christ in and through the Holy Spirit and the shared vision of God's coming shalom is seen not only as a matter for their individuals lives but they also hoped and believed for other people, other communities, and the world. They bear witness to this "shalomic movement of God" and that it can be experienced at the end of life. They described how praying, prayers for others and praying for each other (in words, music, or in silence), are strong practices. Alice, for instance, talked in the context of her comfort vision that after she will have died, she would be able to sit in communion alongside many people at the table with Christ. In such a vision of comfort it is clear that Christian faith is rooted in seeing oneself and the other as part of a wider community brought together in Christ.

The eschatological element in the shalomic movement of comfort is of vital importance. The apostle Paul writes: "Now we see but a poor reflection; then we shall see face to face. Now I know in part; then I shall know fully, even as I am fully known" (1 Cor 13:12). The Bible expresses the conviction that suffering is part of our experience on earth waiting for God's shalom to come in a fully and new way. For biblical authors, suffering is sometimes also a time of change and searching for God on the way towards eschatological fulfillment. David Morris in his observation

---

68. Swinton, *From Bedlam to Shalom*, 60.
69. Swinton, *From Bedlam to Shalom*, 102.

on suffering rightly warns of seeing suffering itself as always evil. "Evil has long been understood by theologians and by popular audiences . . . as the *cause of* suffering. The postmodern era has redefined suffering *as* evil. Suffering becomes one of the few agreed-upon new shapes that evil assumes in the postmodern world."[70] Initially, this sounds understandable, and yet it ignores the complexity of suffering and its causes, as the very attempt to eliminate suffering itself causes other forms of suffering.

Christians believe that the world and the cosmos belong to God, that they are sustained by God, that God has reconciled the world through the death and resurrection of Jesus Christ, and that his work of redemption is still in progress. In faith a person can recognize "that while suffering can be a place of horror, it is also a place where Jesus is and can be found."[71] Such a perspective allows one to understand suffering as a part of human experience without moving into the danger of somehow glorifying it. With this perspective of faith Christians also believe that the world is not the way it should be or the way that God planned it to be. They find comfort in the confidence that God is working against the powers of death in creation. Nicholas Wolterstorff writes in his *Lament for a Son*:

> When the writer of Revelation spoke of the coming of the day of shalom, he did not say that on that day we would live at peace with death. . . . He said that one day "there will be no more death or mourning or crying or pain, for the old order of things passed away."[72]

And John Swinton speaks of an "eschatological imagination" which is inspired by God's promises in Scripture:

> Faithful Christians are called to look beyond our present sufferings and to live among them in the light of that which is to come. . . . To adopt such a faithful stance within the world, we must develop an eschatological imagination. . . . Eschatological imagination is inspired and sustained by God's promises in scripture of how things will be. Such a position presumes that knowledge of Christ and his redemptive movement within history has practical implications for the present and that the ways in which we live in the present have eschatological rhythms and echoes.[73]

70. Morris, "Plot of Suffering," 60.
71. Swinton and Payne, *Living Well*, 125.
72. Wolterstorff, *Lament for a Son*, 38–41.
73. Swinton, *Raging with Compassion*, 55.

A Christian response to suffering, evil, or sin, as discussed before, is the cross of Jesus Christ. This is not a philosophical idea or an abstract concept: the cross of Christ is God's costly solidarity. Some of the findings of the interviews brought that to the surface, such as the comfort Paul got from looking at his picture of the Dalí painting depicting Christ on the cross above the earth. It is an embodied, suffering response on behalf of all humans and of creation.

Interesting for this study in this context of eschatological imagination is the way that Margaret G. Hutchison shows through her narrative what "shalomic" attentive listening at the end of life might look like:

> An elderly lady suffering from dementia, paced the corridors of the nursing home restlessly—repeating over and over, just one word. The staff were disconcerted, but no one seemed quite sure how to calm her and put her mind at rest. In fact, they were at a loss to understand the reason for her distress. The word she repeated over and over again was *God*—and that was all she said. One day a nurse got alongside her and walked with her up and down the corridors until eventually in a flash of inspiration she asked the lady, "Are you afraid that you will forget God?" "Yes, yes!" she replied emphatically. The nurse was then able to say to her, "You know even if you should forget God, He will not forget you. He has promised that." For this lady who was forgetting many things, and was aware of it, that assurance was what she needed to hear. She immediately became more peaceful.[74]

The experience of becoming peaceful was directly connected to the confidence given to the lady at the end of her life by the nurse with her "eschatological imagination" and her conviction that God would not forget the lady. That the theme of being remembered and remembering others is connected to experiences of comfort and peace was a central thought in Blumenberg's philosophical reflections. The pastoral theologian John Patton also emphasizes that remembering is a central theme of pastoral care and pastoral ministry.

> Human care and community are possible only because we are held in God's memory; therefore, as members of caring communities, we express our caring analogically with the caring of God by hearing and remembering one another. God created human beings for relationship and continues in relationship with creation by hearing us, remembering us, and meeting us in our

---

74. Hutchison, "Unity and Diversity."

relationships with one another . . . (pastoral care is) a ministry of the Christian community that takes place through remembering God's action for us, remembering who we are as God's own people, and hearing and remembering those to whom we minister.[75]

The importance of "being remembered and remembering" as comfort and peace can also be described in words of Scripture: "Remember your word to your servant, in which you have made me hope. This is my comfort in my distress, that your promise gives me life" (Ps 119:49–50). For the person who prays, it is important that God has not forgotten his people and holds steadfast to his promises. God remembers as an act of compassionate engagement. In Job 14, the suffering Job can only flee to a God whose memory is that last ground of hope and peace in the realm of death.

> To be remembered by God is to realize that we are of eternal worth and value in God's sight. In remembering someone, we acknowledge the person as worthy of memory, and acceptable as full person. It is easy to forget the word "remember" means re-member. . . . The opposite of remember is not to forget, but to dismember; to take something apart.[76]

As the opposite of re-member is dis-member; to take something apart, so the opposite of peace is hostility, where communication and relations have broken down. At the heart of Christian faith and hope is the conviction that death as an enemy of God is finally defeated in the death and resurrection of Christ. God, not death, is seen as the ultimate reality. Although death is real and tragic, the apostle Paul writes in Rom 8 and 14 that not even dying or death can separate us from the love of God and that our lives and deaths are never just our own but belong to God:

> For none of us lives for ourselves alone, and none of us dies for ourselves alone. If we live, we live for the Lord; and if we die, we die for the Lord. So, whether we live or die, we belong to the Lord. For this very reason, Christ died and returned to life so that he might be the Lord of both the dead and the living. (Rom 14:7–9)

That dying and letting go is not an easy process, is something that Josef Bernardin underlines in his book *The Gift of Peace*. He wrote from

---

75. Patton, *Pastoral Care in Context*, 15.
76. Swinton, *Resurrecting the Person*, 127.

experience. He suffered from cancer and wrote a diary in his last months, including this passage:

> Letting go is never easy. Indeed, it is a lifelong process. But letting go is possible if we understand the importance of opening our hearts and, above all else, developing a healthy prayer life. . . . It is clear that God wants me to let go now. But there is something in us humans that makes us want to hold onto ourselves and everything and everybody familiar to us. My daily prayer is that I can open wide the doors of my heart to Jesus and his expectations of me. . . . I have desperately wanted to open the door of my soul as Zacchaeus opened the door of his house. Only in that way can the Lord take over my life completely. Yet many times in the past I have only let him come in parts of the way. I talked with him but seemed afraid to let him take over.[77]

For Bernardin, the gift of peace was connected to his ability to let himself go and surrender himself to God. "It's in the act of abandonment that we experience redemption, that we find life, peace and joy in the midst of . . . suffering."[78] This corresponds with Brueggemann's description of shalom, which I mentioned earlier, namely, "It is well-being that exists in the very midst of threats."[79] Such well-being is understood holistically as encompassing mind, body, and spirit, even in the presence of illness and brokenness. Thus, it will be helpful in my theological reflection to turn now to the theme of comfort and the body.

Comfort and the "body"

The interview material is rich in describing that comfort and bodily experiences cannot be separated. I recall one interview in which the interviewee, Marion, was holding a cuddly toy sheep and described why and how she felt God's comfort by having different sheep in her room and holding the various ones from time to time close to her body. There are many examples in different research areas which like to focus on embodied experiences of comfort not only at the end of life.[80] Regarding the end of life, however, the ethicist and theologian Joel James Shuman describes the experience of the death of his grandfather and how he, his

---

77. Bernardin, *Gift of Peace*, 3–7.
78. Bernardin, *Gift of Peace*, 48–49.
79. Brueggemann, *Living Toward a Vision*, 16.
80. See, for instance, Bacos and Kim, "Wearable Stories."

family, and the church congregation reacted. In his writing, he questions the understanding of health, body, and person which he most often sees propagated in the modern medicine model. This quote is, I think, a helpful starting point for further discussion and reflection.

> I have come to believe that there is something missing in the way all of us related my grandfather's faith to his sickness and his death. Christian faith should have more to do with sickness and healing than what happens when something goes wrong in the operating room. . . . If one understands the body's ontology to be given by the physical and natural science alone, as modern medicine tends to, then one is left to understanding health in those same essential terms. Health in this view is nothing more—or less—than a certain level of bodily function in the absence of pathology. . . . Such a reductionist account of the body and its good works to isolate the person from her world and from those with whom she shares her life.[81]

What Shuman writes here about the danger of a reductionist account of the body which does not value the wholeness and embeddedness of a person can be shown especially in the interviews which took place after the first COVID lockdown in Switzerland. David, for instance, described the bodily experience of going to church every Sunday as essential for his well-being in old age and despite his physical infirmities. Apart from the disruption to his routine, it was the painful experience of not being allowed to be in bodily communion with his church family and not being allowed to take part in the Lord's Supper that he described as "staying close to Jesus" and "holding on in faith." For David, being part of the church community which meets together every Sunday is a bodily experience which gives him comfort.

Daniela also described her suffering when she as a member of a Christian community was no longer allowed to meet her fellow sisters and they were no longer allowed to sing together. In the first interview she had described her comfort experiences as bound up with being able to pray and sing in the community as a whole body experience, "There comes a stream of peace into my heart, I can feel it through my whole body. I can hand everything over then, including myself" (Daniela). During the COVID-19 crisis, a number of rules were put into place by governments or people in authority, rules which were meant to protect people's health and their bodies, and yet the danger of reducing people's health and well-being

---

81. Shuman, *Body of Compassion*, 82.

to whether they might have a virus or not and taking them forcibly out of community was, I believe, not given enough weight.

Bonnie Miller McLemore takes this up briefly in her article, "This is my body: Christian wisdom on dying in an age of denial" and puts it within a context of the already prevalent technological medical paradigm, "Technology itself creates barriers, limiting touch, mobility, and communication. COVID-19 accentuates the problem and presents unique challenges to attending to the dying."[82] Miller-McLemore took up the theme of embodiment in her previous writings, for instance in "Embodied Knowing, Embodied Theology: What Happened to the Body?"[83] and observed there, within a larger context of searching for understanding around how biology and physicality shape human knowing, different ecclesiological and cultural settings. She points out that the use of one's body in the practice of one's faith is often not much thought about or reflected, but that every church tradition is, obviously, embodied and she poses there the question, "Does it shape how and what one knows or even how one conceives of the divine, especially when one practices certain body motions over a lifetime?"[84]

During the special situation in the COVID-19 lockdown and with the varying regulations regarding communal gatherings, it was of interest within this study that all of those whom I was able to interview a second time after the initial lockdown, described how the changes imposed through regulations had influenced them. David, as mentioned earlier, suffered through not being allowed to go to church and experience communal singing and praying as a physical action. Both Richard and Alice described to me similar painful experiences. And Alice, in not being allowed to go and take part in the Lord's Supper, became very aware that her spirituality was very much part of an embodied faith, something of which she hadn't always been aware before. This was experienced all the more intensely as all the interviewees knew that they were at the end of their lives and that they neither knew when they might die or when the regulations would be lifted. Thus, the comfort dimension of actual physical participation in worship with other Christians became clearer to those I interviewed through the experience of not being allowed to do that.

The theme of comfort and the body is found in a number of places in the Bible: "I will not forget you! I have engraved you on the palms of

82. Miller-McLemore, "This is My Body."
83. Miller-McLemore, "Embodied Knowing."
84. Miller-McLemore, "Embodied Knowing," 750.

my hands" (Isa 49:15–16). Or the biblical expression of "being comforted by God like a mother comforts her child" (Isa 66:13) takes human embodied experience from the end of life to the beginning. Our body is central for being, experiencing, and developing. Eva Simms, a researcher of child development, reminds us how a new-born baby is a being who needs touch and at the same time needs to experience relational life in order to develop. It is interesting that the Bible refers to that experience and can connect it with comfort and consolation in reference to shalom for Jerusalem: "That ye may suck and be satisfied with the breasts of her consolations; that ye may milk out and be delighted with the abundance of her glory" (Isa 66:11). Simms writes further about comfort at the beginning of life, which is pre-reflectively bound up with body experience:

> The mouth that opens when its side is touched . . . orients to and already outlines the shape of the mother's nipples. The newborn's body moulds itself into the mother's arms, fitting along the groove between her arm and abdomen. Newborn eyes can see the perfect distance of twelve inches: the bull's-eyes of the breast's aureole to the maternal face. Infants love to gaze at their mothers, a gaze that is one with the rhythm of breathing, sucking, and swallowing, which are reflexive responses as well. Babies are perfectly made for taking in their mother's milk, calling it forth with the gesture or a cry. The skin as the boundary line between two bodies is breached again and again in the evocation and gift of milk. . . . Perhaps more than any other substance milk is the visible sight of the invisible, the in-between body, the chiasm, the flesh of mother and infant. Its fluidity refuses to belong to one or the other.[85]

In short, all humans who after all can only live and experience the world in an embodied state have initial experiences of comfort which are clearly holistic, and just as much bodily as they are spiritual or mental. Regarding this holistic view of experience the phenomenologist Max van Manen emphasizes: "Just as we cannot separate body from mind, so word and thought or feeling are inseparable."[86] The interviews give witness to the experiences of the participants that their bodies have built up over many years their own embodied memories and wisdom, including comfort experiences. To be comforted is more than an intellectual or cognitive experience, it is just as much an embodied happening or

---

85. Simms, *Child in the World*, 14.
86. Van Manen, *Phenomenology of Practice*, 129.

process, which one experiences with all one's different senses: Aaron's singing inwardly a comfort melody; Daniela looking at and meditating her special Bible verse in her room; Frank touching his broken mug on his desk; Heidi stroking her dog and looking at and touching the flowers in her garden; Ruth touching and moving her blue stone, and so on. Christian comfort experiences as described in the research work show that comfort and embodied experiences are intertwined and cannot be sensibly understood separately. To experience comfort spiritually means also to experience comfort bodily, because we cannot separate the two dimensions.

In the Bible and in the New Testament the body is seen with its limits. In Rom 7 the apostle Paul writes: "Wretched man that I am! Who will rescue me from this body of death? Thanks be to God for Jesus Christ our Lord!" (Rom 7:24–25). The Christian faith tradition has battled for many centuries to understand and interpret Scripture to make it possible to see the body not just as a cage to be escaped from through death in some sort of gnostic sense.[87] It rather underlines through the doctrine of Incarnation that the locus of God's presence and acting is with and within a person, Jesus Christ, and has to be understood as embodied. N. T. Wright emphasizes that personhood from a biblical perspective cannot be divided in some sort of platonic, dualistic sense between body and spirit. For

> when Paul and the gospels use the word psyche, it is clear that they are not using it in the sense we'd find in Plato or Philo, or in the sense which is assumed by many today who advocate what they call dualism. Paul's, and the gospels', usage is far closer to the Hebrew "nephesh," which is the living, breathing creature: God breathed into human nostrils his own breath, the breath of life, "nishmath hayyim," and the human became a living creature, "nephesh hayyah" (Genesis 2.7). When the Septuagint translates this as "psyche zosa," we should not expect psyche here to carry Platonic overtones, though presumably some Jews, not least in Philo's Alexandria, subsequently read it thus. Psyche here simply means "creature," or perhaps even (in modern English) "person." There are several other references indicating the same thing (e.g. 1 Thess 2.8; Phil 1.27; 2.30; Rom 2.9; 11.3; 13.1; 16.4; 2 Cor. 1.23.). All refer to the ordinary human life.[88]

---

87. For a summary of Gnosticism, see, for instance, Churton, *Gnostic Philosophy*.
88. Wright, "Mind, Spirit, Soul."

This holistic view of what it means to be a person from a biblical viewpoint is of relevance while reflecting theologically on comfort. It reminds us not to fall into the traps of various forms of dualism, such as that, for instance, of Cartesian dualism, with its division into *res cogitans* and *res extensa*, in which the mind and thinking are valued more highly than the body or bodily experiences. The theologian Paula Gooder in her book *Body: Biblical Spirituality for the Whole Person* discusses critically such dualism and its historical and philosophical roots and then turns to her understanding of the body in the New Testament with a principal focus on the apostle Paul.[89] There she emphasizes the embodied wholeness of human life while taking up the "Shema Israel" from Deut 6:4–5 and connecting it with the New Testament references Matt 22:37, Mark 12:30, 33, and Luke 10:27. All the words used for heart, soul, mind, might, or strength point to an understanding of personhood which includes the whole person and not just parts. This positive understanding of the whole person includes the body. Thus, an eschatological hope is also an embodied hope and not just something spiritual. She sees this in Paul's writings, where he makes the link between Jesus' resurrection and our own:

> This prompts us to recognize that resurrection of the body—and hence bodies themselves—was central to Paul's theology of bodies. His view of the resurrection of the body was integrally intertwined in his proclamation with the good news of Jesus Christ, who died and rose again. Without bodily resurrection, faith was pointless.[90]

The interviewees drew comfort from the resurrection of Christ and had faith that that bodily resurrection had something to do with their own life after their death. Alice imagined herself, with a smile, sitting around a table with Jesus and with a huge number of other people enjoying a feast of food and drink. Daniela talks about living from Lord's supper to Lord's supper, and how that is a bodily experience which is a foretaste of the heavenly feast. Lydia, having gone through the pearly gates, imagined having a place in the New Jerusalem where she could live in peace and joy.

All of this points to the acknowledgement that we are embodied beings and cannot experience spirituality, hope, or comfort without taking the body seriously.

89. Gooder, *Body*.
90. Gooder, *Body*, 50.

Comfort and "things"

As the findings show, the perception and experiencing of artifacts many of the interviewees found to be comforting and helpful at the end of life. Seeing, hearing, touching, smelling, and feeling are complex bodily experiences for all humans and, as I showed in the previous subchapter about comfort and the body, have a special meaning in end-of-life-care.[91] In the doctrine of the Incarnation in which the locus of God's presence is seen to be within the embodied person of Jesus Christ, a positive attitude to the things of everyday life is necessarily contained. Embodied beings necessarily have a connection with the things which surround them and which they need and use. According to the text in Luke 2, when Christ was born the angel said to the shepherds:

> Do not be afraid. I bring you good news that will cause great joy for all the people. Today in the town of David a Saviour has been born to you; he is the Messiah, the Lord. This will be a sign to you: you will find a baby wrapped in cloths and lying in a manger' (Luke 2:10–12 NIV)

The embodied Messiah was to be found "wrapped in cloths" and "lying in a manger." Neither the cloths nor the manger are of themselves sacred, but they are useful and indeed necessary, because real human persons need real things to make life sustainable. Stephen Pattison puts this in the following way: "The notion of incarnation supports a positive Christian attitude to flesh, embodiment, and the material order in creation."[92] The material order in creation includes artifacts and "things," and Pattison says rightly, I believe, that "there is a need to develop Christian theology and practice that values artefacts, and reflects on relationships with them more carefully and more critically."[93]

Such an approach to "things" resonates with Bonhoeffer's thought in his *Ethics* in chapter five on "Ultimate and Penultimate Things."[94] Because of the incarnation in which in Jesus Christ the ultimate and the penultimate meets, the penultimate (to which "things" in creation belong) can be understood to have meaning because it is that which precedes the ultimate; "something of decisive importance (is) that the penultimate

---

91. See also, for instance, Schulte and Steinebach, *Innovative Palliative Care*.
92. Pattison, *Seeing Things*, 251.
93. Pattison, *Seeing Things*, 258.
94. Bonhoeffer, *Ethics*, 81–99.

must be preserved for the sake of the ultimate."[95] Bonhoeffer sees value in what he regards as penultimate things in that they can be understood as preparing the way for the ultimate, which he then describes as the "entry of grace."[96] Because this "preparing of the way" is necessary, it makes a difference whether the penultimate is respected or not. As the findings from the interviews make clear, some spiritual practices can be seen as penultimate in this regard. Such practices as going to church[97] or meditating on a spiritual painting or even holding a cuddly toy sheep can be useful and good in preparing the way for the ultimate, the entry of grace in Jesus Christ.

Giving the penultimate a certain value in our understanding of God's plan for people does not, however, absolve us from attempting to think clearly and responsibly about the place of "things" in people's lives. These things can become idolatrous and a hindrance to people's spiritual growth. Of interest here is, for instance, Luther's writings to Prince Frederick the Wise, in his *"Tröstungen"* ("Fourteen Consolations"). Luther sent this book to the prince after he fell ill and felt himself to be in crisis. The Prince Elector's court chaplain Spalatin had asked Luther to write a consolation pamphlet for him. Frederick was an avid collector of relics. In 1518, there were an astonishing 17,443 so-called "Heiltümer" (healing objects) in his collections. In this instance, Luther was faced with the task of gently yet clearly directing the sick person's gaze to Christ. Thus, Luther wrote that Prince Frederick shouldn't concentrate on the Saints and "things" (relics) but rather concentrate on Scripture and its comforting qualities. In so doing one could enjoy the goods of life and the gifts of creation, as they were given, he said, but they should be seen in the light of a relationship to Christ, the ultimate comforter.[98]

After the exaggerated value given to things such as relics in the church of the Middle Ages, systematic Protestant theology, with its concentration on "sola scriptura" and "sola fide" tended to diminish the value of "things" in protestant spirituality. In Reformed circles, this meant that generally "things" were banished from sight and out of churches so that people would not be distracted from the essence of God's presence

---

95. Bonhoeffer, *Ethics*, 94.
96. Bonhoeffer, *Ethics*, 97.
97. Bonhoeffer himself uses this example: Bonhoeffer, *Ethics*, 100.
98. Martin Luther, "Tessaradecas Consolatoria pro laborantibus et oneratis," in *Martin Luthers Werke*, 2:115–38 ("Fourteen consolations for those who labor and are heavy-laden," written in 1519 for Frederick the Wise during his illness).

through his word. As a result of this spiritual formation, especially music and Christian hymns, the singing in community as the body of Christ, received a new significance and meaning. This singing and worship as individual praxis and as part of a community was able to touch the hearts of the believers and thus reshape a new orientation of piety, which was in itself embodied. Personal and interpersonal connectedness with God were possible in a new form, without the help of relics or statues, and found a new focus in singing and music. Often the hymns were full of biblical language and Bible verses, and soon after the Reformation the hymn book became important and was, next to the Bible itself, the most widely circulated book amongst pious people. Thus, the hymn book itself became a "thing" of importance, at church as well as at home. The interview material was rich in showing the great significance of music as comfort, especially spiritual Christian music, as well as the importance of the hymn book.

All the interviewees were part of the Swiss Reformed Church and had been formed in this particular spirituality, and they were aware intuitively that "things" had their place. It is interesting that in all the interviews people were aware of some comfort qualities in objects they showed or explained to me, but the interviewees seemed not to be in danger of idolizing these "things" and giving them a quality which one might describe as a dangerous dependency. Things, even comfort things, were personal belongings which had the ability to touch the heart in an encouraging and thoughtful way and to remind the people through them of blessings, beauty, friendship, love, or trust in God. Sometimes, however, the interviewees' relationship to "things" remained somewhat mysterious and in some ways suspicious and thus there was often a shyness in talking about them. "Things" such as images, symbols, paintings, objects etc. can indeed be slippery and difficult to comprehend, and sometimes we don't know ourselves what exactly it is which makes them meaningful to us.[99] Ruth, for instance, spoke shyly of the significance of her blue stone, which she had found one day in the woods. She would look at it often each day and touch it and turn it over, but found it difficult to put into words why it had such significance for her.

Stephen Pattison writes instructively about the diverse meaning people give to things they see:

99. "An image may have a range of material qualities, but it is only when someone uses the image in some way that any of those qualities become activated, as it were, and significant." Rose, *Visual Methodologies*, 220.

> Visual images are in some ways, like verbal images; they are humanly created representations that are "polysemic" and produce symbolic meaning . . . images are representations. . . . This corrects the naïve belief that, in dealing with visual images, what you see is what you get. Insofar as any image is regarded as having significance, its significant representation is bound up with human meaning-making; our vision has been educated and biased in apprehending it.[100]

Such meaning-making and the bias we have in apprehending things would seem to be sometimes intuitive and hidden from our rational gaze. Often it may be a mixture of understood and intuitive significance. Cicely Saunders writes in her book *Watch with Me* that she accompanied different people in great suffering and dying who were comforted by looking at or touching a picture or a crucifix: "I have been impressed again and again at St. Joseph's by the way patients will lie and look at a picture or a crucifix and how much these can then say to them."[101] Visual images can for instance comfort, delight, inform, educate, or worry. They have their own distinctive power that can connect with the emotional part of our personhood, which is sometimes understood and sometimes hidden.

In preparing his book on *Seeing Things*, Pattison interviewed people and asked them about visual images and artifacts. "One person . . . told me that when her mother was dying, she asked for a certain vase to be brought to her and she kept this beside her bed until she finally died."[102] Experiences with visual images and objects, it seems, are not uncommon, but they are rarely spoken of and reflected on, as the interviews in this study show. As the interviewees shared their comfort things and experiences with me, it transpired that people relate to material or inanimate things and that sometimes the relationships are quite intimate, like Marion who shared her feelings about the little sheep and the shepherd that decorated her room in the nursing home. Through seeing and touching the different sheep, she recalled her life story and friendships but above all renewed her faith in God who for her was like a touchable shepherd who was always seeking the lost and the lonely.

To emphasize the spiritual importance of relating to the visual, Paul Tillich's experience is a good example to show the relevance of the discussion for practical theology. Paul Tillich had the experience of being

---

100. Pattison, *Seeing Things*, 67–68.
101. Saunders, *Watch with Me*, 7.
102. Pattison, *Seeing Things*, 112.

physically shaken by Sandro Botticelli's *The Madonna with Singing Angels* when he saw this painting in Berlin after several years of ministering in the trenches of World War I. This moment affected Tillich's entire life, and he experienced it as "giving him the keys for the interpretation of human existence."[103] He could describe the very moment when he was grasped by the divine presence and joy. What he saw gave him a sustained comfort and reassurance of God's presence in the midst of suffering and questions. This single encounter with that painting was enough for him to experience a kind of divine revelation—although he admitted that it was not the most beautiful painting in the gallery.

Coming back to "things" and end of life care, it can be said that seeing or touching things can be helpful in the care of the sick or the dying, and that this "haptic vision" is always connected with our whole personhood and brain activity. It can be useful to listen to different stories and to encourage people to engage with "things" they find helpful and comforting at the end of life. Bringing "things" into a situation with a suffering or dying person as a carer or a visitor is much more difficult. Because relating to "things" is so difficult and complex and personal, a restrained attitude on the part of the carer is important.

The Swiss palliative pioneer Sister Elisabeth Müggler described in an interview that she often offers a very ill or dying person a heart or a cross to hold at nights or when they are suffering particularly much. She is struck by the way even non-Christians respond to this and how helpful they can find it.[104] Yet she is very careful in offering this because there can be a danger that people—both those who visit and the ones who have a relationship to things—fall prey to the mistake of overvaluing objects. Philosopher and theologian Nicolas Wolterstorff explores this misuse of artifacts, criticizing the modern aesthetic tradition of taking art seriously for art's own sake. In aesthetic contemplation, art can become a form of religion, mysticism, and salvation. While taking these concerns seriously, there is also a sensible basis for a positive theological interpretation of "things" and "artifacts."[105]

At the beginning of this section, I took up the incarnation of Jesus Christ from the New Testament as a way of approaching a Christians attitude towards things of a material order. As embodied beings, every person is necessarily surrounded by, needs and uses "things." Having a

103. Tillich, *On Art and Architecture*, 234–35.
104. Holder-Franz and Zinsstag, *In Beziehung sein*, 78.
105. Wolterstorff, *Art in Action*, 47–50.

careful and critical awareness of things and their significance for people is not, I would contend, just an anthropological or psychological issue, but one which is important in practical theology. In this research study I saw this in the way the participants were all able to name and describe things which gave them comfort at the end of life.

Reflecting theologically on these, I could see that some of them led directly to a form of spiritual comfort and strengthened the participant's relation with God and with others. Other forms of comfort were more mundane. And yet, in that they were being experienced by people in faith, they too could be understood by using Bonhoeffer's notion of the penultimate as preparing the way for the ultimate.

5

Envisioning a comfort ministry for the church for those at the end of life

THROUGH THE RESEARCH IN this study so far it can be shown that a comfort-ministry for Christians at the end of life could be something worth considering as part of the different forms of ministry to which the church is called to engage. As I wrote in the introduction, the idea that lies behind this chapter is not to give fixed guidelines or present a training program. But the research can be used to encourage people to reflect with deeper understanding on the care of the sick, old and dying in their churches and to empower gifted Christians to become more involved in such ministry. As I have already written the hermeneutical phenomenological method within qualitative research is one which looks carefully at particular and specific situations and which therefore can only be used with caution in forming a concept regarding the field which has been looked at. There are however, I believe, impulses which result from the research which might resonate with the experience of others in a similar situation. Swinton and Mowat use the phrase "transformative resonance"[1] to describe such impulses and encourage those in the field of practical theology to rethink what impact their research might have for practical ministry in the church.

This chapter, in that it emerges from the theological reflections on my data analysis, takes up such impulses and underlines the importance of a paracletic understanding of a comfort-ministry.

1. Swinton and Mowat, *Practical Theology*, 47.

What I understand by paracletic I attempt to show in the following diagram which shows the grounding of all things in the work of the triune God. Creation, including humankind, which is according to Genesis "very good"[2] is subject to the fall and thus then to the need of redemption. Jesus, the incarnated Son of God, offers redemption through his life, death resurrection and ascension, and promises the Holy Spirit, the paraclete, who is the comforter.[3] The paraclete as comforter I have here described, in reference to chapter one regarding the biblical witness to comfort and consolation and in reference to chapter three regarding the findings of my research, in three main dimensions, that of advocacy, that of encouragement and that of admonishment. In the area of advocacy the comforter might be seen to be working towards justice, righteousness and reconciliation, in the area of encouragement towards peace, friendship, sustaining power and hope, and in the area of admonishment towards the calling of disciples into ministry. These dimensions can be seen as interwoven.

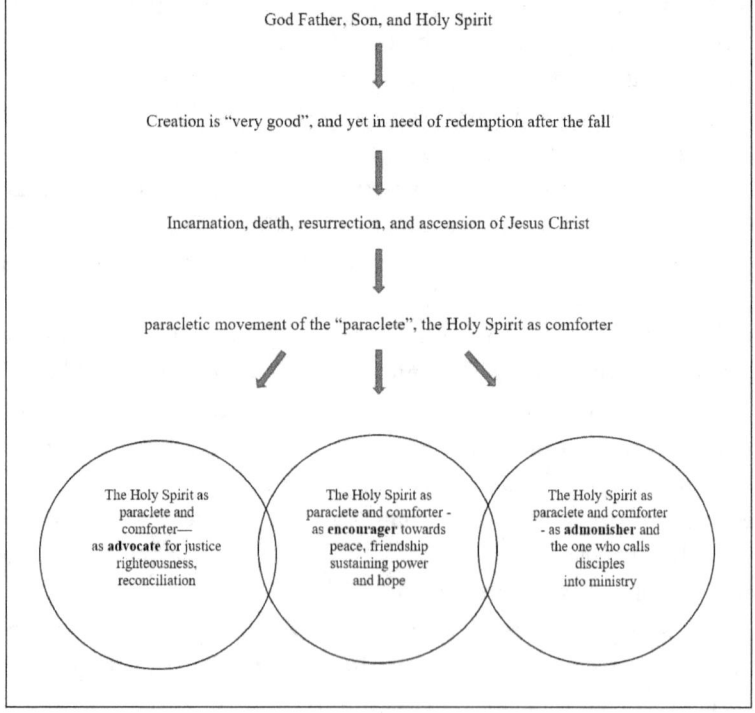

2. Gen 1:31 (NIV).
3. John 14:16 (KJV).

Such a paracletic understanding is useful in all areas of ministry and not just specifically in end-of-life care. As Tacke writes, "Paracletic comforting is the central task of pastoral care. This is about the 'comfort of God' in its correlation to the human who is in need of comfort."[4]

Stanley Hauerwas and Will Willimon in their book *Holy Spirit* choose to translate paraclete as "advocate," and although they mention various other aspects of the Spirit's ministry, such as sustainer, the idea of the Spirit as comforter is not one of them.[5] They do not explain this in the book, but I conjecture (in light of other works by Hauerwas and Willimon) that they want to put a focus on the more communal aspect of the Spirit's ministry, and might see the idea of the Spirit as comforter being too individualistic. If this were the case, I would point out that although obviously comfort and consolation can be seen in quite individualistic terms, they do indeed have important communal aspects, some of which I have shown in this research.

Through the results of my research, it is clear, and I consider it as important, that the meaning of comfort be neither understood in a narrowly individualistic way, in the sense of "cosiness," nor reduced to one of the three aspects mentioned here (advocate, encourager, admonisher). It is precisely in the wide variety of the threefold meanings that practical action can be shaped and developed more concretely. I do not think it is enough to translate paraclete only or mainly with advocate, because the creative ways of experiencing God's presence and sustaining power in the Holy Spirit has to be thought of and imagined with a wholistic approach. The care involved in "παράκλησις/pareklesis" is more than advocacy, even though that is an important part of it. With a threefold meaning of paraclete as comforter in mind, one can deepen an understanding of the Holy Spirit and the work of the Spirit towards humans and creation.

Moving from a general perspective of paracletic ministry towards a ministry of comfort in the church for the sick, old and the dying, it is crucial to look once more at the text to the Corinthian church written by the apostle Paul. Paul combines God's mission for comfort with God being a compassionate God. As already explained in the previous chapter in my reflections on faith and *fiducia*, the apostle Paul reminds the church community that God wants to comfort us in our troubles and sufferings.

---

4. See, for instance, Tacke, *Glaubenshilfe als Lebenshilfe*, 101: "Die parakletische Tröstung ist schliesslich die zentrale Aufgabe der Seelsorge. Es geht um den 'Trost-Gottes' in seiner Korrelation zum trost-losen Menschen."

5. Hauerwas and Willimon, *Holy Spirit*, 18–25.

In Rom 12:7–8 the apostle speaks of different gifts in Christ's body and again uses the verb παρακαλεῖν/parakalein:

> If it is serving, then serve; if it is teaching, then teach; if it is to encourage/comfort, then give encouragement/comfort; if it is giving, then give generously; if it is to lead, do it diligently; if it is to show mercy, do it cheerfully. (NIV with addition of "comfort" to translated ὁ παρακαλῶν, ἐν τῇ παρακλήσει)[6]

When the apostle Paul states here that God wants his people to be comforted, he is not saying that experiencing God's comfort means no suffering. He proclaims the presence and power of God's comfort through the risen Christ in the midst of suffering and reminds the church that some in the body of Christ have a special gift to comfort, a call to a ministry of comfort. There is a particular focus here on the fact that the biblical view of comfort is precisely that God's presence and his working of the Spirit often does not take away suffering, but gives strength and hope in the midst of the challenge of suffering and in illness or weakness.

As I have addressed in the introduction and in my theological response to the data analysis, in the three verses in 2 Corinthians the apostle uses the word παράκλησις/paraklesis or παρακαλεῖν/parakalein six times. There, he is calling church members to be at one and the same time under God's comforting power and part of his ministry of comfort: as part of Christ's body, he calls them into a comfort ministry for each other and for the world, which includes practical help, prayer, Scripture reading, and being together in worship and in communion with each other.

> Praise be to the God and Father of our Lord Jesus Christ, the Father of compassion and the God of all comfort, who comforts us in all our troubles, so that we can comfort those in any trouble with the comfort we ourselves receive from God. For just as we share abundantly in the sufferings of Christ, so also our comfort abounds through Christ. (2 Cor 1:3–5 NIV)

> Εὐλογητὸς ὁ Θεὸς καὶ Πατὴρ τοῦ Κυρίου ἡμῶν Ἰησοῦ Χριστοῦ, ὁ Πατὴρ τῶν οἰκτιρμῶν καὶ Θεὸς πάσης παρακλήσεως, παρακαλῶν ἡμᾶς ἐπὶ πάσῃ τῇ θλίψει ἡμῶν, εἰς τὸ δύνασθαι ἡμᾶς παρακαλεῖν τοὺς ἐν πάσῃ θλίψει διὰ τῆς παρακλήσεως ἧς παρακαλούμεθα αὐτοὶ ὑπὸ τοῦ Θεοῦ. ὅτι

---

6. My own translation. In the Luther translation in German the word "comfort" is used together with admonishing, "zu ermahnen und zu trösten." The old English translations use the word "exhort" and the newer ones "encourage."

καθὼς περισσεύει τὰ παθήματα τοῦ Χριστοῦ εἰς ἡμᾶς, οὕτως διὰ τοῦ Χριστοῦ περισσεύει καὶ ἡ παράκλησις ἡμῶν. (2 Cor 1:3–5)[7]

These verses by the apostle Paul are written for people in different circumstances, and once again it is obvious, they focus not simply on end-of-life issues. But it is also clear that the early church is under threat and that their sufferings are manifold and serious. For example, Paul suggests in Romans, 1 Corinthians, and Ephesians that the church should understand itself as the body of Christ, and thus the sufferings of some are important for the entire body. In this regard, a ministry of comfort for those who are dying and at the end of life is part of this awareness that we as members of that body of Christ are connected to each other.

Before I present some concrete examples from the findings in support of such a ministry of comfort at the end of life, I would like to reflect on some further words of Scripture which I believe are relevant regarding a ministry of comfort in general. That God wants comfort for his people and is ready to send out people for a special comfort ministry can be seen, for instance, in the calling of Isaiah in Isa 40:1: "Comfort, comfort my people, says your God." In this particular situation, God revealed his will, his word of comfort, through a human voice; he was calling humans into comfort ministry for his people. In Luke's Gospel in the New Testament, Jesus himself read words from Isaiah in the synagogue at Nazareth, and proved through this that he had come to comfort his people and saw himself called by God to that ministry:

> He went to Nazareth, where he had been brought up, and on the Sabbath day he went into the synagogue, as was his custom. He stood up to read and the scroll of the prophet Isaiah was handed to him. Unrolling it, he found the place where it is written: "The Spirit of the Lord is on me, because he has anointed me to proclaim good news to the poor. He has sent me to proclaim freedom for the prisoners and recovery of sight for the blind, to set the oppressed free, to proclaim the year of the Lord's favor." (Luke 4:16–19)

Although the word comfort is not used directly in this passage from Luke, it is clear from Isa 61, to which the quote in Luke 4 refers, that Jesus places himself in this comfort ministry and also proclaims himself as the promised messiah, the "menachem."[8]

---

7. Aland and Aland, *Nestle-Aland Novum Testamentum Graece*.
8. See "References to comfort and consolation in the Old Testament" in ch. 1.

At the end of his earthly life Jesus was aware that his disciples needed support and help to stay in the world. They needed help in their calling, namely that of being part of God's ministry of comfort. "But very truly I tell you, it is for your good that I am going away. Unless I go away, the Comforter will not come to you; but if I go, I will send him to you." (John 16:7).

It is the incarnated Son of God himself, the consoler of Israel, who will send the comforter, the paraclete. This was the witness of Simeon at the beginning of Luke's gospel. There, we read that the people were in need of consolation and that Simeon was waiting in the power of the Holy Spirit for the Consoler of Israel: "Now there was a man in Jerusalem called Simeon, who was righteous and devout. He was waiting for the consolation of Israel, and the Holy Spirit was on him" (Luke 2:25). Seeing and touching Jesus was for Simeon identical with embracing God's comfort incarnated. This experience at the end of his life was strong and comforting in a deep sense for Simeon, and not only for himself but also for the people of Israel, to whom he was connected and with whom he suffered.

> Simeon took him in his arms and praised God, saying: Sovereign Lord, as you have promised, you may now dismiss your servant in peace. For my eyes have seen your salvation, which you have prepared in the sight of all nations: a light for revelation to the Gentiles, and the glory of your people Israel. (Luke 2:28–32)

Simeon, old and at the end of his life, was able to let go in peace and be comforted, as he received Jesus into his arms. However, what will a comfort ministry at the end of life look like if, unlike Simeon, we can't actually take Jesus into our arms?

The data analysis from the interviews has shown that comfort ministry at the end of life is not a "big program" or a loud business. It often has to do much more simply and poignantly, with awareness, being present, taking time, listening carefully, and being there. Comfort ministry includes small things, like gestures and an attitude of respect. As the interviewees explained, prayer is a central element to comfort and to be comforted as Christians: prayer for people or sharing in prayer or receiving prayer. The interviewees insist that the end of life can be full of prayer and that very ill and dying people often have a prayer praxis until the very end. It therefore seems to be a false assumption that Christians primarily need prayer as in "prayers for them" (intercession). It is much more likely and true that they welcome prayer *with* them and on their behalf. This opens a way so that they can be part of God's mutual comforting movement, experiencing empowerment through God's Holy Spirit and through that hope and peace in suffering, old age and dying.

At the end of life, the interviewees took certain Bible verses and narratives very close to their hearts. It was not always clear why and how this happened, but with their faith experience and life story they "were nesting," as Frank called it, in specific places of the biblical messages. For the practice of a comfort ministry at the end of life it is valuable to learn to perceive and find which spiritual, biblical concentration points are of importance to a person. Often only through careful listening and the ability to ask good questions are people willing to be open in vulnerable circumstances and have the strength to experience speech, conversation, or spiritual reflection as helpful. Often it is vital to wait until people ask or mention something to a person whom they trust. This can be a friend, a relative, a carer, or a pastor. Yet communication is far more than mere words and speech. A ministry of comfort can learn from other disciplines, such as psychology or different therapies in which nonverbal communication, like a smile or listening to a piece of music together, can be of great value. "Small gestures reveal larger truths."[9] And as Augustine writes, "There is a kind of universal language, consisting of expressions of the face, gestures and tone of voice, which shows whether a person means to ask for something and get it, or refuse it and have nothing to do with it."[10] Gestures and different ways of communication can create an atmosphere of benevolence and trust, so that a comfort dimension can speak for itself or be experienced as helpful and encouraging.

The mystic Theresa of Avila puts this interestingly and with a focus on actual ministry. Although I do not agree with a radical imagination that Christ cannot find other ways to help us humans, I like the vision that we can and are called to do small things for and with Christ for others, and I shall point out some of the possibilities of how to do this, which I understand as emerging from the findings in chapter 5.

> Christ has no body now but yours,
> no hands but yours,
> no feet but yours.
> Yours are the eyes through which

---

9. Morrison, "Poetic *Sling Blade*," quoted in Webb-Mitchell, *Christly Gestures*, 108.
10. Augustine, *Confessions*, 29.

> Christ's compassion must look out on the world.
> Yours are the feet with which
> He is to go about doing good.
> Yours are the hands with which
> He is to bless us now.[11]

When Cicely Saunders, the Christian pioneer of palliative care, looked back on her motivation for the care of the dying, she was able to remember her time in St. Joseph's Hospital in London where, before palliative medicine and care were developed, Catholic nuns cared for the suffering and dying with love and devotion. This showed Saunders that people with a Christian spirituality were seeing in the suffering of the person more than just a patient but above all co-member of Christ's body.[12]

In Saunders's work we can discover interesting details of what comfort ministry for people at the end of their lives might look like. As she developed the concept of her hospice St. Christophers in London, for which she planned for nineteen years before opening it in 1967, she was, for instance, aware of the importance of light in a room, of the effects of colors or the comfort qualities of different activities, like, for instance, walking in creation, writing poems or thoughts or memories, being part of music therapy, and using different materials to express feelings and emotions.

Some of the interviewees, such as Margaret or Richard, for instance, who live in nursing homes, took part in such activities and appreciated them. But speaking about these things to me they said that actual comfort and being comforted had for them a particular connectedness with their Christian faith. They experienced a lot of helpful activities but also a lack of careful awareness that faith and their relationship to God played an important role in everyday life. More than half of the interviewees told me that they can't speak freely or openly about the significance of their relationship to God and Christ with family members, friends, or carers. Thus, that which is really important to them often does not find expression in the way others approach and talk to them. Specifically at the end of life, experience shows that people want to share things of significance, important elements of their life story, but also things to do with guilt or shame. This calls to mind Margaret and Sally in particular

---

11. Teresa of Avila quoted in Rolheiser, *Holy Longing*, 73.
12. Saunders, *Selected Letters*, 12; Saunders, *Selected Writings*, 223–28.

who mentioned that they are thankful to know that "they could talk to God like a friend" and are comforted when they can share their faith with other friends of God. For a comfort ministry, these statements have significance because they show a need to stay in communication not just as carers, but as carers who also understand themselves as members of the body of Christ.

Practical things, however, are also important. Comfort ministry can also mean helping transport a person to a Sunday service so that this person can experience the community and the invitation to the Lord's table again, something Richard said to me: "I need a lot of friendship. (laughing).... Last Sunday I went to the service ... being connected with spiritual friends and the message of the gospel was great" (Richard).

Through the statements by Richard, whose health was very poor, it can be shown that despite his age and weakness, he valued the connection to his church so much that it gave him quality of life and strength for his stay in the nursing home. Without this commitment of others, who fetched him to the service and brought him back to the nursing home, Richard would once again have seen himself "only as old and in need of care" and reduced to his palliative status. This weekly service, in the midst of people of different ages, health conditions or problems, reassured him that in the body of Christ even the sick and soon-to-be-dying have their place, their dignity, and indeed a task to attend to. Although physically very impaired, he wanted to be part of Christ's church, to continue to pray for others, to praise God with others and to continue to share about God's Word with others. He had no doubt that the community is a place of blessing and that those who are sick and soon to die increase the praise of God and thus also strengthen the others and show them how to be Christian, not only at the end of life, but also living in the midst of it. People such as Richard, are witnesses, especially while letting go and dying, of remaining related to Christ and how inner growth is possible until the end. Richard, as a natural scientist, was enthusiastic about the fact that learning does not stop and his great joy was to experience even more of God's grace and fullness with others even at the end of life.

Referring to the interview material again, I also asked the interviewees at the end of the interviews if they had any comments about a "comfort ministry of the church." After a longer conversation, not all of them had the energy to share their thoughts, but the comments are a helpful source to relate the previous reflection to the interview material. In answering my question Frank, for instance, said,

> First of all, it has to do with attention. This is a kind of basic dimension for me. Who is suffering in the church? From what do they suffer? Do I even notice what is happening? . . . I consider it as central that the churches send out and empower people who have the individual and their suffering in view, who visit the individual, take time, listen and can be with them. This is part of a comfort ministry in this world. . . . The churches have to keep the question of God alive. To have services where the gospel can be heard and people meet, pray together, sing together, to share this hopeful and encouraging message is also part of the comfort ministry of the church for this world. (Frank)

I would like to look at the questions at the beginning of the quote. In my view, Frank is right to ask who and what a person is suffering from in the first place. Often, we have information about a disease or a diagnosis, but too quickly this knowledge could narrow our focus towards a medical diagnosis rather than leading us to ask anew and openly who my counterpart is and what questions or experiences of suffering are moving them. The person and their suffering is always more than their medical diagnosis. Again and again, interviewees told of experiences of suffering in their lives and how they shaped by them. Only through retelling could they slowly see how their whole lives, like a woven tapestry, had different colors and patterns of God's presence and encouragement, which was able to comfort them especially at the end of their lives. That which involves suffering at the end of life often cannot be described simply by a diagnosis, but involves the numerous knots and threads woven into the patterns of their life, and which, in the awareness of renewed suffering and the finitude of life, become anew a subject of reflection for them. Why did I have to go through this? What haven't I already endured? How important was this experience to me, even if it was difficult? Through the presence and conversation of another, who "endures" me and listens to me, who takes me seriously and dares to ask questions, it might become possible for horizons and themes to open up, for questions to be asked without the pressure of expectations, for spiritual questions to be shared.

Some of the participants in the interviews in my research study mentioned difficult experiences they had had with others who were trying to explain suffering through a rigid dogmatic Christian lens. For those interviewees it was essential that a comfort ministry be more a space in time to "share and not to explain" (Alice), to "be there even without words" (Sally) and to accept the other as she or he is. Some also mentioned that it is important to be careful about moralizing certain questions, doubts, or suffering experiences. "What is important is to listen well! To take the person seriously and not just to talk to them" (Anne). It was a very strong element in the interviews when they spoke about a comfort ministry of the church "as prayer ministry for one another" (David, Daniela, Alice, Ruth, Paul, Anne) and of the need to encourage people in different ways "to hold on in faith" (David). Richard being an active member in different churches and in various countries reflected on a comfort ministry of the church by noting that: "A comfort ministry of the church has to do with focusing on Christ and trying to live as an example. Christian communities not only tell people what we should do but they try to live it, they should try to be an example" (Richard).

Now I shall attempt to bring together in practical suggestions things which have emerged from this research study, things which might be helpful for thought and practice in regards to a Christian comfort ministry within the church.

POSSIBLE PRACTICAL ELEMENTS OF A COMFORT MINISTRY OF THE CHURCH

Emerging from the data analysis and theological reflection around the particular situation of the interviews I had with people at the end of their lives in the Swiss Reformed Church in this study, a number of elements would seem to be instructive in thinking further, in the sense of "transformative resonance," about a possible comfort ministry of the church. In the data analysis in the fusion of horizons three main areas of comfort for Christians at the end of their lives were identified. These were divine comfort, comfort from friends and family, and comfort from creation, music, art and "things." Approaching these areas of comfort from an understanding of the paracletic movement of the Holy Spirit might involve seeing the one involved in a ministry of comfort as someone who relates to the person at the end of their life as an advocate, as an encourager, and as one who admonishes and calls to ministry. A team of people who visit others in the parishes is an important service and should also be promoted by church leaders to the effect that volunteers are accompanied and well trained for their visiting ministry. Through such a visiting service in cooperation with the pastor or pastors, situations arise in which it becomes clear that people need more or specific spiritual support and pastoral care at the end of their lives. Such comfort ministry doesn't take place just anywhere but understands itself as happening within the body of Christ. Within this framework of faith in Christ an attitude of respect, attentiveness, and careful listening will be a presupposition for a fruitful ministry and something which can be developed and trained. Such an attitude was described by a number of the interviewees as essential for further communication and relationship within any form of comfort ministry. These elements and their connections I attempt to show in the following diagram in which the frame is a symbol for the body of Christ in which a comfort ministry takes place. As noted, both the comforter and the one in need of comfort receive each other as persons connected with each other in the body of Christ. I have noted a number of keywords—respect, attentiveness, and careful listening—which describe a helpful attitude for the relationship. In the middle of the diagram are various pearls of comfort, which symbolise the uniqueness of the experiences of comfort by those relating them. These experiences of comfort cannot be generalized or numbered and will differ from person to person.

Although my research shows that it can be helpful to understand the meaning of comfort by being aware of the three dimensions I have described—divine comfort, human comfort, and comfort through the appreciation of creation, music, art and "things"—nevertheless the unique experience of the different persons remains central, as depicted in the diagram. Because all of these experiences are understood to be taking place within the communal space of the body of Christ, the influence and ministry of the paraclete, the Holy Spirit as a person within the Trinity of God, is understood to be at work as advocate, encourager, and admonisher.

Out of the findings it transpires that all three elements of the paracletic movement in comfort experiences described by the interviewees can be found. These elements are interwoven with each other and are both passively and actively experienced by the participants. Elements of advocacy can be found, for instance, in Richard being taken to worship services or when Anne makes it possible for her disabled friend to be part of a Bible study group. Daniela is comforted by participating in the Lord's Supper as she has faith that in so doing Christ becomes her advocate in a special way. Encouragement is experienced often as visiting, praying with people, singing or reading hymns, reading Scripture, and taking part in worship and in the Lord's Supper. Admonishing is experienced through the "Bible as teacher" (Frank) or when Aaron experienced his pastor admonishing him as a friend. Close relations and friends who are trusted can also act comfortingly as admonishers, such as when Frank's friends refused to allow him to mourn all the time, something which he afterwards described as comforting.

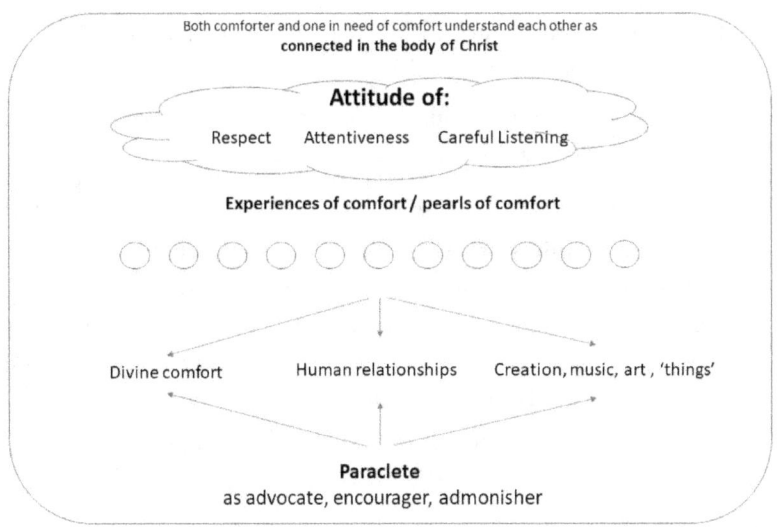

COMFORT SUGGESTIONS FOR CHRISTIANS AT THE END OF LIFE FROM CHRISTIANS AT THE END OF LIFE

From the interview findings I have put together the following suggestions of what may be helpful to give Christians comfort at the end of life. In those instances, in which I have put the names of interviewees at the end of the suggestion, this indicates that those persons made specific comments concerning it.

Keep up a prayer and Scripture reading (or listening) routine (Margaret, Richard, David, Daniela).

- Remember special biblical stories or verses and tell family, friends, and close carers about them (Daniela, Alice, David, Anne, Richard).
- Remember "things" like photos, paintings, crosses, symbols, ordinary things which help you to remember God's love and care for you—perhaps put them very near to you so that you can enjoy them (Frank, Marion, Anne, Heidi, Ruth).

- Try to find out what kind of music you like or which hymns are comforting for you and tell others about it so that they can support you with music and provide the technical assistance you might need—and tell them when you need silence (David, Aaron, Frank, Daniela).
- Be honest and admit, before God and before others, when times are difficult (Marion, Frank, Ruth).
- Ask other Christians to support you in prayer, with psalm readings, and by visiting you (Marion, Anne, Frank).
- Ask other Christians about their comfort experiences (David, Sally).
- Find a pastor/minister/counsellor and bring burdens and mistakes and also good things and gifts of your life to Christ and pray with her or him for peace; if it's possible or helpful, invite others into these times of comfort ministry so that you can experience God's movement towards shalom together (Aaron, Anne).
- Ask for Christians to bless you, or for communion if you desire it (Alice).
- Think of helpful biblical metaphors of Christ and God, such as shepherd, or loving mother, father, or friend (Marion, Lydia, Sally).
- Pray for others or comfort others as well; consider yourself part of the body of Christ, which has a mysterious way of functioning and of experiencing mutual comfort (Marion, David, Paul, Anne).
- Don't think that emotions like fear, anger, or sadness are nothing to you! You can share them with God and others just as you share courage, joy, and laughter (Sally, Marion, Lydia).
- You can have your questions, your doubts; you don't need to hide them from God (Ruth, Lydia, Frank).
- Try to count your blessings every day and try to stay attentive to the beauty of creation and to the joyful little things or moments of your life (Heidi, Daniela).
- Think of God's love as "big"; imagine God's future with the shalom of Christ promised and brought to us through his suffering, dying, and his resurrection (Lydia, Daniela, David).
- Trust in Jesus and in his way for you, and trust that he shares in your suffering and feels with you in your suffering (Ruth, Alice, Aaron).

- Trust that God's power in the Holy Spirit can hold you, even in your dying (Marion, Alice, Richard, Lydia).
- Trust in the Holy Spirit as an active power of God for us throughout our entire lives as children and friends of God (Daniela, Sally, David).

In small gestures Christians can comfort each other in this faithful relationship: being together; sharing bread; singing hymns; praying for each other; reading Scripture for and with each other; offering each other comfort, friendship, and care; remembering each other through different means of communication; and listening carefully with and without words. These gestures and signs are part of a comfort ministry which can allow God's peace to come and shine like a light in the here and now. "Solidarity, comfort and reassurance are not nothing."[13]

At the end of the chapter, I would like to take the liberty of touching on the topic of "things" again, to express an awareness of the fact that many of those interviewed shared that the living out of their Christian spirituality also includes the appreciation of symbols, art or everyday objects. The fact that they also reflect in the conversation with me that they don't want to give these "things" too much weight[14] was of interest. Nevertheless, it is important to me as a researcher in a Protestant Reformed church context that these people have had many experiences, have travelled to various countries, got to know other churches and denominations (for instance Alice and the African Last Supper sculpture or Paul and the Dalí image of the Crucified Christ) and that they have integrated these experiences into their spirituality, which however remains one formed mainly by the Reformed tradition. A cross with a crucifix in the apartment of a Christian of the Reformed Church (Alice) may come as a surprise, but even though she liked concentrating on Scripture and music in her daily spiritual routine, the crucifix was important to her because she and her husband, when he was still alive, put it up together as a symbol of the presence of Christ within their living room.

I think it is important and appropriate to deal more sensitively and attentively with these aspects of visible and embodied signs of faith and not only to regard them suspiciously as imported from other faith traditions, but also to appreciate and reflect on them in one's own tradition. It is inevitable that a critical discourse will be necessary again and again

---

13. Hauerwas, *Suffering Presence*, 178.
14. See above, "Comfort and 'Things.'"

and that it is a strength of the Reformed tradition that is has the potential to make corrections where "things" try to take the place of God's promise and his word. And yet, the "things" are and remain important to us humans, even when we are getting weak, sick or dying. A photo or a cross can give comfort and confidence that we are pilgrims and belong to God's big family, even to a promised new Jerusalem, which is described in Revelation using the picture of pearls. But these will not be the center of the new dwelling, but the triune God will be all in all.

6

Summary and closing thoughts

IN THE FOLLOWING CLOSING thoughts, I reiterate the purpose of the research and the questions that motivated it. I give a brief summary of the findings and an overview of the key contributions of this study. I also discuss the limitations of this project, reflecting on the implications for future research and practice. I suggest that the findings of this research have something important to say to the broader discussion on end-of-life care and church ministry being involved in different areas. I conclude this chapter with some personal reflections.

The research project was motivated by a long and ongoing desire to understand better the phenomenon of comfort and consolation and what it means to experience comfort and consolation at the end of life as a Christian. As discussed in the introduction of the thesis, my interest in the topic was the result of my own experiences first as a child and as a young adult, but also in different social engagements in and out of the church. Because I serve as a minister in the Swiss Reformed Church and I am engaged in accompanying Christians in crisis, sickness, and dying, I had a particular interest in finding out what they experienced as comforting or consoling. Through studying Cicely Saunders's writing and through working within the Swiss palliative network with professionals from many disciplines, I was aware that an understanding of comfort and consolation based on the experience of Christians and which was not located only in the hospital or medical setting had scarcely been discussed or formulated within practical theology.

To explore the phenomenon of comfort as experienced by Christians in my church tradition at the end of life, I decided to work with a specific qualitative research method. In using a hermeneutical phenomenological approach, I was able to combine theological, practical and anthropological reflections alongside insights from a therapeutic and pedagogic praxis. I was enabled to understand comfort experiences of the individual person from different perspectives and could highlight the profound interplay of experiencing divine and human comfort and comfort through creation, music, art, and the material world. The interviewees gave valuable insights and examples of how they experienced comfort in suffering and did so in such a way that God's presence was felt. The interview findings showed that comfort is not only a human experience of the individual but also an experience grounded in community, between humans, and between God and humans. The dialogical structure of being in the need of comfort and being able to comfort needed to be reflected in the findings and in the theological reflections.

By phenomenologically inquiring into lived experiences of practicing Christians at the end of their lives and through the intentional fusion of horizons facilitated between myself and the interviewees, comfort experiences could be described with the help of different themes and subthemes. The third comfort dimension, described in the interviews as "experiencing comfort through creation, music, art and the material world" brought a new dimension into the study which was unexpected and was one that I not considered much at the beginning. Here the advantage of using a phenomenological approach to my research became clearer to me and the method ably opened up a space for the unexpected within my research. It gave me the possibility to experience the dynamic of the hermeneutical circle and to deepen my understanding of how multi-layered such qualitative research is.

I noted in the introduction that theological language in contrast to psychotherapeutic and medical language in the area of palliative care and end-of-life care is rare, and that comfort and consolation are often seen first with a medical pre-understanding. Although the use of the words "comfort" and "consolation" in the Christian tradition and present Christian language is rich and diverse, there is little literature that concentrates on the phenomenon of comfort at the end of life from a Christian perspective, and what is there assigns it to the area of Christian practices for end-of-life care or into the context of a Christian *ars moriendi*.

In my study I have engaged with a number of possibilities to reflect on comfort as an experience and have shown that Christians reflect on the spiritual effects of comfort in a nuanced and fascinating way. The project has drawn to the fore a profound relationship between an anthropological, philosophical and theological understanding of comfort and comfort experiences. What became evident was that former critiques of comfort and consolation, such as those by Freud, Marx, and others, which suggest that Christian comfort and consolation is escapism from the harsh realities of the world,[1] are not sufficient to empty the concept of comfort. Rather, while taking such critique seriously, the research has shown that the interviewees were able to see their suffering reality as it is and yet still rely in trust on and faith in God and be comforted by that and by others at the end of their lives.

In my focus on experiences of comfort by Christians at the end of their lives the research makes a unique contribution to the growing body of pastoral and spiritual care literature which focuses on the end of life and how people can live through the process of letting go and dying. Furthermore, in the particular context of the Swiss Reformed Tradition, a tradition known for its concentration on the Word rather than on "things," it was fascinating to discover the comfort qualities which people associated with some of their artifacts without idolizing them.

Bearing in mind the different findings and conclusions and the unique contributions of the research, I reflect briefly on some of the limitations of the presented study. The first limitation comes out of the specific focus on comfort experiences at the end of life of Christians in the Swiss Reformed Church, as a particular, small ecclesiological setting. This is part of the fascination of qualitative research, in that the specific setting is not a limitation as such but it would have been enriching to include an ecumenical and interdenominational perspective. For practical reasons concerning the size and breadth of the study, this was not possible.

As I mentioned at the beginning that I had difficulties in interviewing dying Christians within a hospice or hospital setting. The time people spend in these specialised units in Switzerland is short[2] and such visits are difficult to fit in if one is not already a member of the staff involved. Often the people at the end of their lives in these units are also so weak

---

1. See Weymann, *Trost?*, 52.

2. The average time dying people spend in a hospice or in a palliative care unit in Switzerland is three weeks. This is largely due to the cost involved.

that longer conversations are impossible. In the sampling process I had help from colleagues who were willing to assist me in finding practicing Christians at the end of their lives at home or in nursing homes to speak to about comfort experiences at the end of their lives.

Another limitation which I realized after the interviews was that I couldn't take up the task of accompanying the people involved further. Because four of the interviewees sent me letters or notes after the interviews, I realized that for some of the people the questions had triggered feelings and thoughts with which they then wrestled. I had informed each of them of the scope of the study and they had all given their consent to that, yet I became even more aware of how delicate doing research in vulnerable situations is.

I was thankful that Aaron brought in the aspect of physical affection and tenderness as an important issue concerning comfort and consolation at the end of life. I realized that that may have been an issue for more of the interviewees, but that they might have been too shy to talk about it without my prompting. Also, it became clear after the first COVID-19 lockdown that people were more open to discussing issues around physical affection. Because of the long crisis around COVID-19 and the issues of loneliness and social distancing it has brought to the surface, it seems vital to me to do more research on how people and also Christians may be in the need of embodied consolation and physical contact at the end of life—or may wish not to be touched.[3]

The aim of this study has not been to make generalizations. The suggestions which came out of the findings for church ministry and my reflections on it should be understood along the lines of "transformative resonance" towards a faithful ministry in the church and for the world. It is fundamental to my methodology that describing the experiences skillfully cannot automatically lead to making generalizations.

Emerging from this process, I suggest that further studies in qualitative research around the same theme but in different cultural and ecclesiological settings could be of value for practical theology. Such studies could be helpful in widening an understanding of what pastoral and spiritual care and the comfort ministry of the church could mean in the area of end-of life-care. Future research on comfort and consolation at the end of life can be a helpful resource to deepen the awareness of the rich spirituality of Christians at the end of their lives. It might be also of

---

3. See Wasner et al., "Bedeutung von Sexualität"; Hjamarsson and Lindroth, "To Live Until You Die."

interest in a future study to compare how different church traditions and contexts appropriate "things" as a form of comfort at the end of life.

To develop a better understanding of mutual communal Christian comfort experiences it is important to focus not only on clinical settings but first and foremost on church communities, their practices and ministry for the sick and dying. This is not intended to diminish the contribution of palliative care and counselling or spiritual care; it simply shows my preference for focusing on the importance of the Christian's life lived in community and being formed by certain kinds of practices.

CLOSING THOUGHTS

To recognize that the research journey has been a transforming experience for me as researcher, I conclude with a few personal thoughts. Throughout this project I had to listen to and be faithfully engaged with people who were in very vulnerable situations. They all agreed to speak with me about their divine and human comfort experiences, and through that opened up to me about experiences of suffering in their lives. It made me humble, and I have often felt grateful that God's presence was felt in so many ways in their lives and that faith and trust was sometimes a battle and sometimes a gift. I learnt from their lives and the way their journeys took them to become aware of the comfort dimensions of relationships, with God, with others, and with things or creation, and was amazed that faith was such a beautiful and mysterious gift even in brokenness and dying. In such a setting, C. S. Lewis's thought seems to ring true: "You never know how much you really believe anything until its truth or falsehood becomes a matter of life and death to you."[4]

Comfort, I learnt, and comfort experiences, don't follow a rhythm or a system. When God's comforting presence comes and moves in a mystical or very human or practical way, it is more like an ever-new epiphany. Perhaps like Elijah on his way to Horeb there is often a longing for comfort, a strange and sometimes painful waiting for God, who is hoped for and in Christ is known as Emanuel, God with us. I like to remember Alice when she said after the first lockdown, "I was not used to inviting the Holy Spirit into my life, but I learnt that being alone for so many days, I can do it and it was a great experience." In Alice's, and my own, church tradition we like to reflect and think about and take God's

---

4. Lewis, *Grief Observed*.

word seriously, and I like that. But there is a danger of being what Miller-McLemore refers to in the Reformed tradition as the "frozen chosen."[5] It is helpful to remember that God's presence is always experienced in an embodied fashion and that the Holy Spirit, the "paraclete," moves us during and at the end of life as a whole person, which includes our bodies, hearts, souls, and minds, even when we are weak and dying.

The interviewees gave me a new understanding of helpful relationships, helpful things, and the comforting quality of creation. I hope that I can encourage other Christians and people responsible for a ministry of comfort in churches or caring institutions that despite the uniqueness of the experiences I have researched here, it is possible to reflect more theologically on comfort and end-of-life care again. Moreover, it is my hope that God's comforting presence can meet people in their suffering and dying, and I trust that I will be surprised one day that God's creativity to do this is beyond my imagination.

I would like to close with a quotation from Cicely Saunders in which she describes her comfort ministry at St. Christopher's Hospice:

> It is the work of Christ in an area of great human need. It is a place where loss is constantly being overcome by creativity and where the continual partings are best expressed: ". . . not fare well, but fare forward, voyagers" (T. S. Eliot, Four Quartets).[6]

---

5. Miller-McLemore, "This Is My Body," 749.
2. Saunders, "Philosophy of Terminal Care," 238.

Appendix

Praying the Psalm 23 differently

Aaron sent me this psalm after the first visit and wrote a short note with it: "This is very comforting; I forgot to show it to you."[1]

IN REFLECTION OF PSALM 23

I pray:
The Lord is my shepherd,
and I feel so abandoned.
And I keep praying
I will lack nothing
and I know I will miss this person
no one can replace her love
I will forever miss her advice and help.
And I keep praying

He feeds me on green meadows and leads me to fresh water
And I think if God has a future in store for me
I don't see that way yet, but if I breathe a sigh of relief now, I'll thank him.

And so I try to keep praying:
He refreshes my soul.
He leads me on the right road for his name's sake.

---

1. My own translation from German into English.

And I think to myself that I'll be tested in my grief
and I ask in my sorrow, what am I sad about?
Am I crying because I lost something or
am I crying because the person I loved has lost their life?

And in my asking I pray:
And even though I wander in the dark valley—and grief is such a valley—
I fear no misfortune—and am not ashamed of my feelings—,
because you are with me
even when I go to the cemetery and when I return to my home.

Your rod and staff comfort me.
And I pray with renewed certainty.
You prepare a table in front of me; and the prayer goes on:
In the face of my opponents.

And if my grief has been able to teach me this:
how unimportant and how lacking in depth my inner battles are,
then, I want to be thankful for the grief that frees me from these battles.
Yes, God, you turn pain into shalom.

Goodness and mercy will follow me throughout my life.
Yes, God, you accompany my life, wherever it goes,
even if I can't feel it yet.

And I will abide in the house of the Lord forever.
Yes, God, I have my home with you.
Amen

Bibliography

Adorno, Theodor W. *Ästhetische Theorie*. Frankfurt am Main: Suhrkamp, 2003.
Aland, Kurt, and Barbara Aland, eds. *Nestle-Aland Novum Testamentum Graece et Germanice. Griechisch-deutsches Neues Testament*. 26th ed. Stuttgart: Deutsche Bibelgesellschaft, 1984.
Arjona, Ruben. "John Calvin on the Lord's Supper: Food, Rest, and Healing for Shivering Souls." *Pastoral Psychology* 66 (2017) 177–190.
Atkinson, David J., and Oliver O'Donovan. *New Dictionary of Christian Ethics and Pastoral Theology*. Westmont: IVP Academic, 1995.
Anselm of Canterbury. *Proslogion: Lateinisch–Deutsch*. Edited and translated by R. Thei. Stuttgart: Reclam, 2005.
Aquinas, Thomas. *Summa Theologiae: Lateinisch–Deutsch*. Vol. 38. Edited and translated by O. H. Pesch et al. Stuttgart: Alfred Kroner Verlag, 1985.
———. *Summa Theologica*. 5 vols. Translated by Fathers of the English Dominican Province. Westminster, MD: Christian Classics, Inc., 1991
Augustine. *Confessions*. Translated by R. S. Pine-Coffin. London: Penguin Classics, 1961.
Bacos, Catherine A., and Kim, Si Jung. "Wearable Stories for Children: Embodied Learning Through Pretend and Physical Play." *Interactive Learning Environments* 31 (2023) 129–41.
Balboni, Michael, and Tracy Balboni. *Hostility Towards Hospitality: Spirituality and Professional Socialization Within Medicine*. Oxford: Oxford University Press, 2019.
Barth, Karl. *The Call to Discipleship*. Translated by G. W. Bromiley. Minneapolis: Fortress, 2003.
———. *Church Dogmatics*. Edinburgh: T&T Clark, 1978.
———. *Fifty Prayers*. Louisville: John Knox, 2008.
———. *Kirchliche Dogmatik*. Zürich: EVZ, 1967.
———. "Witness to an Ancient Truth." *Time*, Apr. 20, 1962.
Bauer, Walter. *Wörterbuch zum Neuen Testament*. Berlin: Alfred Töpelmann Verlag, 1971.
Bayer, Oswald. "Zur Theologie der Klage." *Jahrbuch für Biblische Theologie* 16 (2001) 289–301.
BBC News. "L'Arche Founder Jean Vanier Sexually Abused Women: Internal Report." BBC.com, Feb. 20, 2020. https://www.bbc.com/news/world-51596516.
Bennett, Zoë, et al. *Invitation to Research in Practical Theology*. Oxford: Routledge, 2018.
Bernhardin, Josef. *The Gift of Peace*. Chicago: Loyola, 1997.

Bieringer, Reimund. "The Comforted Comforter: The Meaning of παρακαλέω or παράκλησις Terminology in 2 Corinthians." *HTS Teologise Studies/Theological Studies* 67 (2011).
Bishop, Jeffrey P. *The Anticipatory Corpse: Medicine, Power and the Care of the Dying*. Notre Dame: University of Notre Dame Press, 2011.
Blumenberg, Hans. *Beschreibung des Menschen*. Frankfurt: Suhrkamp, 2014.
Boethius. *De consolatione philosophiae*. Translated by W. V. Cooper. Oxford: BiblioLive, 2009.
Bohren, Rudolf. *Martin Luther, Tröstungen*. München: Kaiser Verlag, 1983.
———. *Sterben und Tod*. Edition Bohren. Waltrop: Spenner, 2003.
Bonhoeffer, Dietrich. *Dietrich Bonhoeffer Works* (DBWE). 17 vols. Minneapolis: Fortress, 1996.
———. *Discipleship* (DBWE 4). Translated by Barbara Green and Reinhard Krauss. Minneapolis: Fortress, 2015.
———. *Ethics*. Translated by Neville Horton Smith. New York: MacMillan, 1967.
———. *Letters and Papers from Prison*. Minneapolis: Fortress, 2015.
Botterweck, Johannes. *Theologisches Wörterbuch zum Alten Testament*. Stuttgart: Kohlhammer, 1970–2000.
Breitbart, William. "Reframing Hope: Meaning-Centred Care for Patients near the End of Life." *Journal of Palliative Medicine* 6 (2004) 979–88.
Brown, Francis, et al. *A Hebrew and English Lexicon of the Old Testament*. Peabody, MA: Hendrickson, 1996.
Browning, Don S. *A Fundamental Practical Theology: Descriptive and Strategic Proposals*. Minneapolis: Fortress, 1991.
———. *The Moral Context of Pastoral Care*. Philadelphia: Westminster, 1976.
Brueggemann, Walter. *Living Toward a Vision*. Philadelphia: United Church, 1976.
———. *The Message of the Psalms*. Minneapolis: Fortress, 1984.
———. *Psalms*. Cambridge: Cambridge University Press, 2014.
———. *Praying the Psalms*. Eugene, OR: Cascade, 2007.
———. *Spirituality of the Psalms*. Minneapolis: Fortress, 2002.
———. *Widerstand und Ergebung: Briefe und Aufzeichnungen aus der Haft*. München, Chr. Kaiser Verlag, 1951.
Brueggemann, Walter, et al. "On Communion." *Mission Catalyst* 2 (2015) 4–6. https://bmsworldmission.org/assets/resources/publications/downloads/mission-catalyst-2-2015-communion-of-sinners-web.pdf.
Buchanan, Jennifer. *A Music Therapy Approach to Life*. Seattle: Hugo House, 2012.
Bühlmann, Matthias. "Heilung durch Gebet." In *Heilen und Heilung*, edited by Susanna Meyer, 43–48. Zürich: TVZ, 2019.
Bultmann, Rudolf. *Der Zweite Korintherbrief*. Göttingen: Vandenhoeck & Ruprecht, 1976.
Cahalan, Kathleen, and James Nieman. "Mapping the Field of Practical Theology." In *For Life Abundant: Practical Theology, Theological Education and Christian Ministry*, edited by Dorothy C. Bass and Craig R. Dykstra, 62–85. Grand Rapids: Eerdmans, 2008.
Churton, Tobias. *Gnostic Philosophy: From Ancient Persia to Modern Times*. Rochester: Inner Traditions, 2005.
Cobb, Marc. *The Dying Soul*. Buckingham/Philadelphia: Open University Press, 2002.

Cobb, Marc, et al. *Oxford Textbook of Spirituality in Health Care*. Oxford: Oxford University Press, 2012.
Coelho, Adriana, et al. "Comfort Experience in Palliative Care: A Phenomenological Study." *BMC Palliative Care* (2016) 15:71. https://doi:10.1186/s12904-016-0145-0.
Chorna, Valentin. "Modern Going Near Creation of In-Hospital Comfort for Patients and Medical Personnel in Psychiatric Establishments of Health Protection." *Journal of the International Academy of Integrative Anthropology* 35 (2019) 48–53.
Csikszentmihalyi, Mihaly, and Eugene Rochberg Halton. *The Meaning of Things*. Cambridge: Cambridge University Press, 1981.
Daaleman, Timothy P. "An Exploratory Study of Spiritual Care at the End of Life." *Annals of Family Medicine* 6 (2008) 406–11.
Dalferth, Ingolf U., and Simon Peng-Keller. *Beten als verleiblichtes Verstehen*. Freiburg: Herder, 2016.
———. *Gottvertrauen*. Freiburg: Herder, 2012.
Denzin, Norman K., and Yvonne S. Lincoln. *Collecting and Interpreting Qualitative Materials*. London: SAGE, 1998.
De Sousa Matos, Ticiane Dionizio, et al. "Quality of Life and Religious-Spiritual Coping in Palliative Cancer Care Patients." *Revista Latino-Americana de Enfermagem* 25 (2017). https://doi.org/10.1590/1518-8345.1857.2910.
Dober, Benjamin. *Ethik des Trostes: Hans Blumenbergs Kritik des Unbegrifflichen*. Velbrück Wissenschaft: Weilerswist, 2019.
Dreyer, Jaco S. "Knowledge, Subjectivity, (De)coloniality, and the Conundrum of Reflexivity." In *Conundrums in Practical Theology*, edited by Bonnie Miller-McLemore and J. A. Mercer, 90–109. Leuven: Brill, 2016.
Ebeling, Gerhard. *Luthers Seelsorge: Theologie in der Vielfalt der Lebenssituationen an seinen Briefen dargestellt*. München: Mohr Siebeck, 1997.
Edwards, A. "The Understanding of Spirituality and the Potential Role of Spiritual Care in End-of-Life and Palliative Care: A Meta-Study of Qualitative Research." *Palliative Medicine* 24 (2010) 753–70.
Engelhardt, H. Tristan, and Corinna Delkeskamp-Hayes. "Der Geist der Wahrheit und die 'Legion' der Spiritualitäten: Ein orthodoxer Blick auf die Klinikseelsorge im religiösen Pluralismus." In *Spiritualität und Medizin: Gemeinsame Sorge für den kranken Menschen*, edited by Eckhard Frick and Traugott Roser, 73–80. Stuttgart: Kohlhammer, 2011.
Eschmann, Holger, and Roser, Traugott. "Vom Trost, der trägt." *Spiritual Care* 11:1 (2022) 1. https://doi.org/10.1515/spircare-2021-0091.
Evangelisches Gesangbuch: Ausgabe für die Evangelische Kirche in Deutschland und ihre Gliedkirchen. Stuttgart: Evangelisches Verlagswerk GmbH, 1993.
Falque, Emmanuel. *The Guide to Gethsemane: Anxiety, Suffering, Death*. New York: Fordham University Press, 2019.
Feld, Steve, and Donald Brenneis. "Doing Anthropology in Sound." *American Ethnologist* 31 (2004) 461–74.
Finlay, Linda. *Phenomenology for Therapists*. Oxford: Wiley-Blackwell, 2011.
Fischer, Clara, and Luna Dolezal. *New Feminist Perspectives on Embodiment*. Berlin: Springer, 2018.
Forcén, Fernando, and Carlos Forcén. "*Ars Moriendi*: Coping with Death in the Late Middle Ages." *Palliative and Supportive Care* 14 (2016) 553–60. https://doi.org/10.1017/S1478951515000954.

Fowler, James. "The Emerging New Shape of Practical Theology." In *Practical Theology: International Perspectives*, edited by F. Schweitzer and J. A. van der Ven, 293–308. Frankfurt: Peter Lang, 1999.

———. "Practical Theology and the Shaping of Christian Lives." In *A Fundamental Practical Theology: Descriptive and Strategic Proposals*, edited by Don Browning, 148–66. Minneapolis: Fortress, 1991.

Frick, Eckhard, and Traugott Roser. *Spiritualität und Medizin*. Stuttgart: Kohlhammer, 2009.

———. "Zwischen Vertröstung und Trost unterscheiden lernen." *Spiritual Care* 11 (2022) 10–18.

Fry, Jane, et al. "Muddying the Waters or Swimming Downstream? A Critical Analysis of Literature Reviewing in a Phenomenological Study Through an Exploration of the Lifeworld, Reflexivity and Role of the Researcher." *Indo-Pacific Journal of Phenomenology* 17 (2017) 1–12. https://doi.org/10.1080/20797222.2017.1293355.

Gadamer, Hans-Georg. *Truth and Method*. London: Bloomsbury Publishing, 2004.

Garg, Rajat, and Vinay Chauhan. "Coping Styles and Life Satisfaction in Palliative Care." *Indian Journal of Palliative Care* 24 (2018) 491–95. https://doi:10.4103/IJPC.IJPC_63_18.

Gehlen, Arnold. *Der Mensch: Seine Natur und seine Stellung in der Welt*. Berlin: Junker und Dünnhaupt Verlag, 1940.

Gerkin, Charles. *The Living Human Document: Re-Visioning Pastoral Counselling in a Hermeneutical Mode*. Nashville: Abingdon, 1984.

Gerstenkorn, Ulrich. *Hospizarbeit in Deutschland: Lebenswissen im Angesicht des Todes*. Diakoniewissenschaft 10. Stuttgart: Kohlhammer, 2004.

Ghaye, Tony. "Into the Reflective Mode: Bridging the Stagnant Moat." *Reflective Practice* 1 (2000) 5–9.

Giske, Tove, and Pamela Cone. "Comparing Nurses' and Patients' Comfort Level with Spiritual Assessment." *Religions* 11 (2020) 671. https://doi:10.3390/rel11120671.

Goldingay, John. *The Theology of the Book of Isaiah*. Downers Grove, IL: IVP Academic, 2014.

Gooder, Paula. *Body: Biblical Spirituality for the Whole Person*. London: SPCK, 2016.

Gregory, Richard, et al. *The Artful Eye*. Oxford: University Press, 1995.

Hall, Amy Laura. *Laughing at the Devil: Seeing the World with Julian of Norwich*. Durham: Duke University Press, 2018.

Hanneke W. M., et al. "Perspectives on Death and an Afterlife in Relation to Quality of Life, Depression, and Hopelessness in Cancer Patients Without Evidence of Disease and Advanced Cancer Patients." *Journal of Pain and Symptom Management* 41 (2011) 1048–59. https://doi.org/10.1016/j.jpainsymman.2010.08.015.

Harasta, Eva, and Brian Brock. *Evoking Lament: A Theological Discussion*. London: T&T Clark, 2009.

Härle, Wilfried. *Dogmatik*. Berlin: De Gruyter, 1999.

Hauerwas, Stanley. *Character and the Christian Life*. Notre Dame: University of Notre Dame Press, 1994.

———. *God, Medicine, and Suffering*. Grand Rapids: Eerdmans, 1994.

———. "Presence and Silence: Lessons from Grief and Suffering." The Table (Biola University Center for Christian Thought), June 2, 2017. https://cct.biola.edu/presence-silence-lessons-grief-suffering/

———. *Suffering Presence*. Edinburgh: T&T Clark, 1986.

Hauerwas, Stanley, and Will Willimon. *Holy Spirit*. Nashville: Abingdon, 2015.
Heidegger, Martin. *Being and Time*. Oxford: Wiley and Sons, 1978.
Hiltner, Seward. *Preface to Practical Theology*. Nashville: Abingdon, 1958.
Hjamarsson, Emma, and Malin Lindroth "'To Live Until You Die Could Actually Include Being Intimate and Having Sex': A Focus Group Study on Nurses' Experiences of Their Work with Sexuality in Palliative Care." *Journal of Clinical Nursing* 29 (2020) 2979–90. https://doi.org/10.1111/jocn.15303.
Holder-Franz, Martina. "Cicely Saunders—Pionierin der Hospizbewegung und der Spiritual Care." *Pastoral-Theologie* 106 (2017) 422–33.
——. "Cicely Saunders—Von Spiritual Pain zu Spiritual Care." In *Spiritual Care im globalisierten Gesundheitswesen*, edited by Simon Peng-Keller, and David Neuhold, 95–118. Darmstadt: Wbg Academic, 2019.
——. "*. . .dass du bis zuletzt leben kannst*": *Spiritualität und Spiritual Care bei Cicely Saunders*. Zürich: TVZ, 2012.
——. "Perlen des Trostes." In "Trost und Vertröstung." Special issue, *Hermeneutische Blätter* 30 (2024) 107–22.
Holder-Franz, Martina, and Maria Zinsstag. *In Beziehung sein: Palliative Care und christliche Verantwortung; 20 Porträts aus der Schweiz*. Zürich: TVZ, 2021.
Houston, James. *The Transforming Friendship: A Guide to Prayer*. Batavia: Regent College, 1989.
Hughes, Gerard J. *Aristotle on Ethics*. London: Routledge, 2001.
Hummel, M. Leonard. *Clothed in Nothingness: Consolation for Suffering*. Minneapolis: Fortress, 2003.
Hunter, Rodney J., et al. *Dictionary of Pastoral Care and Counselling*. Nashville: Abingdon, 1995.
Husserl, Edmund. *Husserl Archiv*. https://www.husserlarchiv.uni-freiburg.de/archiv/Husserlbiographie.
——. *The Shorter Logical Investigations*. London: Routledge, 2004.
——. *Logical Investigations*. London: Routledge, 2001.
Hutchison, Margaret G. "Unity and Diversity in Spiritual Care." Paper presented at the Sydney University Nursing Society First Annual Conference for Undergraduate Nursing Students in New South Wales, Sept. 1997. https://members.tripod.com/marg_hutchison/nurse-4.html.
Jeremias, Jörg. *Aspekte alttestamentalischer Gottesvorstellung*. Neukirchen-Vluyn: Neukirchener Verlag, 1997.
Julian of Norwich. *Revelations of Divine Love*. New York: Dover, 2006.
——. *Showings*. Mahwah: Paulist, 1978.
Kang, Tae-Young. "Spirit and Creation: A Study of Jürgen Moltmann's Pneumatological Doctrine of Creation." PhD diss., University of Heidelberg, 2003.
Kellehear, Allan. "Spirituality and Palliative Care: A Model of Needs." *Palliative Medicine* 14 (2000) 149–55.
Kelly, Ewan. *Personhood and Presence: Self as a Resource for Spiritual and Pastoral Care*. London: T&T Clark, 2012.
——. *Spiritual Care for Healthcare Professionals*. London: Radcliffe, 2011.
Kelly Ewan, and John Swinton. *Chaplaincy and the Soul of Health and Social Care: Fostering Spiritual Wellbeing in Emerging Paradigms of Care*. London: Radcliffe, 2019.

King, Nigel, and Christine Horrocks. *Interviews in Qualitative Research*. London: SAGE, 2010.
Klaasen, John S. "Practical Theology: A Critically Engaged Practical Reason Approach of Practice, Theory, Practice and Theory." *HTS Teologiese Studies/Theological Studies* 70 (2014) a1950. https://doi.org/10.4102/hts.v70i2.1950.
Klein, Rebekka A. "The Phenomenology of Lament." In *Evoking Lament: A Theological Discussion*, edited by Eva Harasta and Brian Brock, 9–24. London: T&T Clark, 2009.
Koch, Sabine C., and Thomas Fuchs. *Body Memory, Metaphor, and Movement*. Amsterdam/Philadelphia: John Benjamin's Pub, 2012.
Koenig, Harold, et al. *Handbook of Religion and Health*. Oxford: Oxford University Press, 2012.
———. "Integrating Spirituality into Medical Practice: A New Era in Medicine." In *Spiritualität, Krankheit und Heilung—Bedeutung und Ausdrucksformen der Spiritualität in der Medizin*, edited by Arndt Büssing, 232–41. Frankfurt: VAS, 2006.
Kübler-Ross, Elisabeth. *On Death and Dying: What the Dying Have to Teach Doctors, Nurses, Clergy, and Their Own Families*. London: Routledge, 2008.
Kvale, Steinar, and Sven Brinkmann. *Learning the Craft of Qualitative Research Interviewing*. London: SAGE, 2015.
Lacan, Jacques. *The Four Fundamental Concepts of Psychoanalysis*. New York: Norton, 1981.
Lazenby, Mark, et al. *Safe Passage. A Global Spiritual Sourcebook for Care at the End of Life*. Oxford: Oxford University Press, 2014.
Leaver, Robi N. A. *Luther's Liturgical Music*. Grand Rapids: Eerdmans, 2007.
Lee, Simon J. C. "In a Secular Spirit: Strategies of Clinical Pastoral Education." *Health Care Analysis* 10 (2002) 339–56.
Lenz, Siegfried. *Über den Schmerz: Essays*. München: Dtv Verlagsgesellschaft, 2000.
Levering, Matthew. *Dying and the Virtue*. Grand Rapids: Eerdmans, 2018.
Lewis, Clive Staples. *A Grief Observed*. London: Faber & Faber, 2013.
———. *The Problem of Pain*. London: Harper Collins, 2006.
Luther, Martin. *Martin Luthers Werke: Kritische Gesamtausgabe*. Weimar: Hermann Böhlau Nachfolger, 1883–2009.
Lyons, Evanthia, and Adrian Coyle. *Analysing Qualitative Data in Psychology: A Practical and Comparative Guide*. London: SAGE, 2007.
MacIntyre, Alasdair. *After Virtue*. London: Duckworth, 1985.
———. *Dependent Rational Animals*. Chicago: Open Court, 1999.
Marcuse, Ludwig. *Sigmund Freud*. Zürich: Diogenes, 2002.
Mason, Jennifer. *Qualitative Research*. London: SAGE, 2004.
McKinnish Bridges, Linda. "Paul's Words of Comfort in First Thessalonians." *Review and Expositor* 96 (1999) 211–32.
McKeon, Richard. *The Basic Works of Aristotle*. New York: Random House, 2001.
McLeod, John. *Qualitative Research in Counselling and Psychotherapy*. London: SAGE, 2011.
McNeill, Donald P., and Douglas A. Morrison. *Compassion: A Reflection on the Christian Life*. New York: Doubleday, 2005.
Merleau-Ponty, Maurice. *Phenomenology of Perception*. London: Routledge, 1962.

———. *The Primacy of Reception: And Other Essays on Phenomenological Psychology, the Philosophy of Art, History and Politics.* Evanston, IL: Northwestern University Press, 1964.

———. *Signs.* Evanston, IL: Northwestern University Press, 1964.

———. *The Visible and the Invisible.* Evanston, IL: Northwestern University Press, 1968.

Migliore, Daniel. "Death." In *Dictionary of Pastoral Care and Counseling*, edited by Rodney J. Hunter, 502–27. Nashville: Abingdon, 1990.

Milbank, John. *Theology and Social Theory: Beyond Secular Reason.* Cambridge: Blackwell, 1990.

Miller, Daniel. *The Comfort of People.* Cambridge: Polity Press, 2017.

———. *The Comfort of Things.* Cambridge: Polity Press, 2008.

Miller-McLemore, Bonnie J. "Embodied Knowing, Embodied Theology: What Happened to the Body?" *Pastoral Psychology* 62 (2013) 743–58. https://doi:10.1007/s11089-013-0510-3.

———. "'This Is My Body': Christian Wisdom on Dying in an Age of Denial." *Practical Theology* (2021) 472–75. https://doi.org/10.1080/1756073X.2021.1889766.

———. *The Wiley Blackwell Companion to Practical Theology.* Oxford: Oxford University Press, 2014.

Möller, Christian, and Christa Lauter. *Seelsorge in Einzelportraits.* Göttingen: Vandenhoek & Ruprecht, 1994.

Moltmann, Jürgen. *The Crucified God.* London: SCM Press, 1974.

———. *The Open Church: Invitation to a Messianic Lifestyle.* London: SCM, 1978.

Morris, David B. "The Plot of Suffering: Aids and Evil." In *Evil after Postmodernism: Histories, Narratives and Ethics*, edited by Jennifer L. Geddes, 56–75. London: Routledge, 2000.

Morrison, Bill. "Poetic *Sling Blade* Cuts to the Truth." *News and Observer* (Raleigh, NC), Feb. 14, 1997.

Murray, Derek. *Faith in Hospice: Spiritual Care and the End of Life.* London: SPCK, 2002.

Murray, Levine. "Prayer as Coping: A Psychological Analysis." *Journal of Health Care Chaplaincy* 15 (2009) 80–98.

National Cancer Institute. "Faith and Spirituality with Cancer." Cancer.gov, Nov. 13, 2024. https://www.cancer.gov/about-cancer/coping/day-to-day/faith-and-spirituality.

Neslon, Wesley. "The Pastor as Comforter." In *Baker Dictionary of Practical Theology*, edited by Ralph Turnbull, 297–302. Grand Rapids: Baker Academic, 1967.

Norman, Donald A. *Emotional Design.* New York: Basic, 2005.

Nouwen, Henri, J. M. *Bread for the Journey: A Daybook of Wisdom and Faith.* New York: Harper Collins, 1996

———. *The Inner Voice of Love: Journey Through Anguish to Freedom.* New York: Image, 1996.

———. *A Letter of Consolation.* San Francisco: Harper & Row, 1982.

———. *Out of Solitude.* Notre Dame: Ave Maria Press, 1974.

———. *The Way of the Heart: Desert Spirituality and Contemporary Ministry.* New York: Seabury Press, 1981.

———. *The Wounded Healer.* London: Darton, Longman & Todd, 1990.

Van Oorschot, Jürgen. "Leben/naefaesch (AT)." WiBiLex: Das wissenschaftliche Bibellexikon im Internet, Nov. 2020. https://bibelwissenschaft.de/stichwort/80314/

Opitz, Peter. "Evangelium als Befreiung zum Vertrauen bei Huldrych Zwingli." In *Gottvertrauen*, edited by Ingolf U. Dalferth and Simon Peng-Keller, 182–208. Freiburg: Herder, 2012.

Osmer, Richard. *Practical Theology: An Introduction*. Grand Rapids: Eerdmans, 2008.

Otto, Rudolf. *Das Heilige*. München: C. H. Beck, 2014.

Pascal, Blaise. *Pensées*. New York: E. P. Dutton & Co, 2006.

Pattison, Stephen. *Seeing Things: Deepening Relations with Visual Artefacts*. London: SCM, 2007.

———. "Stuff Pastoral Theology." *Practical Theology* 154 (2007) 6–14. https://doi.org./10.1080/13520806.2007.11759081.

Patton, John. *Pastoral Care in Context*. Louisville: John Knox, 1993.

Peng-Keller, Simon. *Klinkseelsorge als spezialisierte Spiritual Care*. Göttingen: Vandenhoeck & Ruprecht, 2021.

———. "Spiritual Care als theologische Herausforderung." *Theologische Literaturzeitung* 140 (2015) 455–67.

———. "Symbolisierung des ultimativen Abschieds zum Bilderleben Sterbender." *Swiss Archives of Neurology, Psychiatry and Psychotherapy* 167 (2016) 81–87.

Peng-Keller, Simon, and David Neuhold. *Spiritual Care im globalisierten Gesundheitswesen*. Darmstadt: Wbg Academic, 2019.

Pfenninger, Michael, and Stefanie Koch. "Trost und Vertröstung." Special issue, *Hermeneutische Blätter* 30 (2024).

Pinto, Sara, et al. "Comfort, Well-Being and Quality of Life." *Porto Biomedical Journal* 2 (2017) 6–12.

Piper, Hans-Christoph. *Gespräche mit Sterbenden*. Göttingen: Vandenhoeck & Ruprecht, 1977.

Plessner, Helmut. "Die Stufen des Organischen und der Mensch: Einleitung in die philosophische Anthropologie." In *Gesammelte Schriften*, 4:385–417. Frankfurt am Main: Suhrkamp Verlag, 1981.

———. *Philosophische Anthropologie*. Frankfurt: Suhrkamp, 2019.

Powell, John. *How Music Works: The Science and Psychology of Beautiful Sounds, from Beethoven to the Beatles and Beyond*. London: Little and Brown, 2011.

Puchalski, Christina M., et al. "Improving the Quality of Spiritual Care as a Dimension of Palliative Care: The Report of the Consensus Conference." *Journal of Palliative Medicine* 12 (2009) 885–904. https://doi.org/10.1089/jpm.2009.0142.

Puchalski, Christina M., and Betty Ferrell. *Making Health Care Whole: Integrating Spirituality into Patient Care*. West Conshohocken, PA: Templeton, 2010.

Reinders, Hans. *Receiving the Gift of Friendship: Profound Disability, Theological Anthropology, and Ethics*. Grand Rapids: Eerdmans, 2008.

Resch, Claudia. *Trost im Angesicht des Todes: Frühe reformatorische Anleitungen zur Seelsorge an Kranken und Sterbenden*. Tübingen/Basel: A. Francke Verlag, 2006.

Reumer, Stefanie. "Was ist dein Trost im Leben und im Sterben? Eine Untersuchung zur Dimension des Trostes im Kontext der Beerdigung." PhD diss., University of Basel, 2019.

Riede, Peter. *Trost, der ins Leben führt: Ein Beitrag zum Menschen- und Gottesverständnis des Alten Testament*. Biblisch-Theologische Studien. Neukirchen-Vluyn: Neukirchener Verlag, 2013.

———. "Trost/Tröster/trösten." *Wissenschaftliches Bibellexikon zum Alten Testament*, Aug. 2014. http://www.bibelwissenschaft.de/stichwort/36214/.

Riggs, John W. *The Lord's Supper in the Reformed Tradition*. Westminster: John Knox, 2015.
Rilke, Rainer Maria. *The Garden of Olives*. New York: Norton, 1938.
Roberts, Tom Aerwyn. *The Concept of Benevolence: Aspects of Eighteenth-Century Moral Philosophy*. Berlin/Heidelberg: Springer, 1973.
Rolf, Sibylle. *Vom Sinn zum Trost*. Münster: Lit Verlag, 2003.
Rolheiser, Roland. *The Holy Longing: Teresa of Avila*. New York: Doubleday, 1999.
Rose, Gillian. *Visual Methodologies: An Introduction to the Interpretations of Visual Materials*. London: SAGE, 2007.
Roser, Traugott. *Spiritual Care*. Stuttgart: Kohlhammer, 2007.
Rosner, Brian S. *The Consolation of Theology*. Grand Rapids: Eerdmans, 2008.
Rotelle, John. *The Works of St. Augustine: A Translation for the 21st Century*. New York: New City Press, 2000–2004.
Rothschild, Babette. *The Body Remembers*. New York: Norton, 2017.
Rubin, Lilian B. *Just Friends*. New York: Harper Collins, 1985.
Rumbold, Bruce. "Spiritual Assessment and Health Care Chaplaincy." *Christian Bioethics* 19 (2013) 251–69.
Saarelainen, Suvi-Maria, et al. "Religious Experiences of Older People Receiving Palliative Care at Home. " *Religions* 11 (2020) 336. https://doi.org/10.3390/rel11070336.
Saunders, Cicely. "And from Sudden Death." *Frontier* 4 (1961) 39–41.
———. *Beyond the Horizon*. London: Longman and Todd, 2003.
———. "Current Views on Pain Relief and Terminal Care." In *The Therapy of Pain*, edited by M. Swerdlow, 179–92. Lancaster, UK: MTP, 1976.
———. *Der Horizont ist nur das Ende unserer Sicht*. Zürich: TVZ, 2015.
———. "The Philosophy of Terminal Care." In *The Management of Terminal Malignant Disease*, edited by Cicely Saunders, 232–41. 2nd ed.. London: Edward Arnold, 1984.
———. "The Problem of Euthanasia." *Nursing Times* 72(36) (1976) 135–36.
———. *Selected Letters*. Oxford: University Press, 2003.
———. *Selected Writings*. Oxford: University Press, 2006.
———. *Sterben und Leben*. Zürich: TVZ, 2018.
———. *Watch with Me*. Sheffield: Mortal Press, 2003.
Scarry, Elaine. *The Body in Pain*. Oxford: University Press, 1987.
Schäufele, Wolf-Friedrich. "Fiducia bei Martin Luther." In *Gottvertrauen*, edited by Ingolf U. Dalferth and Simon Peng-Keller, 163–81. Freiburg: Herder, 2012.
Schmid, Magnus. "Die Kunst des Sterbens als Lebenskunst: Von der Ars moriendi des Mittelalters zu wahrer und falscher Sterbehilfe heute." *Ärztliche Praxis* 28 (1976) 497–50.
Schneider-Harpprecht, Christoph. *Trost in der Seelsorge*. Stuttgart: Kohlhammer, 1989.
Schrock, Chad D. *Consolation in Medieval Narrative*. New York: Palgrave Macmillan, 2015.
Schulte, Volker, and Christoph Steinebach. *Innovative Palliative Care*. Bern: Huber Verlag, 2014.
Schulz, Heiko. *Theorie des Glaubens*. Tübingen: Mohr Siebeck, 2001.
Selman, Lucy. "Research Priorities in Spiritual Care: An International Survey of Palliative Care Researchers and Clinicians." *Journal of Pain and Symptom Management* 48 (2014) 518–31.

Seybold, Klaus. *Introducing the Psalms*. London: Bloomsbury, 2000.
———. *Poetik der Psalmen*. Poetologische Studien zum Alten Testament 1.1. Stuttgart: Kohlhammer, 2007.
Shogren, Gary Steven. "Consolation." *Baker's Evangelical Dictionary of Bible Theology*. Grand Rapids: Baker, 1996. https://www.biblestudytools.com/dictionary/consolation/.
Shuman, Joel James. *The Body of Compassion*. Oxford: Basic Books, 1999.
Silverman, David. *Doing Qualitative Research*. 6th ed. London: SAGE, 2021.
———. *Interpreting Qualitative Data*. London: SAGE, 2010.
Simmel, Georg. *Fragmente und Aufsätze aus dem Nachlass und Veröffentlichungen der letzten Jahre*. Munich: Drei Masken Verlag, 1923.
Simms, Eva M. *The Child in the World: Embodiment, Time and Language in Early Childhood*. Detroit: Wayne State University Press, 2008.
Singer, Peter A., et al. "Quality End-of-Life Care Patients' Perspectives." *Journal of Palliative Medicine* 3 (2000) 403–5. https://doi.org/10.1089/jpm.2000.3.4.403.
Smeet, Wim. *Spiritual Care in a Hospital Setting*. Amsterdam: Colofon, 2006.
Smucker, C. "A Phenomenological Description of the Experience of Spiritual Distress." *Nursing Diagnosis* 7 (1998) 81–91. https://pubmed.ncbi.nlm.nih.gov/8716949/.
Sölle, Dorothee. *Suffering*. Philadelphia: Fortress, 1975.
Struthers Malbon, Elizabeth. "No Need to Have Any One Write? A Structural Analysis of 1 Thessalonians." *Semeia* 26 (1983) 71–92.
Swift, Christopher. *Hospital Chaplaincy in the Twenty-First Century: The Crisis of Spiritual Care in the NHS*. 2nd ed. Farnham, UK: Ashgate, 2014.
Swinton, John. *Dementia: Living in the Memories of God*. Cambridge: Eerdmans, 2012.
———. *From Bedlam to Shalom*. New York: Peter Lang, 2000.
———. *Raging with Compassion*. Grand Rapids: Eerdmans, 2007.
———. *Resurrecting the Person: Friendship and the Care of People with Mental Health Problems*. Nashville: Abingdon, 2000.
Swinton, John, and Harriet Mowat. *Practical Theology and Qualitative Research*. London: SCM, 2006.
Swinton, John, and Richard Payne. *Living Well and Dying Faithfully: Christian Practices for End-of-Life Care*. Cambridge: Eerdmans, 2009.
Tacke, Helmut. *Glaubenshilfe als Lebenshilfe*. Neukirchen-Vluyn: Neukirchener Verlag, 1975.
———. *Mit den Müden zur rechten Zeit reden*. Neukirchen-Vluyn: Neukirchener Verlag, 1989.
Teilhard de Chardin, Pierre. *The Divine Milieu*. Mahwah: Paulist Press, 2007.
Thayer, Joseph. *Thayer's Greek-English Lexicon of the New Testament*. Peabody, MA: Hendrickson, 2000.
Tiemeyer, Lena-Sophia. *For the Comfort of Zion*. Oxford: Brill, 2010.
Tillich, Paul. *On Art and Architecture*. New York: Crossroad, 1989.
———. *Systematische Theologie*. Berlin/Boston: De Gruyter, 2017.
Tornøe, Kirsten Anne, et al. "The Challenge of Consolation: Nurses' Experiences with Spiritual and Existential Care for the Dying; A Phenomenological Hermeneutical Study." *BMC Nursing* 14 (2015) 62–67. https://doi.org/10.1186/s12912-015-0114-6.
Turnbull, Ralph. *Baker's Dictionary of Practical Theology*. London: Morgan and Scott, 1968.

Ursinus, Zacharias. "Heidelberger Catechism, 1563." German Translation by Otto Weber. *Der Heidelberger Katechismus*. Gütersloh: Gütersloher Verlags Haus, 1996.
Van de Geer, Joep. "Training Spiritual Care, Palliative Care in Teaching Hospitals in the Netherlands: A Multicentre Trial." *Journal of Research in Interprofessional Practice and Education* 6 (2016) 1–12.
Vanier, Jean. *Becoming Human*. Toronto: Anansi, 2001.
———. *Be Not Afraid*. Toronto: Griffin House, 1975.
———. *From Brokenness to Community*. Mahwah, NY: Paulist, 1992.
Van Manen, Max. *Phenomenology of Practice*. London: Routledge, 2014.
———. *Researching Lived Experience*. London: Althouse Press, 2016.
Van Manen, Max, and Catherine Adams. "Qualitative Research: Phenomenology." In *International Encyclopedia of Education*, edited by E. Baker et al., 6:449–55. Oxford: Elsevier, 2010.
Van Laarhoven, H. W. M., et al. "Coping, Quality of Life, Depression, and Hopelessness in Cancer Patients in a Curative and Palliative, End-of-Life Care Setting." *Cancer Nursing* 34 (2011) 302–14.
Van Oorschot, Jürgen. *Wissenschaftliches Bibellexikon zum Alten Testament*. Stuttgart: Deutsche Bibelgesellschaft, 2009.
Von Balthasar, Hans Urs. *Mysterium Paschale*. San Francisco: Ignatius Press, 2012.
———. *A Theological Anthropology*. Eugene, OR: Wipf & Stock, 2010.
———. *Theologik*. Einsiedeln: Johannes Verlag, 1985–87.
Vos, Cas J. A. *Theopoetry in the Psalms*. Edinburgh: T&T Clark, 2005.
Wagensommer, Georg. *Klagepsalmen und Seelsorge*. Münster: Lit Verlag, 1998.
Ward, Pete. *Introducing Practical Theology*. Grand Rapids: Baker Academic, 2017.
Wasner, Maria, et al. "Bedeutung von Sexualität und Intimität für Palliativpatienten." *Zeitschrift für Palliativmedizin* 9 (2008). https://doi:10.1055/s-0028-1088432.
Webb-Mitchell, Brett. *Christly Gestures: Learning to be Members of the Body of Christ*. Grand Rapids: Eerdmans, 2004.
Weber, Beat. *Werkbuch Psalmen*. Vol. 1: *Die Psalmen 1 bis 72*. Stuttgart: Kohlhammer, 2001.
Wehrle, M. "Being a Body and Having a Body: The Twofold Temporality of Embodied Intentionality." *Phenomenology and the Cognitive Sciences* 19 (2020) 499–521. https://doi.org/10.1007/s11097-019-09610-z.
Weiher, Erhard. *Das Geheimnis des Lebens berühren*. Stuttgart: Kohlhammer, 2009.
Welter-Enderlin, Rosmarie, and Bruno Hildenbrand. *Resilienz—Gedeihen trotz widriger Umstände*. Heidelberg: Karl-Auer-Systeme Verlag, 2006.
Welz, Claudia. "Trust and Lament." In *Evoking Lament: A Theological Discussion*, edited by Eva Harasta and Brian Brock, 116–36. London: T&T Clark, 2009.
Wendland, Heinz Dietrich. *Das Neue Testament: Die Briefe an die Korinther*. Göttingen: Vandenhoeck & Ruprecht, 1968.
Werkander, Carina et al. "Guilt and Shame in End-of-Life Care." *European Journal of Cancer* 49 (2013) 376–77.
Wertz, Frederick J. *Five Ways of Doing Qualitative Analysis*. New York: Guilford, 2011.
Weymann, Volker. *Trost?* Zürich: TVZ, 1989.
Wilkes, Paul. *Beyond These Walls*. New York: Image, 2000.
Wils, Jean-Pierre. *Ars moriendi*. Frankfurt: Insel Verlag, 2007.
———. *Sterben*. Paderborn: Brill, 1999.

Wolterstorff, Nicholas. *Art in Action: Towards a Christian Aesthetic.* Carlisle: Send The Light, 1997.

———. *Lament for a Son.* Grand Rapids: Eerdmans, 1987.

Woodward, Walter, and Stephen Pattison. *Pastoral and Practical Theology.* Oxford: Blackwell, 2000.

Wright, N. T. "Mind, Spirit, Soul and Body: All for One and One for All; Reflections on Paul's Anthropology in his Complex Contexts." Paper delivered at the Society of Christian Philosophers: Regional Meeting, Fordham University, Mar. 18, 2011. https://ntwrightpage.com/2016/07/12/mind-spirit-soul-and-body/.

Zenger, Erich. *Psalmen.* Freiburg: Herder, 2011.

Zimmermann, Markus, and Jürg Steiger. *Das Lebensende als gesellschaftliche Herausforderung.* Synthesebericht NFP 67. Bern: Schweizerischer Nationalfonds, 2017. https://www.snf.ch/SiteCollectionDocuments/nfp/nfp67-synthesebericht-de.pdf.

Zwingli, Huldrych. *Huldreich Zwinglis Sämtliche Werke.* Edited by E. Egli et al. Berlin: C. A. Schwetschke und Sohn, 1905–.

———. *Zwinglis Schriften.* Vol. 3. Edited by T. Brunnschweiler and S. Lutz Zürich: TVZ, 1995.

www.ingramcontent.com/pod-product-compliance
Lightning Source LLC
Chambersburg PA
CBHW051639230426
43669CB00013B/2369